PURITAN AND ANGLICAN

PURITAN AND ANGLICAN

STUDIES IN LITERATURE

BY

EDWARD DOWDEN

Essay Index Reprint Series

 BOOKS FOR LIBRARIES PRESS
FREEPORT, NEW YORK

First Published 1901
First Reprinting in this Series 1967
Second Reprinting 1969

INTERNATIONAL STANDARD BOOK NUMBER:
0-8369-0386-2

LIBRARY OF CONGRESS CATALOG CARD NUMBER:
67-23208

PRINTED IN THE UNITED STATES OF AMERICA

PREFACE

THE first article in this volume is reprinted from *The Contemporary Review*; the rest of the volume has been hitherto unpublished. The Puritan writers with whom I deal are such as to render the title "Puritan and Anglican" not inexact, although many of the Puritan party were loyal members of the Anglican Communion.

In choosing my subjects I have been influenced by two things: first, I have spoken only of writers with whom I have dwelt long and intimately; and secondly, among such writers I have spoken only of those who move me to speak through some personal interest which I feel in the men or their work. Hence without scruple or regret I omit many great names, being here content to indulge my own likings.

I have desired to remain close to my subjects. In many passages, for example, of what I have written on Herbert and Vaughan, it is Herbert and Vaughan who are in fact the speakers; but I did not think it necessary to encumber my pages with a crowd of references to scattered poems from which their thoughts and phrases have been collected.

I write not as a controversialist but as a student of literature. Literature, however, and especially what is most valuable in seventeenth-century literature, cannot be studied without reference to the history of religion. All these writers, except Hooker, belong to the seventeenth century; and the influence of Hooker, who died in 1600, was in great measure posthumous.

CONTENTS

I.

II.

III.

VII.

VIII.

Contents

PURITANISM AND ENGLISH LITERATURE

I

THE greatness of Elizabethan literature arose from the unity of the national mind, in which the streams of the Renaissance and the Reformation had met and mingled. The enthusiasm of the years that followed the destruction of the Spanish Armada fused together powers which often work in opposition or apart. Reason, passion, and imagination co-operated one with another, and through their co-operancy gave substance and form to the poetry of Shakespeare and of Spenser, to the prose of Bacon and of Hooker. The literature of pleasure had never before attained to such seriousness in beauty, the literature of knowledge had never before been so infused with imaginative power. In such works as " Hamlet," " Measure for Measure," and " The Tempest " there is a depth of reflection equal to their heights of poetical vision. Spenser is at once a weaver of dreams and a teacher of truth. Hooker cannot discuss the sign of the cross in baptism or the rites of burial until he has first expounded his magnificent conception of the universe under a reign of law. The scientific writings of Bacon—later as these are in date—are the utterances of a great imaginative seer rather than of a fully equipped scientific student. If his nature was lacking in passion of other kinds, he had assuredly an unbounded passion for universal knowledge, and for the power to enhance the worth of human life which knowledge confers. But gradually in the history of our literature there was a descent from the heights. The unity of the national mind was broken or impaired. Passion in large measure transferred itself from literature to the affairs of politics and religion. Reason, confronted with urgent practical problems, grew perplexed. Imagination waned, and often yielded to the seductions of easy and vulgar pleasure. A period of doubt and difficulty followed a period of steadfast and daring advance. Two doctrines in religion arrayed themselves each against the other. Two parties in the State entered upon a great contention. Two theories of life and conduct stood opposed. All things tended towards a vast disruption ; and in the strife of King and Commonwealth, of Puritan and of Anglican, that disruption was accomplished.

The chief glory of Elizabethan literature was the drama, with the deepest passion and the most heroic actions of humanity for its theme. It had its basis in what is most real in the life of man, and what is real was interpreted into the highest meanings by imagination. During the later years of the reign of James I. and during the reign of Charles the drama lost touch with reality ; it was cut off from its true basis of supply. It advanced with a showy gallantry, but its strength and solidity of movement were gone. It relied too often, as with Massinger and Fletcher, on overstrained, fantastic motives. It deserted the substantial ground of national history. It endeavoured to excite a jaded imagination with extravagances of romantic passion or even of unnatural lust. It sought for curiosities of prettiness in sentiment and imagery. It supported its decline by splendours appealing to the senses ; vast sums of money were expended upon the masque. It grew shallow in true passion and meditative wisdom. It grew rhetorical ; its moralities are often those of eloquent periods. And if at times less rudely gross than the earlier drama, it was infected with a subtler and a baser spirit of evil. Nor do other forms of poetry compensate the decline of the drama. While much in the Jacobean and Caroline lyric poetry is admirable in its kind, a charming intermixture of nature with art, of grace with gay effrontery, it does not often deal with the great lyric themes in a spirit of serious beauty ; it ceases to be in any large sense an interpretation of life.

To us, looking back upon the period, the literature of pleasure may be worth far more than its theological treatises or its political pamphlets : grace and gaiety are always welcome gifts, fresh and living, while the theological and political controversy of the seventeenth century concerns us chiefly as a matter of history. The questions so fiercely debated then are not the questions which concern us to-day, or at least they require for our uses to be re-stated in modern terms. But to a man of serious mind, living in the years which preceded the struggle between the King and the Parliament, the poetry of the time would have appeared as no more than a decorative fringe ; the warp and woof of thought would have been found by him in those folios and quartos on which the dust now gathers in our libraries. The same cannot be said of the contemporaries of Shake-

speare or of Spenser: for them the poetry of the
time was a large and true interpretation of life. And
science and theology were then a genuine portion of
literature.

Was there a check, an interruption, of the higher
intellectual life of England ? Yes—to a certain extent.
The Renaissance influence in literature, separated from
the serious temper of the Reformation, dwindled and
suffered degradation ; the spirit of liberty, entangled
with politics, set itself to resolve urgent, practical problems, and lost some of its nobler ideality. Human
freedom—that indeed was still sought ; but freedom
came to mean deliverance from an unjust tax or from
an inquisitorial bishop. The spirit of the Reformation
separated from the Renaissance influence lost some of
its more liberal temper in a narrow Scripturalism and
in pettinesses of moral rigour. But the political and
religious questions could not be put aside ; they, too,
supplied a stern discipline for the intellect ; in their
solution an effort was made on behalf of liberty of
thought, narrowed in its meaning though liberty of
thought might be by the exigencies of the time. The
more enlightened Puritanism contained within it a
portion of the spirit of the Renaissance. The mundane spirit of the Renaissance, in its lower form of
commercial interests, by degrees allied itself with
Puritanism. The higher tendencies of the Renaissance re-emerged in the great scientific movement of
the second half of the seventeenth century. Through
the strife of parties and the tangle of interests a real
progress is discernible.

Poetical literature, in the years of growing trouble had in some degree, as has been said, lost touch with reality. The Cavalier poets produced their gallant songs of pleasure, of fancy, of delicate melody ; but they do not, and they did not, sway the life of man. Two things, however, became more real and gravely earnest. One of these concerned the corporate life of the nation —the great contention between King and people. The other concerned primarily the inner life of the individual soul. In Elizabethan literature these two things had not fallen apart. Spenser's "Faërie Queene" deals essentially with the life of the soul and its combat with the various foes and tempters which beset that life ; but it is also a poem concerning the honour and well-being of England. It is a moral or spiritual allegory ; but at the same time it is an historical allegory. Gloriana is at once the glory of God and the Queen of England ; St George is at once the knight of Holiness and the patron saint of England. Shakespeare can search the mysteries of the solitary soul in Hamlet, but he can also celebrate the glories of his country at Agincourt, and raise his chant of patriotic triumph. Such poetry became impossible in the days of James and of Charles. Men who were interested in public life were putting on their armour for an internecine struggle. Men who were concerned for the life of the soul, if they did not carry that concern into the public strife and become the zealots of a party, were tempted to retreat from the world of action, like the devout company at Little Gidding or certain of the Puritan fugitives to America, and they nourished the spirit of religion in secret or in little com-

munities.   The highest Elizabethan literature is at once
mundane and, in the truest sense of the word, religious.
At a later time the mundane literature became wholly
mundane, often even frivolously or basely mundane ;
the religious literature, when it ceases from controversy,
often ceases to regard the affairs of earth, which is but
a City of Destruction or a Vanity Fair, and has its gaze
intensely fixed upon another world, where the Saint will
attain his Rest.

II

One of the first effects of the Protestant Reformation
was a quickening of self-consciousness in matters of
religion.   External rites, ordinances, and ceremonies
seemed for many devout men and women to lose much
of their virtue.   To some they became matters of indifference ; to others they appeared hostile to the true
life of the soul.   The realm of sense was viewed as if
it were separated by a deep gulf from the realm of the
spirit.   There have, indeed, always existed the two types
of mind which we may call the Catholic and the Puritan,
to one of which the visible and the invisible are only
different aspects of one great reality,while to the other they
stand apart as sundered or even as antagonistic powers.
In a review of Newman's "Phases of Faith," written many
years ago by the most venerable of recent thinkers,
Dr Martineau endeavours to distinguish between these two
conceptions of life and the world and of God's relation to
it in a passage which it is worth while to quote at some
length.   According to the Catholic conception the two
spheres of sense and spirit seem to melt into each other

under the mediation of a kind of divine chemistry; "hence," he goes on, "the invariable presence of some physical element in all that Catholicism looks upon as venerable. Its rites are a manipular invocation of God. Its miracles are examples of incarnate divineness in old clothes and winking pictures. Its ascetic discipline is founded on the notion of a gradual consumption of the grosser body by the encroaching fire of the spirit; till in the ecstatica the frame itself becomes ethereal and the light shines through. Nothing can be more offensive than all this to the Evangelical [or, as we may put it, the Puritan] conception, which plants the natural and the spiritual in irreconcilable contradiction, denies to them all approach or contact, and allows each to exist only by the extinction of the other. . . . This unmediated dualism follows the Evangelical into his theory as to the state of each individual soul before God. The Catholic does not deny all divine light to the natural conscience, or all power to the natural will of unconverted men : he maintains that these also are already under a law of obligation, may do what is well-pleasing before God, and by superior faithfulness qualify themselves to become subjects of grace ; so that the Gospel shall come upon them as a divine supplement to the sad and feeble moral life of nature. To the Evangelical, on the contrary, the soul that is not saved is lost. . . . So, again, the contrast turns up in the opposite views taken of the divine economy in human affairs. The Evangelical detaches the elect in imagination from the remaining mass of men, sequesters them as a holy people, who must not mix themselves with the affairs of Belial. . . . The

Catholic, looking on the natural universe, whether material or human, not as an antagonist but as the receptacle of the spiritual, seeks to conquer the World for the Church, and instead of shunning political action, is ready to grasp it as his instrument."

The tendency to the one or the other of these religious conceptions, adds Mr Martineau, marks the distinction between two great families of minds. How, we may inquire, does each conception adapt itself to literature and especially to the literature of imagination? We can at once perceive that what has been named the Catholic conception more readily finds that sensuous vehicle for its ideas which literature and art demand. It interprets the invisible by the visible ; it does not suspect beauty or colour or the delight of life, but seeks to inter-penetrate these with what is divine. The danger is that it may mistake what is arbitrary, artificial, or merely traditional for that which is natural, and so may con-struct a body of factitious symbolism instead of discovering the veritable play of what is spiritual in and through what is sensible. Such factitious symbolism debars or diverts the mind from the genuine sources of light ; at best it serves as a receptacle for truth or passion trans-ferred to it from the mind itself. In this large sense of the word " Catholic " we might name Wordsworth in some of his earlier poems a true Catholic, discovering, as he does, the ideal in the real, the divine in the natural, the invisible in the visible ; and we might name Keble, in certain of his verses, a pseudo-Catholic, applying, as he sometimes does, a factitious or a traditional symbolism to sanctify what in reality is sacred in itself.

For the Puritan, on the other hand, using the word to describe a type of mind, the natural and the supernatural exist in an unmediated dualism, and it is a difficulty with him to clothe the naked idea—religious or ethical—in any sensuous medium or body. Hence Puritanism in itself is ill fitted to produce a great art. Yet the inward life of the soul may be intense, and the more intense because it does not readily distribute itself through appointed forms; and absorbing thoughts and passions cannot fail in some way to discover or to create that outward vehicle through which alone they can secure a complete self-realisation.

In the Fourth Part of "The Saints' Everlasting Rest" Baxter considers the aids which the senses can afford to the spirit. It is a point of spiritual prudence, he says, to make friends of powers which are usually our enemies; our senses and their objects would not have been given to us by God if they might not be serviceable in His own praise; the Holy Ghost in the phrase of Scripture sets forth the excellences of things spiritual in imagery borrowed from the objects of sense; the Son of God assumed our human nature "that we might know Him the better." Are we, then, to think heaven to be made of gold and pearl? Or picture Christ, "as the Papists do," in such a shape? Or believe that departed saints and angels do indeed eat and drink? Or hold that God actually is moved by human passions? Not so: we are to accept such notions as aids to our infirmity, but they cease to be aids when we take them for a literal presentation of the facts; the condescending language of the Spirit is so designed that we may "raise suppositions

from our bodily senses," and so elevate our affections
towards things invisible.

"Suppose with thyself thou hadst been that Apostle's
fellow traveller into the celestial kingdom, and that thou
hadst seen all the saints in their white robes, with palms
in their hands; suppose thou hadst heard those songs
of Moses and the Lamb; or didst even now hear them
praising and glorifying the living God. If thou hadst
seen these things indeed, in what a rapture wouldst thou
have been? . . . I would not have thee, as the
Papists, draw them in pictures, nor use mysterious, significant ceremonies to represent them. This, as it is a
course forbidden by God, so it would but seduce and draw
down thy heart; but get the liveliest picture of them in
thy mind that possibly thou canst."[1]

Thus the imaginations of a Michael Angelo or a Raphael
are forbidden to serve their fellows, unless they can employ, like Baxter himself, the medium of written words
instead of the more suitable language of colour and of line.

In his criticism of English Puritanism, Matthew
Arnold strangely misconceived its essential character
and its governing idea. Puritanism, he told us,
existed for the sake of certain doctrines derived mainly
from an imperfect interpretation of the writings of
Paul — the doctrines of predestination, original sin,
imputed righteousness, justification by faith. The
historical answer is sufficient: these doctrines, though
truly Puritan in their tendency, were held by many
members of the Church of England who were outside
of the Puritan party and were even opposed to it

[1] "Saints' Everlasting Rest," Part IV., section ii.

The ceremonial controversy preceded the controversy concerning theological dogma; it was independent, in a large measure, of the controversy as to Church government. To discover the dominant idea of Puritanism we must look beyond dogma to something common to every phase of the great contention. And undoubtedly the unvarying central element was this— Puritanism maintained, as far as was possible, that the relation between the invisible spirit of man and the invisible God was immediate rather than mediate. It set little store by tradition, because God had spoken to man directly in the words of revelation. It distrusted human ceremonies, because these stood between the creature and his Creator; the glory of the Christian temple is the holiness of the living temple which rises in the heart of the child of God. The pretensions of an ecclesiastical hierarchy are an estrangement of the adopted son of the Father; every lay Christian is himself a royal priest. The Calvinistic doctrines, on which Matthew Arnold laid extreme and exclusive stress, were maintained because they were held to be Scriptural, and also because they seemed to bring the divine agency immediately into every part of human life : predestination meant the presence of God's foreknowledge and God's will in every act and thought that pulsates on the globe; imputed righteousness meant that Christ and His faithful follower were regarded by the Father as one ; and through faith, which justifies the believer, that union is effected.

Such was the central idea of Puritanism. Its cardinal error, which in many directions tended to defeat its own

purpose, lay in a narrow conception of God as the God
of righteousness alone, and not as also the God of joy
and beauty and intellectual light. The higher Puritanism has been preached in our own day by Browning :

> "no beauty, nor good, nor power,
> Whose voice has gone forth, but each survives for the melodist
> When eternity affirms the conception of an hour."

It was taught by Goethe in "Wilhelm Meister," where
the uncle of the devout lady, in the eighth book, instructs
his niece that the lit lamp and the girt loin are needful
for other things than the culture of the religious spirit.
But among the Puritans of the seventeenth century few
besides Milton, who was more than a Puritan, had that
coherent conception of human life and human culture
which recognises the Divine Spirit as present and operative in all the higher strivings of man. Scholarship,
knowledge, beauty, art appeared to Milton to be sacred
things ; means by which the "ruins of our first parents"
may be repaired ; means, therefore, by which we may
recover the image of God, and possess our souls in true
"virtue" in its widest sense, "which, being united to
the heavenly grace of faith, makes up the highest perfection."

Religious ideas and religious emotions, under the
influence of the Puritan habit of mind, seek to realise
themselves not in art, but, without any intervening
medium, in character, in conduct, in life. It is thus
that the gulf between sense and spirit is bridged : not
in marble or in colour is the invisible made visible, but
in action public and private—"ye are the temples of
the Holy Ghost." In an ordered life, an ordered house-

hold, an ordered commonwealth, according to the ideal of Puritanism, the spirit is to be incarnated. Let the praise which Virgil gives to the Roman people be translated into Evangelical meanings and it applies accurately enough to the Puritan ideal :

> " Others, I ween, to softer form shall mould
> The breathing bronze, shall win the living face
> From marble, plead the cause with happier skill,
> Map out the skies, and name each rising star.
> Roman ! be thine to rule the tribes of men ;
> These be thy arts ; the discipline of peace,
> To raise the fallen, to lay low the proud."

Through what was practical in the Puritan spirit, when seen at its highest, a noble ideality breaks forth. Its canticles of joy and thanksgiving, if heard meanly in the church or chapel, are heard nobly on the battlefield. If Puritanism did not fashion an Apollo with the bow or a Venus with the apple, it fashioned virile Englishmen.

" We that serve you," writes Cromwell to the Speaker of the Parliament immediately after the amazing victory of Dunbar, " beg of you not to own us—but God alone. We pray you own this people more and more; for they are the chariots and horsemen of Israel. Disown yourselves ;—but own your authority ; and improve it to curb the proud and the insolent, such as would disturb the tranquillity of England, though under what specious pretences soever. Relieve the oppressed, hear the groans of poor prisoners in England. Be pleased to reform the abuses of all professions :—and if there be any one that makes many poor to make a few rich, that suits not a Commonwealth. If He that strengthens your servants to fight, please to give you hearts to set upon these things, in order to His glory, and the glory of your Commonwealth,—besides the benefit England shall feel thereby, you shall shine forth to other nations, who shall emulate the glory of such a pattern, and through the power of God turn-in to the like."

Hæ tibi erunt artes.

And since the instinct of beauty works indefatigably in man, other arts may be looked for in time to grow upon the foundation of a life of righteousness. Continental, if not English, critics have recognised the fact that a Puritan strain has entered into much that is most characteristic in our literature. It is present in the "Faërie Queene" as well as in "Samson Agonistes"; in the "Vision of Sin," the "Palace of Art," the "Idylls of the King"; in the poetry of the author of "Dipsychus" and the poetry of the author of "Christmas Eve and Easter Day"; in the prose of "Sartor Resartus." And though Matthew Arnold said hard things, and some of them not without good reason, of English Puritanism, the son of Thomas Arnold could not escape from an hereditary influence; the Hellenic tendency in his poetry is constantly checked and controlled by the Hebraic tendency as it had been accepted and modified by the English mind.

III

Fortunately for Puritan art in the seventeenth century there was a great body of literature which was regarded as sacred. Puritanism may have suspected the literature of Greece and Rome; it may have cast some scorn upon the glory of Mediæval art; but it venerated the Old and

the New Testaments. Not with a fully enlightened
intelligence ; not, certainly, in the way of modern criticism ; but it found in the Bible a rule of life and a
storehouse of ideas ; it fed its passions with the passions
of the Hebrew singers and prophets; its imagination
adopted the antique garb, not in the manner of mumming
or disguising, but as proper for the uses of the day ; it
found in narrative and vision and parable a vehicle,
already sanctified, for the invisible ; it carried the genius
of the Scriptures into the very heart and soul of England.

The moral rigour and the anti-ceremonial spirit of
Puritanism in their immediate effects were unfavourable
to a generous development of art ; in their indirect
effects, quickening as they did the spiritual consciousness,
bracing character in a period of relaxation, and intensi-
fying the individual temper in matters of religion, they
were not wholly unfavourable. In the second half of
the seventeenth century, from amid the literature of
moral licence, when the imagination of the time, out-
wardly graceful and humane, was inwardly gross—

> " To vice industrious, but to nobler deeds
> Timorous and slothful "—

rise those creations to which the Puritan spirit contributed
—" Paradise Lost," " Paradise Regained," the "Pilgrim's
Progress " ; and, apart from the Puritan influence, such
works are inexplicable. The great intellectual fact of
the age was the scientific movement : it liberated the
minds of men from the bondage of a narrow Scripturalism ;
but who shall say that the large part which England
took in the scientific movement—itself a European
rather than an English phenomenon—was not aided by

the habit of the loins girt and by the lit lamp, by the seriousness of spirit, now transferred from Scripture and the moral world to external nature, which Puritanism had encouraged and sustained ? In Newton and his fellow inquirers of the Royal Society the seriousness of the Protestant Reformation was reunited with the exploring intellect of the Renaissance.

In the appalling loss of a living authority which should declare infallible doctrine, it was fortunate that men could in some degree steady themselves by the support of the infallible written Word. Puritanism helped the Protestant Reformation, in its more extreme developments, to define itself both in its weakness and its strength. The entire ecclesiastical polity was to be modelled on the Scriptures ; some thinkers desired to model on Biblical example the entire polity of the State. When Milton would justify the deposition and condemnation of the King, he proves from Scripture that kings and magistrates hold their authority from the people : " David first made a covenant with the elders of Israel, and so was by them anointed king; Jehoida the priest, making Jehoash king, established a covenant between him and the people. When Roboam, at his coming to the crown, rejected those conditions which the Israelites brought him, they answer him, ' What portion have we in David, or inheritance in the son of Jesse ? See to thine own house, David.' " It was the unqualified reference of all forms of religious order and duty to Scripture that Hooker set himself to oppose and to correct. Every rite or ceremony, every garment worn, unless it could be justified by a precedent or a text of the

Bible, was condemned as unwarrantable. The persuasions of the Oxford and Cambridge Professors of Divinity, who happened to be two foreigners, Peter Martyr and Bucer, were needed to induce Hooper to wear his consecration robes ; once he preached in the questionable garb, and never again. The ring in marriage, the cross at baptism, the posture at Holy Communion, the music of organ-pipes, were causes of serious doubts and scruples. Somewhat later the controversy turned chiefly upon matters of Church government and discipline ; but still the central question was the same—Could this or that be justified by the authority of Scripture ? Finally, in the reign of James I., when the Arminian High - churchmen became dominant in the Anglican communion, the questions grew of deeper import — they concerned doctrine, which Hooker himself would have determined alone by the written Word.

A new race of schoolmen—Protestant schoolmen of the Reformation — arose. Elaborate systems of theology were constructed, and the substance of those of the school of Calvin may still be found operative in the Westminster Confession of Faith and the Longer and Shorter Catechisms. An admirable intellectual gymnastic they afford to a certain class of minds, and one who has mastered even his Shorter Catechism will have all the advantages (and the disadvantages) which attend a resolute effort to interpret the whole of things as a coherent scheme. The Holy Scriptures were, of course, accepted as the sole basis of the faith. An attempt was made to define the

nature of God, to set forth His attributes ; and the
body of Calvinistic theology, with the precise plan
of salvation, was exactly laid down. All was as de-
finitely mapped out as the structure of the heavens
in the Ptolemaic astronomy. That sense of awe and
mystery derived from the Unknown and the Unknowable, in which some thinkers have found the
essence of religion, was present only in a subordinate
degree. Things the angels desire to look into might
be boldly scrutinised by the theologian, for were they
not revealed in the written Word ? The source of
religious emotion was not the unknown but the
known ; and this was methodically arranged so as to
present it with the utmost precision to the intellect.
But in what had been ascertained were many things
wonderful, many things capable of inspiring solemn
awe, the brightest hope, the most overwhelming terror.
God's eternal decree by which, for the manifestation
of His glory, some men are predestined to everlasting
life and others are foreordained to everlasting death,
the creation of the world out of nothing, the constant, wise and holy providence of the Creator over
His work, man's fall, God's covenant with the human
race, the inheritance of sin, the mediation of Christ,
the irresistible nature of grace, the effectual calling
and final perseverance of the saints, the endless joy
of heaven, the endless gnashing of teeth in hell—
these were themes for passionate contemplation, sources
of agony, sources of rapture. Undoubtedly the whole
scheme of belief, if imposing on some a burden which
they were not able to bear, was one which helped

to form certain eminent types of character, to regulate conduct, to prompt steadfast and heroic action. No believer could suppose that he lived in a world of chaos or blind chance. A just, intelligent, inflexible Ruler presided over the material world, over human society, over the course of individual lives. At the lowest the body of doctrine was a translation—in part, perhaps, a mistranslation—into supposed objective facts, of the monitions and premonitions, awful or blessed, of man's moral nature, with such additions and modifications as seemed to be required by the statements of revelation.

And as there were schoolmen of the Reformation who built up a huge fabric of doctrine, so there were Protestant moralists and casuists who drew out to the utmost detail a corresponding system of conduct. From the Puritan theologians, Perkins and Ames, the study of casuistry passed to the hands of Sanderson, Hall, and Jeremy Taylor. The " Christian Directory, or Sum of Practical Theology and Cases of Conscience," by Richard Baxter, passes from Christian ethics, or the private duties of Christians, to economics or family duties, and so proceeds to ecclesiastics, or Church duties, and Christian politics, or duties to our rulers and neighbours. The catalogue of duties and the catalogue of breaches of duty are elaborated with a minuteness which may lose something of the amplitude of a free and generous loyalty to good, but which undoubtedly exhibits conscience as presiding over every act of human life.

" After discussing thirty tongue-sins and twenty

questions for the conviction of drunkards; eighteen
necessary qualifications of lawful recreation; eighteen
sorts that are sinful; and twelve convincing questions
to those who plead for such pastimes; thirty-six
questions about contracts; twenty about buying and
selling; sixteen respecting theft; and one hundred
and seventy-four about matters ecclesiastical, he yet
regrets that the want of his library at the time
when he composed the work prevented him from enlarging his enumeration of cases." [1]

With the aid of those keen scenters, "Sayrus,
Fragosa, Roderigues, Tolet," the rat-hunt for sins
might have yielded better sport. The excessive inwardness of the Puritan spirit quickened the mental
eye for every detail that tended to moral good or
evil. The genius of Duty which carries in its head
the thirty tongue-sins and one hundred and seventy-
four questions concerning Church affairs may not be
exactly the Duty invoked in Wordsworth's ode:

> " Flowers laugh before thee in their beds,
> And fragrance in thy footing treads."

Nevertheless, in a time of careless living and declining
morals, the error of too scrupulous self-superintendence
is not the most grievous error.

IV

We know sufficiently through the caricatures of
dramatists and novelists the grotesque side of Puritan
morals and manners—the affectations of the precisian,

---

[1] Principal Tulloch in his study of Baxter; and Orme's "Life and
Writings of Baxter," ii. 175.

the scruples with regard to things innocent, the casuistry
by which self-indulgence was sanctified, the Hebraic
phraseology, the danger of moroseness of temper. Among
the various bodies of sectaries exploring their way with
little guidance, roused to all manner of extravagances of
feeling, interpreting the words of Scripture by an inner
light, intolerant in their rival orthodoxies, there was
ample material for a caricature. But among the Puritans
were not a few men and women who added to purity
of morals and the happiness of domestic affections,
guarded as sacred, the best graces of culture and refinement. The Puritan gentleman might surprise a nineteenth-century drawing-room by certain peculiarities of
manner and of speech, but he would not offend by
brutal licence. His temper might be grave rather than
buoyantly gay, but he would possess within certain
springs of happiness which do not sap the genuine joy
of human life. He might be a scholar, a lover of music,
a lover of letters. Cromwell's chaplain, Peter Sterry,
who was an adviser in the purchase by the State of books
from Ussher's collection, was a lover of the work of
Titian and Vandyke. We remember the early home of
Milton, the house of a London scrivener of Puritanic
faith and Puritanic habits, where the father would join
in madrigals of his own composing, and the boy, by his
father's desire and through his own passion for learning,
would remain till midnight busy with his poets of
Greece and Rome and his French and Italian studies.
It was of a Puritan divine, Thomas Young, that Milton
afterwards wrote : " First, under his guidance, I explored
the recesses of the Muses, and beheld the sacred green

spots of the cleft summit of Parnassus, and quaffed the
Pierian cups, and, Clio favouring me, thrice sprinkled
my joyous mouth with Castalian wine." We think of
the beautiful record of her husband's life written by
Lucy Hutchinson. This Puritan soldier, son of one who
also took the side of the Parliament, " was apt," so his
wife tells us, " for any bodily exercise ; . . . he could
dance admirably well, but neither in youth nor riper
years made any practice of it ; he had skill in fencing
such as became a gentleman ; he had a great love of
music, and often diverted himself with a viol, on which
he played masterly ; and he had an exact ear and judgment in other music ; . . . he had great judgment in
paintings, 'gravings, sculpture, and all liberal arts, and
had many curiosities of value in all kinds ; . . . he was
wonderfully neat, cleanly, and genteel in his habit, and
had a very good fancy in it ; but he left off very early
the wearing of anything that was costly, yet in his
plainest, negligent habit appeared very much a gentleman ; . . . his conversation was very pleasant, for he
was naturally cheerful, had a ready wit and apprehension ;
. . . everything that it was necessary for him to do he
did with delight, free and unconstrained."

" He was," writes his wife, " as kind a father, as dear
a brother, as good a master, as faithful a friend as the
world had."

Colonel Hutchinson, the regicide, was a member of the
first two Councils of the Commonwealth. It may at
first sight appear a strange inconsistency that the Puritan
party, possessed as many of its members truly were by a
spirit of inwardness, and looking as they did, to another

country, that is, an heavenly, should yet have taken a passionate interest in mundane affairs. There were doubtless material concerns which deeply moved them—unjust taxation, the exercise of arbitrary power in the State; there were ecclesiastical concerns—the offence of ceremonialism, the infringement of the claim to liberty of worship in the way their conscience dictated. But it is a mistake to suppose that such a faith as theirs should weaken or impair activity in mundane affairs. Not through sacred symbol, not through the glories or the pomps of art was their faith to find an outward manifestation, but through conduct and public action. The belief that the order of the world is a divine order, that each man has his allotted part in maintaining it, that a great contention is in progress between the powers of darkness and of light, that the victory will be the Lord's, but through His human instruments, nerves the believer to put forth all his strength on behalf of what he holds to be the cause of his Supreme Ruler. The creed of Calvinism is called by Mr Froude a creed of intellectual servitude, but he has hardly exaggerated the fact when he declares that it was able to inspire and sustain the bravest efforts ever made by man to break the yoke of unjust authority. In proof of his assertion he cites the names of William the Silent, Knox, Andrew Melville, the Regent Murray, Coligny, Cromwell, Milton. If obedience to the will of God be man's highest duty, a part of that duty must be to make the will of God prevail on earth, to widen the borders of light, and co-operate, as far as a human creature may, in driving back the edge of darkness. The Puritan had hitched his waggon to a star ; whether a star of bale or benison remained to be proved.

Here was something to counterbalance the inwardness of the Puritan spirit, something to maintain a just equipoise of character. And if in taking the Bible as their guide they often read into it their own meanings, often gave it passionate misinterpretations, often applied to modern life what was of transitory significance, still in the Bible they had a veritable manual of moral wisdom and high common sense. It has been truly said that from the Bible the noblest minds among the Puritans imbibed not merely the great enthusiasm which it expresses, but also the strong practical sagacity and broad right-mindedness of which it is the emphatic teacher.[1] The passion for righteousness could ally itself with a spirit of prudent and patient opportunism. "If ever there was a man who suffered fools gladly, who sought to influence and persuade, and who was ready to get something tolerable done by consent rather than get something better done by forcing it on unwilling minds, that man was Cromwell."[2]

We have seen some of the formative influences from which a Puritan literature might arise. But we must bear in mind the fact that Puritanism was only for a short time triumphant. Except for a few years, Puritanism was militant or Puritanism was depressed. We can only conjecture whether a great literature would have developed on a Puritan basis if the

[1] J. L. Sanford, "Studies and Illustrations of the Great Rebellion," p. 81.
[2] S. R. Gardiner, "Cromwell's Place in History," p. 48.

Commonwealth had existed even for one entire generation ; we can only surmise on the question whether
righteousness would have flowered in beauty and severity
have worn the garments of joy. Mantegna's "Triumph
of Cæsar" and Raphael's cartoons (which Charles II.
was ready to sell) were saved for the nation by
Cromwell. Two organs stood in the great hall at
Hampton Court, and a pupil of Orlando Gibbons was
the Protector's organist. At the wedding-feast of the
Protector's daughter Frances forty-eight violins dis-
coursed excellent music, and the company frolicked
and danced until five o'clock of the November morning.
For his daughter Mary's marriage Andrew Marvell
furnished songs, a pastoral in which Oliver was introduced as Menalcas, and a dialogue between Endymion
and Cynthia, representing the bridegroom and the
bride. Modest as were Cromwell's ways of private
living, in State ceremonial, as Protector of England, he
could be magnificent.[1] Although Mrs Mary Netheway
implored that the bronze statues of Venus and Cleopatra
and the marble statues of Adonis and Apollo in the
garden at Hampton Court, "monsters which are set
up in Privy Gardens," might be demolished, there the
monsters remained. But the strife of parties during
the Commonwealth made it inevitable that the graver
mind of England should in the main occupy itself with
practical work of immediate importance. Theological
folios and political pamphlets may now slumber on

[1] See Mr Frith's article, "The Court of Cromwell," in the *Cornhill
Magazine*, Sept. 1897 ; and Mr St Loe Strachey's "From Grave to Gay,"
pp. 152, 153.

dusty shelves, but some of these in their day were instinct with fire; they were living forces helping to form character, to regulate conduct, to shape public action. If few of them deserve the name of literature, they yet stirred the soil from which a literature might have sprung. And certain works remain to us which serve as more than an indication of the possibilities of a Puritan literature. We have the impassioned exhortations of "The Saints' Rest"; we have the epic of seventeenth-century theology—the poems of the loss of Paradise by man and its recovery by a greater Man; we have the Puritan drama of God's afflicted champion obtaining victory by obedience unto death; we have the story, ardent, tender, humorous, of the Pilgrims' wayfaring from the City of Destruction to the Celestial City. And what else in the literature of the period can outweigh these gifts of Puritan passion and Puritan faith?

V

In the Puritan inwardness of spirit, in its vivid realisation of the unseen, if only these could find a suitable medium of representation and vehicle of expression, lay important possibilities for literature. If Hellenism served to broaden, Hebraism served to deepen the national consciousness of England. The inward drama of the spiritual life became more tragically earnest; its lyrical cries of hope and fear, of anguish and joy, became more poignant. God and the soul were the chief actors in the drama, but for the Puritan imagination a world of magic lay around the human

soul—blessed angels, demons of the pit, special inter-
positions of Providence, miraculous words of Scripture,
preternatural voices echoing in the heart. In the
introspective habit which scrutinised and searched the
soul for intimations of loss or gain there were grave
dangers ; it might pass into a diseased fascination ; but
it might also be a great discipline ; it might discover
a world of marvellous phenomena hidden from those
accustomed only to turn the eye outward on the world
of action.

Again, in the doctrine of Puritanism was a body of
inspiring ideas, an inspiring conception of the life of
man, which humbled and at the same time exalted.
He was the creature of a passing moment, yet a spirit
moving in a world at present only realised in part
and formed for eternity. Already his destiny was
sealed, yet—appalling mystery—free and responsible,
he became his own doomsman. As this conception was
made real and living, human existence—the existence
even of the meanest child of earth—grew in dignity,
since to it belonged the most awful, the most blessed
issues. Our threescore years and ten—an atom in
eternity— acquired a grandeur as the moment of a
solemn test and trial. Everything that seems to careless eyes trivial and accidental was in truth part of
a divine order ; but this order included the sudden
interventions of the law-maker. Man, mysteriously
endowed with free will, was no estray wandering in a
realm of chance ; rather was he a subject, loyal or
disloyal, of a stern and beneficent Ruler. He had his
appointed station in a vast warfare, his appointed place

in a mighty scheme. Fallen, indeed, he was, bound
under sin by the transgression of our first parents, condemned by the law, a defaulter under the covenant of
works ; but a door of escape, a radiant avenue of hope,
had been opened under a covenant of grace. Through
disobedience Adam fell : through perfect obedience to
the divine will a way of salvation had been wrought
out. In these ideas, not all peculiar to Puritanism, but
realised by the Puritan temper with peculiar intensity,
Milton found the themes for his epic of the Fall and his
epic of Redemption. They were no mere part of a
theological system ; they entered profoundly into life
and into literature.

But obedience and loyalty to the divine will does not
consist solely in passive submission ; they breathe forth
or flame forth in an active co-operancy with that will.
One who has himself become a part of the heavenly
order in the world cannot but seek to extend that order
into regions not yet reclaimed. And this he may strive
to do in either of two ways—by appeals to the individual souls of men, or by action in the social and
political sphere. Hence arose a literature of passionate
exhortation, the pleadings of the preachers ; hence also
arose the zeal and energy of public reform, which in
literature found expression in such works as the prose
writings of Milton. Of the hortatory literature, in
which meditation passes naturally into appeal, " The
Saints' Rest " is a conspicuous example. It was written,
as Baxter himself tells us, for his own use, in the time
of his languishment, when God took him from all public employment. He was ill, and alone in the country,

given over by the physicians to death. "I began," he writes, "to contemplate more seriously the everlasting rest, which I apprehended myself to be on the borders of." "To despise earth," he said, "is easy to me, but not so easy to be acquainted and conversant in heaven."[1] But it was impossible for Baxter to meditate for himself alone ; he was nothing if not a preacher, and he preached from what he believed to be his dying solitude. He pleads with men as if tears were in his voice. In the "Epistle to the Reader" prefixed to his "Poetical Fragments" (1681), Baxter justifies passion and sense against the invasion of Rationalism, which already was opening a way for the spirit of the eighteenth century :

"I am assured that God made not passion in vain ; and that reason is a sleepy, half-useless thing, till some passion excite it. . . . I confess, when God awakeneth in me those passions which I account rational and holy, I am so far from condemning them, that I think I was half a fool before, and have small comfort in sleepy reason. Lay by all the passionate part of love and joy, and it will be hard to have any pleasant thoughts of Heaven. In short, I am an enemy of their philosophy that vilify sense. . . . The Scripture that saith of God that He is life and light, saith also that He is love, and love is complacence, and complacence is joy; and to say God is infinite, essential love and joy is a better notion than, with Cartesians and Cocceians, to say that God

---

[1] These words must have been in Wordsworth's mind when he wrote in "The Excursion," Book IV. :
> " 'Tis, by comparison, an easy task
> Earth to despise ; but to converse with heaven—
> This is not easy."

and angels and spirits are but a thought or an idea. What is Heaven to us if there be no love and joy ? "

The Epistle from which these words are quoted is solemnly dated " London, at the Door of Eternity."

For the maintenance of high passion the habit of moral restraint is in the long run more favourable than the habit of moral relaxation. It may take the lifetime of a whole generation to produce the consequences in literature and art of base morals, but no law is more inevitable than that what is sown must in due time be reaped. The worst effect of a corrupt society upon literature is not, perhaps, the deadness of the senses to what is gross and repulsive ; this indeed comes gradually and inevitably, but the odour of the sink warns off any passer-by who has breathed clean air. Far more danger- ous is the false homage of baseness to a virtue which, in the deadness of true passion, it has lost the very power of conceiving aright ; the substitution of factitious, romantic, overstrained heroics for the plain and modest realities of righteous living. It is not the facile licen- tiousness of the plays of Fletcher that chiefly offends a reader ; the lascivious imagination of puberty, it is true, in the lapse of time will necessarily lose its gay colours and youthful vivacity, and will sink into the cynical brutality of Wycherley. But we are more offended by the spurious moral ideality of Fletcher, by his fantastic code of heroism, his extravagant gallantries, his indecent celebration of chastity. And Fletcher's spurious ideality prepared the way for the high-pitched heroics of certain Restoration dramas. The one indicates the decline, the other indicates the death of genuine passion. The

Puritan regard for righteousness in its lower forms was injurious to literature and art as inducing a dull didactic tendency. Wither has shown how it is possible to be exceedingly moral and excessively dull during many pages. In its higher forms the passion for righteousness tempers an instrument for breathing music of the Dorian mode. It was the great Puritan poet who wrote those well-known words, which, if rightly interpreted, convey an ascertained law of art :

"I was confirmed in this opinion that he who would not be frustrate of his hope to write well hereafter in laudable things ought himself to be a true poem ; that is, a composition and pattern of the best and honourablest things ; not presuming to sing high praises of heroic men or famous cities, unless he have in himself the experience and the practice of all that which is praiseworthy."

Milton does not mean that great art will be, in the common meaning of the word, didactic art. He means that heroic music can be adequately breathed only through a noble instrument. He means that there is a music which teaches nothing, but by its very tones can "raise to height of noblest temper," can "breathe deliberate valour," can "mitigate and swage with solemn touches troubled thoughts," and that the faculty for producing such music diminishes in proportion to the loss of such noblest temper by the musician himself. In a corrupt society the art of the Dorian and the Phrygian modes is lost, or is heard only from some survivor of a more strenuous age. And when they are lost art recovers itself commonly, not by a great enthusiasm, but by good sense, modera-

tion, and those common decencies which are found to
be needful for the very existence of human society.

Among the factors determining the character of a
Puritan literature must be reckoned the popular
sympathies which informed the movement for ecclesiastical and civil reform.   Milton, indeed, its chief
representative—although he, like Hooker, would de-
rive all political authority from the consent of the
people—was essentially aristocratical in his intellect,
and became the advocate of an oligarchy not of birth
but of merit.   He honoured heroic individuals, a
Christ in the wilderness, a Samson in captivity, a
Fairfax at the siege, a Cromwell in the council and
in the field; he could speak more scornfully than
Burke ever spoke of the wayward and variable multitude.   But, in a large way, Puritanism was a movement of the people, with not a few leaders from
among the aristocracy.   For a time its temper was
high and courageous, hopeful and even audacious in
new experiments.   Its religious spirit tended to
abolish or to abate social distinctions: all mortal
men were alike sinners before God, and, peer or
peasant, if true members of the congregation, were
equally saints.   Its favoured ecclesiastical schemes
and platforms were of a democratic kind.   Its political ideal was not a loose and incoherent democracy;
it aimed at vigour in government, and was willing to
confer immense powers upon chosen individuals; but
its political culmination was a Republic.   A literature
informed by popular sympathies may lose much that
is of high worth; it may, on the other hand, gain

some things—a homely strength, a genial warmth, a respect for man as man, a breadth of human interest, a humour that is not supercilious, a pity which is not condescending. Some of these qualities are manifest in both Parts, perhaps especially in the Second Part, of the "Pilgrim's Progress."

With these various possibilities for literature, Puritanism still felt the difficulty of mediating, as art should mediate, between the spiritual and the material, the difficulty of finding an imaginative body for theological dogma and the deepest experiences of the soul. It was partly solved by Milton with the aid of an imagination educated among classical models. The influence of the Renaissance came to aid him in his dealing with the Puritan abstractions. But the solution was not absolutely successful. There is still a portion of theological doctrine in "Paradise Lost" which is not vitalised for the imagination, and remains doctrinaire. It is true that God the Father and His Son discuss the scheme of salvation too much in the manner of school-divines. The Hebraic ideas and the classical garb do not always perfectly correspond each with the other. We cannot assert that Milton entirely succeeded in finding an imaginative vehicle to convey his Puritan conceptions. Bunyan, perhaps, succeeded better; but in allegory the idea has a certain detachment from its body of sense; it dwells within, but it is never indissolubly incorporated. In prose Bunyan could drop more easily than Milton could in his verse from narrative to the exposition of doctrine. The pilgrims in their talk by the way are as frankly theological or

C

hortatory as if they were worthy Nonconformists of real life crossing the fields from Elstow to Bedford. Bunyan, as compared with Milton, had no slight artistic advantage in the fact that his starting-point was a personal experience. What he beheld in vision he had known in a cruder form as a fragment of actual life. Perhaps it was also an advantage that, being unlearned in the culture of Greece and Rome, he drew no robe of Hellenism around his Hebraic ideas. The "Pilgrim's Progress" is derived from only one of the two antiquities; it is the prose-epic of English Hebraism.

SIR THOMAS BROWNE

I

" ALL divinity," writes Donne in one of his poems,
" is love or wonder." If we accept Donne's definition
we must think of Sir Thomas Browne as among the
greatest of English divines. Contemplative charity ;
illuminated wonder — these were his possessions, or
rather by these he was possessed. With nothing
unsocial or inhospitable in his disposition, these made
him in his best moments a solitary—Thomas Browne,
" the only one." In an age of violence and strife, he
moved serenely, or abode in the cloudy tabernacle of
his own mind. In an age when religious ceremonial
was strenuously enforced for the sake of uniformity, he
valued ceremony—of diverse kinds—for its emotional
or imaginative suggestions. In an age when dogma
hardened into systems, and the sense of mystery departed, as all truth was made definite in schemes and
plans dovetailed together from Scripture by the schoolmen of Protestantism, he gazed into what Bishop
Berkeley described as the arcane part of divine wisdom,
and amid the humblest circumstance of our daily lives
he discovered something shadowy and arcane. While
others were alarmed by the terrors of religion, he was
rapt by its harmonies of beauty and of wonder.

In the affairs of state Browne's sympathies were

with the Royalist cause; in matters ecclesiastical he
professed himself a loyal son of the English Church.
Yet in truth he stands somewhat apart from the movements of his own day. Or if we are to connect him
with any of the public interests of the seventeenth
century, it must be with the research for scientific
truth. The great scientific movement of the period
which followed the Restoration was in the hands of
a younger generation than that of Browne. His
position was between the old view of the world and
the new. The fabulous natural history, the popular
folk-lore, the fictions of geographical speculation, the
mediæval legends preserved in pictures, the strange
Rabbinical interpretations of Scripture interested his
imagination ; they had the support of antiquity and
of authority ; they led him into a curious labyrinth ;
they made him, as he says, a wanderer in " the America
and untravelled parts of truth " ; and such wanderings
in the virgin continent pleased him. He could indulge a scholarly scepticism without any apprehension
that in exposing popular errors he was diminishing
his territory of wonder. To explode a vulgar delusion
was only to open an avenue for some finer apparition
of the marvellous. His imaginative faith discovered
under every roof of Norwich and in his own soul
mysteries more moving than the legends of the
basilisk, the phœnix, and the mandrake.

Apart from the confessions and betrayals of his
mind, we can form some acquaintance with Browne and
his surroundings. His life extended from 1605, the
year of the Gunpowder Plot, to the year 1682, when

Monmouth made his popular progress and Shaftesbury
retired to Holland. It was, amid all the national
struggle, a scholar's life of tranquillity ; when Fairfax
advanced to Oxford, and the King quitted the city
in disguise to place himself in the hands of the
Scottish commissioners, Browne published his folio
on Vulgar Errors ; in the year of the Protector's death,
when dangers threatened and the army plotted against
his feeble successor, Browne was discoursing ou the
sepulchral urns lately found in Norfolk, and on the
quincuncial plantations of the ancients.   By birth
a Londoner, he became an Oxford student, accompanied
his stepfather to Ireland on a visitation of military
defences, travelled in France and Italy, resided for
a time at Montpellier and again at Padua, returned
through Holland, and received his doctorate of medicine at Leyden.   The "Religio Medici" was surrepti-
tiously published when he was thirty-seven, and
Browne became famous.   At Norwich he practised
medicine during upwards of forty years ; in 1641
he married a lady of good family, and "of such
symmetrical proportion to her worthy husband," writes
his friend Whitefoot, "both in the graces of her
body and mind, that they seemed to come together
by a kind of natural magnetism."   With her he
lived happily for forty-one years ; she bore him twelve
children, of whom four survived their parents.   Browne
was the friend of John Evelyn, Sir William Dugdale,
and other distinguished persons whose interest in
science or in antiquities drew them towards him.   In
1671 he was knighted at Norwich by Charles II.

Eleven years later, after a short illness, he died on his seventy-seventh birthday.

Some minutes for Browne's life were set down at the request of his widow by his friend Whitefoot, the rector of Heigham. His complexion, and the hair, which fell curling upon his shoulders, were, says Whitefoot, "answerable to his name"; the hair was still auburn when in 1840 the coffin-lid was accidentally broken by the pick-axe of a workman in St Peter Mancroft. He was of moderate stature, neither meagre nor of disproportioned bulk. In dress he studied simplicity. He was by the habit of his mind introspective—"a singular observer of everything that belonged to himself"; yet at the same time he loved to explore for curious knowledge all the visible universe and the world of books, eagerly observed the stars, had a most exact acquaintance with the geography of the globe, and was a student of plants and flowers. Evelyn visited Norwich on the occasion when Browne received the honour of knighthood; he found the physician's house and garden "a paradise and cabinet of rarities," chosen with good judgment, "especially medals, books, plants, and natural things." So Browne balanced his introspective tendency with the study of nature and the world of past generations of mankind; indeed his scrutiny of the world of his own mind, the microcosm within, was a kind of objective observation; he explored his spirit as a singular fragment of nature, finding there the choicest rarities to add to his collection. Except in the passion of contemplation, the soaring or sinking in his meditative rapture, he knew no great disturbances of mood. " He had," Whitefoot tells us, "no despotical power over his affections and passions . . . but as large a political power over them as any stoick or man of his time. The strongest that were found in him, both of the irascible and concupiscible, were under the control of reason." The face familiar to us in the portrait of the Bodleian confirms his friend's statement ; its dominant expression is that of a calm and sweet reflectiveness. " Of admiration," says Whitefoot, and the word includes the idea of wonder, ". . . he had more, and less, than other men, upon the same account of his knowing more than others ; so that, though he met with many rarities, he admired them not so much as others do." Browne's faculty of imaginative wonder did, in fact, not cling to material objects ; a curiosity in his collection was in itself of small account ; it was precious chiefly as the starting-point of that sense of mystery which soon wandered forth on a flight of its own. He was never seen to be transported with mirth or dejected with sadness ; but a sensitive delicacy of feeling brought ever and anon a blush to his face like that of youth. His friend proceeds to speak of Sir Thomas Browne's liberality in everything except his time, of his devotion to study, of his acquaintance with classical and modern authors : " he was excellent company when he was at leisure, and expressed more light than heat in the temper of his brain." He could not be eager in dispute, when he gazed through the matters of controversy to something beyond them and remote, where all contention was lost in contemplative quietude or contemplative awe.

If we knew Sir Thomas Browne only through his
solitary musings and his ingenuities of learning we
might wonder what manner of man this hermit spirit
was in his home and among his children.   Happily a
considerable number of his letters remains with us.   No
one was a truer father and friend to his sons and
daughters.   Edward Browne, the elder of two sons
whom we meet in the correspondence, followed his
father's profession, and like his father travelled over
Europe.   He had inherited or acquired a curiosity for
various knowledge, in some respects like that of the
elder Browne; the element of genius, the passion of
contemplation was not transmitted to the son.   A
perfect friendship existed between the old and the
young physician.   On his continental wanderings
Edward Browne wrote frequently to Norwich, giving
his father such remarkable scraps of information as
he knew would be welcome, and assuring the modest
student of an English provincial city that his fame
was great throughout Europe.   The information was in
general connected with science or with scholarship, but,
knowing as he did, Sir Thomas's mingled credulity and
scepticism, he sometimes ventured to report, in a spirit
of doubt, certain supernatural marvels.   He has been
assured that the great sorceress of Bohemia, Libussa,
had foretold many things concerning the mines of
Cottenberg, but for his own part he believes little in
such matters.   " In the mines of Brunswick is reported
to be a spirit; and another at the tin mine at Slacken-
wald in the shape of a monk, which strikes the miners,
singeth, playeth on the bagpipe, and many such tricks.

But I doubt if I go thither I should find them as vain
as Montparion's drum." When Edward Browne, distinguished as a London physician, delivered medical
lectures at Surgeons' Hall, his father gladly advised
and assisted him; his sister Betty, who was skilled
with her pencil, made drawings of the kidney and
heart of a *vitulus marinus* or seal; Dame Dorothy,
his mother, considerate of creature comforts, sent him
the receipt for orange cakes. Sir Thomas cautions
his son against the error of undue modesty, the error of
hiding his talents; exhorts him to take with him to
church a Greek Testament or the Septuagint, so that
he may learn two good things together; and on the
occasion of his marriage recommends a wise frugality, a
prudent disposal of his money, the choice of a good
house, and of apparel moderately rich.

The second boy, named after his father, was all that
a gallant English boy should be. Had he lived, he
might have been one of England's great sea-captains,
for assuredly he was of the same breed as theirs. Did
he inherit his joy in action from Dame Dorothy Browne?
Entirely unlike his father in temperament as he was,
the relations between the two were delightful in their
cordiality. At the age of fourteen young Thomas
Browne was so far trusted to his own care that he
travelled in France without a companion or attendant.
He entered the Royal Navy in 1664, took part in the
Dutch war, and received such commendations for his
courage, skill, and generous temper as highly delighted
his father. He thought lovingly of the Norwich
household, and was careful that his old pensioner, John

More, a scavenger and a centenarian, received his
weekly allowance. He was all on fire when a "grand
action" was in prospect, longing extremely for that
thundering day. "It is impossible," he writes, "to
express unto another how a smart sea-fight elevates the
spirits of a man, and makes him despise all dangers."
At Bergen the dying gunner Blanchot left his boy in
Browne's care, and great was his joy on obtaining a
pension for Will. His own pieces of eight were always
ready for the aid of sailors whose pay was in arrears.
"While I have a penny I cannot but relieve them of
whose fidelity and valour I can give so good testimonie."
His father writes to "honest Tom" with an exultant
pride: "God hath given you a stout but a generous
and merciful heart withal, and in all your life you
could never behold any person in misery but with
compassion and relief; which hath been notable in
you from a child." The heroic lad was like his father
a lover of learned studies. He read the "noble
straynes" of Lucan while his ship lay in Plymouth
Sound. It pleased his father that Tom was "not only
Marti but *Mercurio*," and had found time at sea not
only to practise his violin and his foils, but to read
divers books, especially "Homer and Juvenal with
Lubine's notes." The only danger the elderly physician
feared was from his boy's desperate courage. He had
instructed his young navigator in Aristotle's definition
of fortitude; *laborare* is well, but *tolerare* is no less a
duty. Tom should consider the arguments against
blowing up his ship and her crew in extremity; to be
made prisoner at overpowering odds is no disparage-

ment; let him remember the examples thereof, even of the worthier commanders, in his beloved Plutarch. In the summer of 1667 the name of young Thomas Browne disappears from the household chronicles, and from a later letter we learn that his gallantry and generosity had passed away from earth. Another Tom —the son of Edward Browne—"little Tommy," came to cheer his grandfather's elder days. Like a good boy he chose Dame Dorothy and his Aunt Betty for valentines; he came home laden with presents from the fair; sometimes he was taken to see a play; and if "begging books and reading of them" is a promise of scholarship, Tom gave early pledges that he would be a man of learning. The records of a happy home, over which the wisdom and gracious temper of Sir Thomas Browne presided, are of worth as throwing light upon his character; his curious erudition and retired speculations did not sequester him from the beloved humanities of the hearth.

II

The *Religio Medici* was written about 1635, when Browne, having returned from his continental wanderings, was living near Halifax, before he settled at Norwich. It was not intended for publication, being a "private exercise," a monologue directed to himself. He wrote with what seemed to him the disadvantage of absence from a library, and hence the book is rather a meditative overflow than like other writings of Browne, a piece of architectural construction into which the marble, brick, and rubble of erudition are laboriously built. Browne did not aim at defining and establishing a four-square system of theology ; there were theological systems enough, and more than enough; nor did he plead with the soul and seek to incite new fervours of piety. The " Religio Medici" is rather of the nature of a philosophic poem, the expression of an unique mind and its musical moods, a mind occupied with itself, and with external things as beheld in its own magic mirror, a series of lyrical confessions, in which philosophy is quickened by being made personal, and what is personal is refined and clarified by the infusion of philosophical ideas. As a transcript from its author's spirit at the age of thirty, it must not be taken in a literal sense ; he plays around his own mind, and discerning a germ of feeling here, a suggestion of thought there, he develops these and refashions the whole substance of his being in an ideal mould. In a period of religious excitement he discourses on religious subjects in a luminous serenity ; he is free from such personal terrors, such spasms of fear, such cold and hot fits as attacked Bunyan ; sometimes when he soars in his flights of imaginative faith, he soars so smoothly that we hardly discern the quiver of a wing.

Browne's manuscript pleased the friends to whom it was lent ; transcripts were made, and from one of these the text of the surreptitious edition of 1642 was obtained. In the following year, and in self-defence, he published a "true and full copy." A book, personal and intimate in its origin, had proved to be of interest to many readers. In truth, he had elevated the personal and historical self into an ideal self ; he had made this self the centre of

his universe of thought; he had not pronounced the
ponderous phrase, "relativity of human knowledge," but
he had found in a purified and idealised *ego* the interpretation of all things; the microcosm of his own frame
was that he cast his eye on; as for the macrocosm of
earth and planets and spheres, "I use it," he says, "but
like my globe, and turn it round sometimes for my
recreation." The essentials of his faith are accepted by
him on the authority of Scripture and of the Church;
these form a citadel from which he sallies forth on
adventures of the soul. Even as regards the beliefs
which he accepts on authority, he ranges at will, above
and around them, gazing into their mysteries until his
imagination and his feelings are kindled, so that the
statements of the Bible and the councils are for him
not so much statements as living powers, instinct with
spiritual fire and mysterious light.

When Browne wrote his "Religio Medici," Laud was
engaged in harrying the Puritan clergy; he hoped in
the end to secure unity within the Anglican communion,
and the first step towards this object was to enforce external uniformity. His method was to work from without inwards; let certain postures of the body of religion
be required (at the cost, if need be, of Christian or human
charity) and the soul of religion will by degrees adapt
itself to those postures. The "five busy points of Ar-
minius" occupied the minds of Churchmen who thought
more of dogma than of ceremony. Both the High Church
and the Puritan parties stood on their defence against
the counter-Reformation of the Roman communion. Amid
these conflicts there was a certain growing liberality of

thought, but though it drew its lines of toleration a little wider than had been customary, it drew them in the same manner of hard and exact precision. Browne's confession is not moulded on the articles of a creed, but is far more the exposition of a religious temper ; it concerns itself with the Christian graces ; the first Book of the " Religio Medici " deals with Faith and the Hope which attends on Faith ; the second Book considers the grace of Charity, and indicates certain extensions of charity little thought of in his own day.

As to ceremony, to which a spirit so humanly catholic as his could not be indifferent, he viewed it less as a symbolism of dogma than as a vehicle of religious emotion. His tolerance was a form not of intellectual comprehension but of human sympathy ; through the diversities of creeds he felt rather than argued his way to the deep communities of religious sentiment. He declares himself a sworn subject of the Church of England, which, with its temperate wisdom and its seemly ordinances was, as it were, framed to his particular devotion ; but holy-water and crucifix, " dangerous to the common people," did not disturb his piety. A transcendentalist may be a ceremonialist, but he cannot attach supreme importance to any particular set of forms ; wherever the spirit dwells in form, he reads the meaning of the hieroglyph ; " I could never hear an Ave-Mary bell without an elevation ; . . . at a solemn procession I have wept abundantly." The common satires and invectives of the pulpit did not confirm his faith ; many persons, he thought, through an inconsiderate zeal for truth, had too rashly charged the troops of Error.

He had learnt by his own experiences that unauthorised opinions may lodge in certain brains that are naturally framed to receive them, and may fade away if they are not fixed and supported by opposition. He had held, as Milton afterwards held, that the soul perishes with the body, to be miraculously raised with it at the last day; it was an opinion natural to one who, as a physician, reflected much on the intimate connection between what is spiritual and what is material in man. He had believed in the final salvation of all men, and in the lawfulness of prayers for the dead ; if these were heresies, they were the indiscretions of charity, and, being neither discussed nor defended, they had passed away insensibly as his trust in the Divine wisdom had enlarged its bounds. As for the deeper mysteries in Divinity and "airy subtleties in religion," his mind moved among them as in its natural element. Argument lapsed away, and a sacred awe filled his spirit : " I love to lose myself in a mystery, to pursue my reason to an *O altitudo* ! " Miracles were superfluous for his faith ; he rejoiced that he believed and saw not. He loved to let his thoughts play at the utmost verge of human speculation, close to God's abyss, and if they threw themselves forward with closed eyes, he was assured that some angelical powers would bear them up in their hands—*Certum est, quia impossible est.* Above all, he stretched and confounded his intellect with the idea of God—a circle whose centre is everywhere and circumference nowhere ; he brooded on the thought of God's unsearchable wisdom and incomprehensible eternity—a duration which is " one permanent point, without succession, parts, flux, or division." The

wisdom of the Creator he sought to trace particularly in
His creatures—such is part of a physician's piety—and,
seeing in the visible world an image of the invisible, he
believed that in the study of nature he was in truth
deciphering the supernatural :

> Give Thou my reason that instructive flight,
> Whose weary wings may on Thy hands still light.

Even in the nineteenth century the mystic and the
man of science may be united ; matter may disappear in
force or in motion ; and the scientific intellect may lose
itself in the darkness or the light of the unknown cause
of motion.   In Browne's day, with cruder conceptions
of science and a mysticism more emotional and imaginative, the combination had a shimmer of colour and of
fantastic strangeness that has passed away.

The study of final causes may be discredited by
modern science, or at least may have been driven to
indirect methods ; it was especially final causes, as
leading him through narrow channels to the ocean of
Divine wisdom, that Browne, as he says, groped after
in the works of nature.   This goodly habitation, the
earth, seemed thus to grow more luminous ; what was
opaque became transparent ; the quaint hieroglyphic of
the forms of beast and reptile and plant ceased to be
merely grotesque, as the hidden significance of each
emerged to view ; what was most trivial to the eye of
sense might give access to an abyss of intellectual light.
The flux and reflux of the sea, the waning and increase
of the Nile produced in the mind of Browne no deeper
sensation of awe than did the skill of the little citizens
of a hive.   Beauty and what is ignorantly termed

deformity alike served the ends of the supreme Artist. Art itself is only the perfection of nature, and nature, everywhere significant of ideas, is no other than the art of God.

Seeking in all directions for a Divine presence, unsatisfied until he had found spirit interpenetrating the whole framework of things, and filling all the interstices of existence, Browne loved to trace out the meanders of Providence in what men misname fortune. When the faculties of man—intellect, passions, and the energies of faith—are justly poised, when each aids the others, it is not difficult to commune with the soul of things. When we are ourselves harmonical, we give a spontaneous response to the harmonies of the world. The essentials of a spiritual creed naturally evolve themselves from a spirit at one with itself, while many questions merely curious, or worthy of consideration, but of no vital import, may remain unanswered. In his highest moments Browne—anticipating Wordsworth's mood—seemed to commune with some universal soul of Nature, but, whether this were so in reality or not, he could not doubt that some common spirit, which no man can properly call his own, plays in and through everyone of us like the breeze in an Eolian harp : " Whoever feels not the warm gale and gentle ventilation of this Spirit, though I feel his pulse, I dare not say he lives ; for truly, without this, to me there is no heat under the tropic, nor any light though_ I dwell in the body of the sun."

This wonderful universe becomes yet more wonderful when we know that it is tenanted by noble invisible

D

guests — tutelary angels of countries and provinces,
guardian angels of man, woman, and child ; while, on
the other hand, evil spirits roam abroad by permission,
infuse melancholy into susceptible minds, communicate
secrets of unholy knowledge, delude the credulous as
phantasms of the dead, and possess the unhappy bodies
of witches. Truly, a world full of wonders, where the
Genius of Middlesex may be superintending the crowd
that flows morning and evening through the city, or a
demon may be gazing at you through the eyes of some
Rose Cullender or Amy Duny.[1] Browne's imaginative
wonder is free from perturbation ; he could sooner pity
the great fallen archangel than be terrified by his
malice ; God's affable ministers approach us with no
waving of fiery swords or blast of doom, but rather on
gentle wings and with "courteous revelations."

A great scale of creatures ascends and descends from
the meanest worm to the loftiest of the cherubim ; in
this scale man has his place as a kind of amphibious
being, existing partly in a material and partly even
now in a superterrestrial sphere. Of death, therefore,
Browne had no fear ; are we not already half in the
sanctuary of spirits ? Only through a natural bashfulness, he thought with a certain remorse of the ignominy
of the body after its great change. Not by the vulgar
contemplation of cross bones and a skull is the true
theory of death to be attained. He meditated rather
on life than on that cloudy portal through which we
pass from life to life. If he mused on heaven, no

[1] The names of those unhappy women whom Sir T. Browne's evidence
in 1664 helped to send to execution on a charge of witchcraft.

Apocalyptic dream came to him of emeralds, chrysolites, and streets of paven gold; he looked within to those highest moments when the boundless appetite of the spirit seems to be satisfied : " The soul of man may be in heaven anywhere, even within the limits of his proper body." Fixing his contemplations on such attainments and foretastes of joy, he had little regard for those terrors of hell which filled the imagination of so many of his contemporaries ; gross fancies of corporal torture by fire did not afflict him ; the hell which he sometimes seemed to discover lay, like heaven, within his own heart : " Lucifer keeps his court in my breast, Legion is revived in me." Such thoughts, however, were quickly encountered by thoughts of the abyss of God's mercies, and even judgments put on the countenance of mercies. He was not the master of his own destiny; that was provided for by a higher Power ; his future had been all determined for him before the world was : " Thus was I dead before I was alive ; though my grave be England, my dying place was Paradise, and Eve miscarried of me before she conceived of Cain." And so, with a flight of the intellect and imagination towards eternity and the Divine will, Browne's confession of faith attains a resting-place, and settles there in a calm of wonder and of love.

III

The second part of the " Religio Medici " considers the grace of charity, without which faith is a mere notion. In a poem of Cardinal Newman's a warning is uttered against the easy dreams of an otiose ami-

ability; true love has rigour at its heart; hatred
and zeal and fear are its awful consorts and companions. In Browne's day zeal was not lacking in
either of the contending religious parties; the zeal
of Laud was encountered by the zeal of Laud's opponents; Browne distrusted the piety of fiery indignation against the alleged enemies of heaven: "no
man can justly censure or condemn another, because
indeed no man truly knows another." Which of us,
indeed, truly knows himself? Perhaps, after all, a
natural disinclination to unreasonable repugnances and
aversions is favourable to the growth of that plant
that springs from no mortal soil—divine charity. True
charity is not a weak commiseration for our fellows;
it is part of the energy of our love of God. But
petty instincts of hostility to any fragments of God's
world—to beast, or reptile or plant—do not predispose
us to the reception of His highest grace. Browne
has pleasure in thinking that he is not palisadoed
with the sharp stakes of prejudice or bastioned in
idiosyncrasy, but lies open to every diversity of enjoyment: "I have no antipathy, or rather idiosyncrasy, in diet, humour, air, anything. . . . I could
digest a salad gathered in a churchyard as well as
in a garden. I cannot start at the presence of a
serpent, scorpion, lizard, or salamander"—why should
he, who chose rather to decipher these odd hieroglyphs
of God?—"at the sight of a toad or viper I find
in me no desire to take up a stone to destroy them."
If there was anything which raised his scorn, it was
that disorganised rabble — no true people — which

Burke afterwards named " the swinish multitude," a hydra-headed beast, humanity forfeiting through madness and impiety, its true prerogative; but his disdain was not a class-feeling, an aristocratic insolence towards those rude mechanicals, at whose mingled folly and shrewd sense Shakespeare smiled; he discovered his rabble among the gentry also, plebeian heads, however dignified by rank or birth. Differences of opinion, difference of race or nationality he could hardly conceive of as alienating men from one another. There were but differences of degree in his universal charity; God, his country, his friends he embraced as his closest kin; and after them all those his fellows to whom he could render any human service.

At thirty years of age Browne had not yet felt that " natural magnetism " which afterwards drew him to Mistress Dorothy Mileham. The fascination of ideas had preserved him from the passion for any creature of flesh and blood. Not, indeed, that he who regarded a toad or salamander without hostility could be "averse from that sweet sex"; rather he was naturally amorous of all that is beautiful. But the harmony which he saw in the marriage-union reached him, entered into him, became a part of himself in other delightful ways, and ways less cumbered with material interests; it ravished him in the organ tones and the voices of a church; " even that tavern-music, which makes one man merry, another mad, strikes in me a deep fit of devotion, and a profound contemplation of the First Composer." We may suppose that when Thomas Browne pleaded his cause with Mistress Mileham in some pleached arbour of the Burlingham garden, he represented to her that he affected all harmony, and that to him the harmonical composition of her soul was an hieroglyphical and shadowed lesson of the whole world.

It was, in fact, in this noble manner that Browne conceived the art of music, rather as a disciple of Plato or a foreseer of Beethoven than as a seventeenth - century lover of light airs and recollected terms arranged for the lute and youthful voices; he recognised in music the interpreter of nature and an ambassador of the divinity; the consonance of the microcosm of man's soul echoes with a music akin to that of the spheral concord. He feared by perturbations, even by indignations that might seem righteous, to disturb the inner harmony of the spirit, by which he was a part of the vast symphony of God. Yet how could he greatly mar that "undisturbed song of pure concent," when God's abyss of mercy encircled all his existence? "As for my life, it is a miracle of thirty years, which to relate were not a history but a piece of poetry, and would sound to common ears like a fable." "Surely," exclaimed Johnson in the spirit of eighteenth-century common sense, "a man may visit France and Italy, reside at Montpellier and Padua, and at last take his degree at Leyden, without anything miraculous." The standing miracle—as indeed Johnson remembered—is life itself, with that secret labyrinth of Providence which entangles and resolves the least remarkable of human stories. To Browne every soul of man was a fragment of the great wonder, and the humblest no less than the greatest: "There is surely a piece of Divinity in us, something that was before the elements, and owes no homage unto the sun." The progress of each ordinary day was to him miraculous—darkness and light, the mystery of sleep, the mystery of waking, the flight of thought, the flame of love, the harmony of the soul, the play of God in the human spirit. Browne was learned, and, according to the standards of his earlier days, a man of science; but erudition and science drop away when he contemplates the primary facts of the soul and of life; the mystic, on whom the scholar and the man of science had been engrafted, alone remains, and with the prayer of a mystic for the total subjugation or abolishment of self, his book concludes—"Thy will be done, even in my own undoing."

IV

Browne's type of mind, so curious in its research for recondite facts, so elusive of facts in its meditative climbings, is of rare occurrence, and among English writers of his day it was unique. He was sceptical of many things commonly believed; credulous of many things which others doubted. Chief among his gifts to us is that gift of genius—the quickening of our sense of awe and solemn wonder in presence of the familiar phenomena of daily life, in presence of the external world and the world of our own souls. Mr Theodore Watts-Dunton, in his article on Dante Rossetti contributed to the "Encyclopædia Britannica," has spoken of the

movement of recoil in literature from eighteenth-century
materialism as the Renascence of the spirit of wonder in
poetry and art, of which, he says, Rossetti became the
acknowledged protagonist. But the wonder derived from
romance is shallow or fragile compared with the wonder
in reality. A Blessed Damozel or a Rose Mary appears
as a pale and shadowy marvel of art-wizardry if set
beside a peasant woman nursing her infant at a cottage
door or an old man breaking stones by the roadside.
Pandora and Proserpina and Beata Beatrix are figures
of visionary power; but they evoke a sense of wonder
less large and sane than what we feel in view of Millet's
plain heroic sower casting his seed into the common clay.
The true protagonist of the nineteenth-century Renascence of wonder was neither Rossetti nor Coleridge, but
Wordsworth. And though Browne generalises rather
than individualises, though he troubles the simplicity of
feeling with paradox and with quaintness, something of
that same illumination which is part of the natural magic
of the " Highland Girl of Inversnaid " and of " Stepping
Westward " touches us as we read the eloquent periods
of the " Religio Medici "; we are startled out of the
dream of custom ; we look around on Mother Earth as if
we were her first-born and none had lived before us.

Browne's " Christian Morals " is of a much later date
than the " Religio Medici," and was not published until
after the writer's death. The " Religio Medici " is a
confession uttered in solitude, a meditation, sometimes
a rapt contemplation ; " Christian Morals " is didactic in
its purpose, a series of brief exhortations addressed to
others. It was in lonely musings that Browne attained

his clearest altitudes ; yet the " Christian Morals " contains not a few striking passages on which he has
impressed his characteristic sign manual. This, for
example, on the conquest of the passions :

" Make the quarrelling Lapithytes sleep, and Centaurs
within lie quiet. Chain up the unruly Legion in thy
breast ; lead thine own captivity captive, and be Cæsar
within thyself."

And this on the mystery of the divine nature :

" Where imitation [of God] can go no further, let
admiration step in, whereof there is no end in the wisest
of men. . . . Even the most winged thoughts fall at
the setting-out, and reach not the portal of Divinity."

And this metaphor declaring the course of the sins
named deadly :

" We are carried into the dark lake, like the Egyptian
river into the sea, by seven principal ostiaries."

And this beautiful word on the peace of submission :

" Guide not the hand of God, nor order the finger of
the Almighty unto thy will and pleasure ; but sit quiet
in the soft showers of Providence."

And this on the joyful close of life for one who has
escaped the sins of youth :

" He that hath not early suffered this shipwreck, and
in his younger days escaped this Charybdis, may make
a happy voyage, and not come in with black sails into
the port."

" Christian Morals," itself probably a tesselated arrangement from Browne's note-books, bears well to be represented by fragments. A few more sentences may be
added :

" Lose not the advantage of solitude, and the society
of thyself, nor be only content but delight to be alone
and single with Omnipresency.   He who is thus prepared, the day is not uneasy nor the night black unto
him.   Darkness may bound his eyes, not his imagination.
In his bed he may lie like Pompey and his sons in all
quarters of the earth, may speculate the universe, and
enjoy the whole world in the hermitage of himself."

" To enjoy true happiness we must travel into a very
far country, and even out of ourselves ; for the pearl we
seek for is not in the Indian but in the Empyrean ocean."

" [*Of one who has reached old age.*] Having been long
tossed in the ocean of this world, he will by that time
feel the indraught of another, unto which this seems but
preparatory, and without it of no high value."

With one more passage these citations may close—that
which brings the first part of " Christian Morals " to a
conclusion ; we may, if we please, indulge the fancy that
when Sir Thomas Browne described the " true heroick
English gentleman," he thought of what his own sailor
lad might have been had he fulfilled on earth the promise
of his boyhood.   " Where true fortitude dwells, loyalty,
bounty, friendship, and fidelity may be found.   A man
may confide in persons constituted for noble ends, who
dare do and suffer, and who have a hand to burn for
their country and their friend.   Small and creeping
things are the product of petty souls.   He is like to be
mistaken who makes choice of a covetous man for his
friend, or relieth upon the reed of narrow and poltroon
friendship.   Pitiful things are only to be found in the
cottages of such breasts but bright thoughts, clear deeds,

constancy, fidelity, bravery, and generous honesty are the gems of noble minds, wherein (to derogate from none) the true heroick English gentleman hath no peer."

V

" The Garden of Cyrus," first published three years before the Restoration, is the most conspicuous example of Browne's spider-like architecture of ingenious gossamer webs. To brush it away would be harsh ; to trace its reticulations is a bewilderment of the brain. In speaking of the doctrine of the Trinity in the " Religio Medici " Browne confesses that he had often admired the mystical way of Pythagoras and the secret magic of numbers. Before we of the present day can be caught in the meshes of his mystical mathematics, we must dismiss more of our intellectual sanity than is quite convenient. We are forced, for our own part, to regard the exposition of nature and art, and the mysteries of the universe in the light of the quincunx and the number five as a kind of game ; but the quincuncial game is somewhat laborious and is somewhat long. Browne had doubtless more than a half faith in his Pythagorism, but at the same time he had something of a sportsman's joy in hunting his prey through the heavens and the earth, until at length earth and heaven so thicken with quincuncial forms that the chase becomes a mystical battue. Only in the concluding page, which haunts the memories of all who have once read it, does Browne charm us into credulity ; and at that point he is prepared for sleep and oblivion of quinary arrangements : " To keep our eyes open longer were to act our Antipodes. The huntsmen are up in

America, and they are already past their first sleep in
Persia." An excellent and a poetic reason for moving
bedward—the wave of sleep is washing round the globe,
the tide that has ebbed from one hemisphere invades the
other, and should we not be in harmony with nature.[1]
The reader may, if he please, slumber also, and when
he awakes think that he has dreamed of floral and
starry quincunxes or is dreaming still, exclaiming with
Demetrius in Shakespeare's comedy—

> Are you sure
> That we are awake ?   It seems to me
> That yet we sleep, we dream.

And indeed the Puck that misleads night-wanderers
had some acquaintance with the learned physician of
Norwich.

Highly characteristic of its author is the "Letter
to a Friend upon the occasion of the death of his intimate friend," which was probably written immediately
after "Christian Morals," but remained unprinted until
1690. Some portions of the letter were conveyed
from "Christian Morals," which was still in manuscript,
to form an edifying close, so that the *memento mori*
might lead to a final "Think of living." The mystery
of death is always potent with Browne's imagination
and his familiarity as a physician with all its physical
details leads to that conjunction of definite fact with
visionary imaginings, which gave the two sides of
his genius their appropriate play. Already, when he

---

[1] Coleridge seems to see only the oddity in Browne's plea for sleep:
"Was there ever such a reason given before for going to bed at midnight ?"

wrote, the departed friend had been in the grave
some little time; he was already "no puny among
the mighty nations of the dead," to whose dark
society every hour adds a thousand. No dreams or
airy nuncios had announced to his correspondent their
common loss, and the physician takes up his pen
to make a full report of the case. The young sufferer,
whose disease was a consumptive wasting away, had
died in May, and when Browne, as his medical
adviser, had first visited him, he perceived at once
that the end was not very far off: "He was not
like to behold a grasshopper, much less to pluck
another fig." [1] The attenuated features—"I never
more lively beheld the starved characters of Dante
in any living face"—showed that fatal symptom of
assuming the aspect of elder kinsfolk. Change of
climate was useless for one on whom death had set
his broad arrow; the Morta, deity of fate, had impressed "her hard seal" upon his temples. But his
departure was soft, as if the rest of sleep had seized
him. With that noting of curiosities which was
characteristic of Browne, he observed that at the
hour of death the moon was in motion from the
meridian, "at which time an old Italian long ago
would persuade me that the greatest part of men
died." Some were of opinion that he would breathe
his last upon the approaching day of his nativity—
it was Browne's own case some years later—"the tail

---

[1] The grasshopper would have been a burden; the fig is perhaps
named because Hippocrates had observed that the time of the year is
mortal when the fig-leaf resembles a daw's claw.

of the snake returning into its mouth "; but he
lingered a little longer. The patient's female friends,
desiring some omen of life, were irrationally curious
to examine his dreams: " He was now past the
healthful dreams of the sun, moon, and stars, in their
clarity and proper courses. 'Twas too late to dream
of flying, of limpid fountains, smooth waters, white
vestments, and fruitful green trees." The sick man
dreamed of the dead; but to dream of the dead,
" so they appear not in dark habits and take nothing
away from us," is, as Hippocrates explains, of good
signification. As we read the letter we assist at the
bed-side of the unknown youth — one of many such
unknown—and see the light of his spirit shining
through the almost translucent frame, like the gleam-
ing of a lamp circled by porcelain. From one ignoble
infirmity of some who approach their end the sufferer
was wholly free — he had not grown self-absorbèd,
narrow-minded, or tenacious of the things of earth;
nor, though he felt for the world a " sober contempt,"
did he ever fall into a cynic's mood, understanding
well that for the very reason that the felicities of this
world do not satisfy the soul, we may accept them,
so to soften the stream of our lives. " To be dissolved
and be with Christ was his dying ditty," yet Browne
temperately adds that to be content with death may
be better than to desire it. His years were few;
but if we reckon up only our best days, a life of
many decades may be only a span-long, and thus youth
may have a longer term than old age. With such
consolations as these Browne communicates the mourn-

ful tidings, from which he passes on to those ethical and religious reflections that are also embodied in his " Christian Morals."

VI

No theme better fitted to evoke Browne's various powers can be imagined than that suggested by the discovery in Norfolk of certain sepulchral urns, several of small dimensions, one more capacious. The urns were in themselves objects of curiosity, which excited his interest as an antiquary and led him into paths of strange learning; higher mysteries of darkness and of light, of mortality and of immortality encompassed them. All the burial customs of mankind from the interment of Adam, perhaps near Damascus, perhaps on Mount Calvary, to the funeral rites of comparatively recent times are recited. Indian Brahmins, Chaldeans, Jews, Egyptians, Scythians, Parsees, Mussulmans, Christians, Greeks, Romans, Britons defile before us on their way to the pyre or to the tomb. But Browne was more than an antiquary. There was much virtue for his meditative passion and his imagination in these sad pitchers silently expressing the ruins of forgotten times, filled with ashes half-mortared to the sand and sides, and having some long roots of quich or dog's-grass wreathed about the bones. To which of the great nations of the dead did they belong? Who laid them in their silent retreat beneath the soil ? Did they contain the relics of warriors, or priests, or children, or lamented women ? Such questions gave his speculation pause, and then pushed it onward into

the obscure. Above these poor jars of human dust
rose the mysterious powers of Life, and Love, and
Death, rose the bright mystery of fire, rose Time
the shadow, and the deep illumination of Eternity.
Readers of Browne's "Hydriotaphia" are apt to pass
lightly over its antiquarian lore, and to dwell long
on the eloquence of its closing pages; but the curious
pillars of his structure support the cloudy vault; the
matter-of-fact details, lit ever and anon by some
gleam of romance, are needful as a basis for his impassioned contemplation. The material pomps and
ceremonies of death lead up to the sublime meditation
on its spiritual mystery; the long procession conducts
us to an altar of worship.

The Norfolk urns were discovered but a little way
below the surface of the soil. Time lightly conceals
the varieties of which it has a number without end
in the heavens and in the earth. Great and small are
brought together by the abstracting power of imagination. Wordsworth, watching a butterfly poised upon
a flower, finds a parallel for its motionless life in
breadth of frozen seas as motionless. Browne makes
a sudden transit from the handful of dust to new-found
stars and to that great antiquity, America, which lay
buried in an unexplored ocean for thousands of years.
In these rural urns of Norfolk no lamps, no sealed-up
oil or wine, no lachrymatories or tear-bottles were
found. Yet it was customary with the ancients to
burn or bury things of worth, "either as farewells unto
all pleasure or vain apprehension that the departed
might use them in the other world." Witness "the

gem or beryl-ring upon the finger of Cynthia, the
mistress of Propertius, when after her funeral pyre
her ghost appeared unto him "—so Browne loved to
light up the gloom with some touch of romantic
beauty or wonder. These vessels were composed of
unadorned clay, but Browne was unwilling to believe
that they entered their graves naked, without "the
old habit of flowers." Many fragments of skulls lay
close together; he speculates on the possibility of a
passionate attachment between some who would not
be separated even in their dust: "The ashes of
Domitian were mingled with those of Julia; of
Achilles with those of Patroclus. All urns contain not
single ashes; without confused burnings they affec-
tionately compounded their bones, passionately en-
deavouring to continue their living unions. And
when distance of death denied such conjunctions,
unsatisfied affections conceived some satisfaction to
be neighbours in the grave, to lie urn by urn, and
touch but in their *manes.*" To seek out such nobler
magic that sleeps in mortal relics is the way to quell
the diseased curiosity for that petty magic attributed
by sorcerers to the ashes of the dead. Highest magic
of all is the hope that dwells in them of resurrection
which, indeed, is the life of the grave and "sweetens
our habitation in the land of moles and pismires."

"In that 'Hydriotaphia,'" exclaimed Coleridge, "how
earthly, how redolent of graves and sepulchres is every
line ! . . . the gayest thing you shall meet with shall
be a silver nail or gilt *Anno Domini* from a perished
coffin top." It is not so; gaiety, indeed, and the grave

E

are only forced into companionship by insensibility or by the humour of fantastic melancholy, by Hamlet or by the rude churchyard knave. Sir Thomas Browne discovers love in kinship with grief, and life in an indissoluble alliance with death. He yields to the sublime attractions of the grave, finding there our finest memories and our highest hope. He thinks with tenderness of the rites of sorrow, and of their passion or their grace; how the mother wrapped the little bones in linen, and dried them in her bosom, " the first fostering part and place of their nourishment," or how sweet blossoms were strewn. In the requiem music and funeral chaunts he finds a symbolical expression of the harmony of the soul, which had departed to enjoy the primitive harmony of heaven, from whence it first descended. The supine position of the corpse is an emblem of the repose of profound sleep. The survivors sucked in the last breath of their expiring friends, through some Pythagorical opinion that the spirit passed from one body into another in the desire for endless union. Oil was poured upon the pyre to facilitate the ascension of the soul. " That in strewing their tombs the Romans affected the rose, the Greeks amaranthus and myrtle; that the funeral pyre con- sisted of sweet fuel, cypress, fir, larix, yew, and trees perpetually verdant, lay silent expressions of their surviving hopes." No criticism can be wider of the mark than that which describes the " Hydriotaphia " as merely redolent of graves.

His lore as an antiquary ended, Browne rises to that concluding chapter in which light contends with darkness and remains the victor. The opening sentence strikes a chord of majestic harmony : " Now since these dead bones have already outlasted the living ones of Methuselah, and in a yard underground and thin walls of clay, outworn all the strong and spacious buildings above it, and quietly rested under the drums and tramplings of three conquests, what prince can promise such diuturnity unto his relics ? " [1] With every appeal to the imagination and an organ-like solemnity of utterance Browne urges his central thought—that our memorials on earth must pass away as a dream : " Oblivion is not to be hired." Yet we shall not utterly perish. Having removed all hope of terrestrial immortality, Browne looks upward, and perceives the dawn of a deeper light than that of earth ; and this so glorifies human nature that it almost justifies the celebrations of the tomb : " Man is a noble animal, splendid in ashes, and pompous in the grave, solemnising nativities and deaths with equal lustre, nor omitting ceremonies of bravery in the infamy of his nature." Pyramids and obelisks are but " wild enormities," when judged by the Christian hope. The writer's sympathy with the passion

---

[1] De Quincey in commenting on the sentence enters into rivalry with Browne in the splendours of elaborate rhetoric : " What a melodious ascent," he writes, " as if a prelude to some impassioned requiem, breathing from the pomps of earth and from the sanctities of the grave ! What a *fluctus decumanus* of rhetoric ! Time expounded, not by generations or centuries, but by vast periods of conquests and dynasties ; by cycles of Pharaohs and Ptolemies, Antiochi and Arsacides ! And these vast successions of time distinguished and figured by the uproars which revolve at their inaugurations : by the drums and tramplings rolling overhead upon the chambers of forgotten dead—the trepidation of time and mortality vexing, at secular intervals, the everlasting sabbaths of the grave ! "

of religious mysticism carries him away; already some
on earth have known the transit from death to life and
the rapture of immortality : " If any have been so happy
as truly to understand Christian annihilation, . . . the
kiss of the spouse, gustation of God, and ingression into
the divine shadow, they have already had a handsome
anticipation of heaven." To one in whom there lives
such evidence of things unseen, monuments are vain :
" 'Tis all one to lie in St Innocent's churchyard as in
the sands of Egypt. Ready to be anything in the
ecstasy of being ever, and as content with six foot as
the *moles* of Adrianus."

Such is Sir Thomas Browne's stateliest prose-poem,
enriched with all curious learning, and passing from
erudition to wonder and to faith. Its poles are
mortality and immortality ; it moves from darkness to
light. The clods of the valley are sweet to the writer's
brooding imagination ; but above earth and its mourning
trains, and fall of tears, and requiems of lament, rises,
as it were, the illimitable heaven of a day in mid-
summer. Mortality is swallowed up in life.

It cannot be said that Browne contributed any idea
of capital importance to seventeenth-century thought;
he ascertained no new truth ; he confirmed no old truth
by an original dialectic. His gift has been one for the
emotions and the imagination ; he felt the wonder of
the world ; he widened the bounds of charity ; his
divinity is composed of these two elements—wonder
and love.

RICHARD HOOKER

I

THE Anglican position at the close of Elizabeth's reign is defined in the writings of Hooker; more than this, the best temper of English thought is exemplified in his work. The spirit of the Renaissance is brought into harmony by him with the spirit of the Reformation; he is serious, reverent, devout; with seriousness and reverence he does honour to human reason; a grave feeling for beauty moulds his elaborate periods; he can soar and circle aloft in a wide orbit, yet all the time he remains in living relation with concrete fact and the realities of human life; he is at once humanist and theologian.

Through Izaac Walton's delightful biography we are familiar with the man. Walton, with much seeming simplicity or naïveté of style, was an artist in his craft; he had formed a definite conception of what Hooker was, or what he ought to be for the purposes of biography. A great scholar and thinker, his greatness was to be enhanced by something like insignificance in his outward aspect. Not that he was in any sense really insignificant, but his exceeding meekness and humility, together with a bodily presence which was not impressive, are used by Walton's art to throw out his intellectual and moral greatness. Keble, in his edition

of Hooker's works, qualifies Walton's view by adding
that meekness and patience were by no means constitutional with Hooker: "Like Moses, to whom
Walton compares him, he was by nature extremely
sensitive, quick in feeling any sort of unfairness, and
thoroughly aware of his own power to chastise it; so
that his forbearance . . . must have been the result
of strong principle and unwearied self-control. Again,
Walton or his informants appear to have considered
Hooker as almost childishly ignorant of human nature
and of the ordinary business of life: whereas his writings throughout betray uncommon shrewdness and
quickness of observation, and a vein of the keenest
humour runs through them." We cannot quite be
brought even by an editor's enthusiasm to regard the
author of "The Laws of Ecclesiastical Polity" as an
Elizabethan humourist, but he was master, when he
pleased, of a certain restrained irony. Let us think of
him, among his fellow-divines of the Anglican communion, as the Elizabethan incarnation of that stranger
who in the days of the Oxford movement reappeared as
Newman's guest and lives for us in Newman's sonnet:

> Courteous he was and grave—so meek of mien
> It seem'd untrue, or told a purpose weak;
> Yet in the mood he could with aptness speak,
> Or with stern force, or show of feelings keen,
> Marking deep craft methought, or hidden pride:
> Then came a voice,—"Saint Paul is at thy side."

But Hooker's logic is less emotional than the true Saint
Paul's, and he never glows with as bright an ardour of
charity.

Hooker's complexion, says Walton,—and we must

attend to such hints of a rude physical psychology—
was sanguine with a mixture of choler; yet even in
youth his speech and movements were grave and deliberate. As a boy he was distinguished by the union
of a questioning intellect with habitual modesty and
" a serene quietness of nature." He was never, Walton
declares, known to be angry, or passionate, or extreme
in any of his desires ; he was never heard to repine or
dispute with Providence. No man, he would say, ever
repented him upon his death-bed of moderation, charity,
humility, obedience to authority, peace to mankind.
" There will come a time," wrote Hooker, " when three
words uttered with charity and meekness shall receive
a far more blessed reward than three thousand volumes
written with disdainful sharpness of wit." In reply to
the violence of a controversial adversary his word is
formidable in its moderation : "Your next argument
consists of railing and of reasons ; to your railing I say
nothing ; to your reasons I say what follows." Begging
to be removed from the Mastership of the Temple, " My
Lord," he wrote to the Archbishop, " when I lost the
freedom of my cell, which was my college, yet I found
some degree of it in my quiet country parsonage ; but
I am weary of the noise and oppositions of this place,
and indeed God and nature did not intend me for con-
tentions, but for study and quietness." His desire, he
says, was to keep himself in peace and privacy, to
behold God's blessing spring out of his mother earth,
and to eat his own bread without oppositions.

To conduct a campaign of controversy in the interests
of peace — it is a rare achievement ; to possess the

magnanimity which does not seek to score points
against an antagonist, which does not triumph in putting an opponent to shame—it is a high distinction.
The rage of theologians in the sixteenth and seventeenth centuries strikes our ear as terribly as that
hollow burst of bellowing "like bulls or rather lions"
which alarmed Shakespeare's conspirators on the enchanted island. Hooker was deeply concerned on
behalf of the cause which he had undertaken to
defend ; he gave his whole mind to the great debate ;
his love of peace was not a lethargic complacency or a
dull wooing of ease ; but he desired to bring his opponents, if possible, to an honourable surrender ; he saw
the questions in dispute in relation to first principles
on which an agreement might be possible, and which
made the personal passions of controversy dwindle ;
possessed by a profound reverence for order, he felt
that intemperance or breach of charity would ill become
one who attempted to expound the divine idea of order.

This magnanimous combatant in his quiet parsonage
at Canterbury was already famous. Scholars, as Walton
tells us, turned out of their way to see the man whose
life and learning were so much admired—no stately
personage to look on, but "an obscure, harmless man ;
a man in poor clothes, his loins usually girt in a coarse
gown or canonical coat ; of a mean stature, and stoop-
ing, and yet more lowly in the thoughts of his soul ;
his body worn out, not with age, but study and holy
mortifications." In the pulpit he was never vehement ;
he used no graceful gestures of the orator ; his dim eyes
remained, from first to last, fixed upon one spot ; "he

seemed to study as he spake "; his voice was grave and tranquil; "his style," says Fuller, "was long," that is, involved, "and pithy, drawing on a whole flock of several clauses before he came to the end of a sentence," so that to some hearers he seemed tedious and obscure. To the close of his life Hooker remained the student and the thinker. When during his last illness robbers plundered his house, the sick man's inquiry was, "Are my books and papers safe?" The property inherited by his wife and daughters, to the value of a thousand pounds, was in great part made up by his library. His friend Dr Saravia, standing by the bedside, asked what was now occupying his mind (for Hooker's face wore its contemplative aspect), "to which he replied that he was meditating the number and nature of angels, and their blessed obedience and order, without which peace could not be in heaven; and oh, that it might be so on earth!" In another of Walton's familiar records it is the humanist rather than the theologian who is presented; former pupils of Hooker visiting him found their master tending his small allotment of sheep, with a book—the "Odes of Horace"—in his hand. A contemporary of Shakespeare and Spenser and of that choir of singers who made tuneful the closing years of Elizabeth's reign, Hooker was no stranger, we are assured, "to the more light and airy parts of learning—as music and poetry."

The marriage into which Hooker unwisely allowed himself to be drawn was not fortunate, but Walton, to exalt his meek hero, seems to make the worst of what he had learnt by hearsay. The gravest charges that can be brought against Hooker's wife are that she perhaps allowed her Puritan friends to tamper with the papers entrusted to her—who was she to doubt their superior learning and wisdom ?—and that, after a fashion not without precedents in her day, she posted with speed to a second marriage. She was guilty, indeed, of the high crime and misdemeanour of calling upon Richard to rock the cradle. Richard could not have had a sweeter employment; he was precisely in the place assigned to him in the divine order of the universe, as rightly interpreted by Mistress Joan ; and while he lulled his infant daughter to sleep, Richard might appropriately have meditated on the number and the order of the Holy Innocents. The wife of an exalted scholar cannot always maintain the adoring attitude assumed by her husband's passing admirers. Hooker had besides a sufficiently distinguished consort in the aged Queen, who trusted her "little black husband" with the very secrets of her soul, and would never eat flesh in Lent without her black husband's license. The only authentic portrait of Hooker is the bust in the parish church where he lies buried. "It is," wrote Dean Stanley, "of the same style and form as the nearly contemporary one of Shakespeare in the church of Stratford-on-Avon. Unlike that more famous monument, this has the good fortune to have retained the colour without whitewash. . . . It represents Hooker in his college cap, his hair black, without a tinge of grey, his forehead high and broad and overhanging, lively, piercing eyes, deepset beneath it, his cheeks ruddy, and a powerful mouth,"

II

We need not follow Walton through his record of the events in a scholar's uneventful life. The only incident that must be noted is the controversy with Travers which gave its origin to the "Laws of Ecclesiastical Polity." When in 1584 Richard Alvey, Master of the Temple, died, it was expected that according to his wish the afternoon lecturer, Walter Travers, a good and learned man, a popular preacher and a leader among the Puritans, would have been appointed as his successor. Archbishop Whitgift, who had himself been engaged in controversy with Cartwright, was no favourer of Puritanical discipline. The Mastership was given, by way of a compromise between contending parties, to Hooker. Travers was still the evening preacher, and an unseemly dissonance, doctrinal rather than personal, arose in the teaching at the Temple ; " the pulpit," in the often quoted words of Fuller, "spake pure Canterbury in the morning and Geneva in the afternoon." The congregation ebbed from Canterbury and flowed to eloquent Geneva. "What Mr Hooker delivered in the forenoon, Mr Travers confuted in the afternoon. At the building of Solomon's temple neither hammer, nor axe, nor tool of iron was heard therein ; whereas, alas ! in this Temple, not only much knocking was heard, but (which was the worst) the nails and pins which one master-builder drave in were driven out by the other." The Archbishop therefore took energetic action : on the ground that Travers had received orders from the Presbytery

of Antwerp, that he preached without a license, and
engaged in controversies against an order of Her Majesty,
he was peremptorily silenced. When about to go into
the pulpit, he received from the hand of a sorry fellow
the letter of prohibition. Travers calmly explained the
matter to the assembly, which dispersed, not without
frowns and murmurs, and shakings of the head. A
petition of Travers to the Privy Council was overborne
by Whitgift's influence. In the controversy which
arose between him and Hooker neither lost respect for
the other or self-respect. Travers quitted London to
receive the provostship of Trinity College, Dublin, and
Hooker began to meditate his great treatise on the
authority and order of the Church.

A word is necessary to explain the state in which
the "Ecclesiastical Polity" has reached us. It was
designed to consist of eight Books; of these, four were
published by the author as a first instalment, probably
in the year 1594; the fifth Book, which is longer than
the preceding four taken together, appeared with the
advantage of Hooker's superintendence in 1597. Three
years later Hooker died. The so-called sixth Book and
the eighth were first published half a century afterwards in 1648; the seventh was issued under the care
of Bishop Gauden in 1662. The history of Hooker's
manuscripts reminds us of that of the sermons of
Bossuet. The sixth Book, which was to have dealt
with the subject of lay eldership, is in fact lost; what
is called "Book VI.," though derived from Hooker's
notes, forms in the main no true portion of the
"Ecclesiastical Polity." The seventh Book undoubtedly

comes from Hooker's hand, but it is mutilated, thanks, perhaps, to the pious care of Mrs Hooker's Puritan friends and relations. The eighth and last Book was presented in editions which precede that of Keble in an imperfect condition ; by Keble's diligence it was reconstructed and restored on the basis of manuscripts in Oxford, Cambridge, Lambeth, and Trinity College, Dublin. Thus to the close of the fifth Book we are on safe ground ; in reading the later Books there is necessarily some sense of insecurity ; even if through them we come to know Hooker's mind on the subjects of which they treat, it is still open to question whether his whole mind is there expressed.

The development of the English Church of the Reformation, like that of the English constitution, was historical rather than logical. No great theological and ecclesiastical systematiser, like Calvin, presided over its early years. In this there were sources of weakness, but also sources of strength. Shaped to a considerable extent by a kind of opportunism, political as well as religious, it could not possess entire logical self-consistency and perfect coherence. But it had a unity of life, if not an absolute unity of idea. It did not wholly break with the old faith; it did not reject new developments; it received influences from tradition and the past; it received influences from Luther; it received influences from Calvin. At its best the Church of England has been of the nature of a federal union between groups of believers in a common Christianity, whose diverging opinions in detail are wholly incapable of logical

conciliation ; at its worst it has attempted to establish the unity of an idea, a theory, or a system,
and has denied the right of citizenship to its lawful
children, shedding large portions of its population to
found those colonies, disdainfully named sects, which
constitute a no less genuine part of the religious
life of the nation. We are assured by recent ecclesiastical historians that Calvinism is irreconcilable with
the idea of the Church ; as a historical fact the
Church of England has been Calvinist, and Arminian,
and Latitudinarian, and Evangelical, and Sacramen-
tarian. Its unity has been not the unity of an idea
but that of a living organism. Burke has spoken
somewhere of the " clumsy subtlety " of the French
constitution-mongers of the period of the Revolution.
A theory — Calvinistic or Anglo-Catholic — may be
elaborate and ingenious, but still it may be clumsy
as compared with the incalculable complexity of life.
Let the rival doctrines be as uncompromising as
doctrine needs must be ; compromises do not really
conciliate. The life of the national Church as a
federal union can embrace both ecclesiastical Tory
and ecclesiastical Whig. " Bishop is not like bishop,"
wrote Newman, " more than king is like king, or
ministry like ministry," and therefore he could feel
no interest " of any kind in the National Church,
nor put any trust in it at all from its past history,
as if it were, in however narrow a sense, a guardian
of orthodoxy." The fact, as stated by Newman, is
historically true ; and therefore we feel the deeper
interest in the National Church, and put the fuller

trust in it as a guardian of one great portion of the religious life of the English people.

Keeping a middle way of its own, the Church of England moved between two systems which seemed each to have greater coherence and more of logical consistency — the Roman Catholic system and the system of extreme and rigid Puritanism. The spirit of Puritanism, like that of the French Revolution, was the reverse of historical. But whereas the theorists of the French Revolution based their new constitutions on ideas or supposed ideas of the reason, Puritanism sought for its basis, and indeed its super-structure also, in the written Word. Not only was all sound doctrine to be derived directly from the infallible Book, but all lawful discipline was to be found within the covers of the Old and the New Testaments. All merely human expediencies in matters ecclesiastical were in theory (though not in fact) re-jected as illegitimate. At every point, in theory at least, an appeal was made to the law and to the testimony. With a deep sense of the inwardness of religion, Puritanism regarded the external apparatus, which to the Catholic seemed avenues and inlets for the Divine influence, not as avenues but as barriers. With a deep sense that religion is an affair between the individual and his awful Creator and Judge, Puritanism conceived the Church as an assemblage of elect and sanctified souls, each in direct and personal relation to the invisible, rather than as a great in-corporation of those who had been baptised in the sacred names. The Elizabethan Church, maintaining

a balance between powers never perhaps completely
harmonised, was a Reformed Church, but it preserved
continuity with the past; it was a Protestant communion which claimed to be Catholic; it asserted the
right of private judgment, but it respected authority;
it appealed to Scripture, but it also recognised the
living voice of the Church; it possessed a strong element of individualism, but it restrained caprice and
the extravagance of private inspiration. In a word,
if it had not the unity of a logical system, it had
the comprehensiveness of a rich and varied life. The
scriptural dogmatism of the Puritan party is powerfully expressed in the writings of Whitgift's erudite
antagonist, Cartwright. The more liberal spirit of
the Anglican communion is reflected in the pages of
the "Ecclesiastical Polity."

The special characteristic of Hooker's intellect is
its comprehensive grasp of a large body of truth.
The controversy of the time dealt much with matters
of detail—the vestments of the clergy, the dedication,
the naming, the sumptuousness of churches, the form
of the liturgy, the length of the service, the petition
for deliverance from sudden death, the prayer that
all men may find mercy, the sign of the cross in
baptism, the rites of burial, the authority of bishops,
and a hundred other questions. Hooker does not
decline the consideration of questions small or great.
He goes perhaps even too laboriously into detail;
but all these details connect themselves in his mind
with large, general principles. He is capable of system, but, being in contact with concrete fact, he is

systematic without rigidity. He does honour to human
reason as a source of truth, yet he has none of the
arrogance or the dogmatism of some rationalists. He
has a deep feeling of the inwardness of religion, yet
he does not disregard its external forms, finding in
the senses powers which may be auxiliar to things
divine. He reverences the past, and would build to-
day on the foundation of yesterday, yet he leaves
space and scope for the new developments of to-
morrow. He condemns superstition, yet he finds that
truth is often intertwisted with error ; he seeks for
general truths, but, like Edmund Burke, he is a
diligent observer of circumstances, " the loose regard
whereof is the nurse of vulgar folly " ; his temper,
like the temper of Burke, is that of a liberal con-
servatism.

III

The cardinal principle of Hooker's Puritan opponents
was the sole and exclusive authority of Scripture; all
laws found in Scripture are of permanent and universal
force ; no law derived from any other original can be of
permanent obligation. The cardinal principle of Hooker,
as Dean Church correctly expressed it, is the concurrence
and co-operation, each in its due place, of all possible
means of knowledge for men's direction. "Take which
you please," Dean Church goes on, "reason or Scripture,
your own reason or that of others, private judgment or
general consent, one *presupposes*—it is a favourite word
with Hooker—the existence of others, and it is not
intended to do its work of illumination and guidance

without them; and the man who elects to go by one alone will assuredly find in the end that he has gone wrong." The position is eminently reasonable; far more reasonable than the Puritan position. But we can readily understand how Protestantism in the appalling loss of the infallibility of Rome threw itself, through the instinct of a supreme need, upon the infallibility of Scripture, and was compelled to add as a corollary the declaration of Luther that the Bible " so far as is necessary for salvation is clear enough," and that it " belongs to each and to every Christian to know and to judge of doctrine." And it was natural that this acceptance of Scripture as a final authority in doctrine should extend itself to discipline and to ceremony.

Before proceeding to discuss any matters of detail, Hooker sets himself to consider the ground and origin of all law, the nature of that order which presides over the universe, over the external cosmos and human society, and to determine the principle which renders certain laws of permanent and others of temporary obligation. The first Book, accordingly, is rather philosophical than theological; it presents a majestic conception of the world as existing under a reign of law—law not arbitrary but an expression of the Divine reason. Hooker's method is not that of wrangling over texts, but of first grasping general principles, and afterwards of viewing particulars, with a full regard to circumstances, in the light of those principles. It is not the shortest way of controversy; but Hooker is more than a controversialist; he is a master-builder. He admits that such delving and diving towards the roots and foundations of things may be ob-

jected to as involving the thinker in obscurity; but it
becomes necessary in order that the whole edifice may
be well based and secure. " The stateliness of houses,
the goodliness of trees, when we behold them delighteth
the eye ; but that foundation which beareth up the one,
that root which ministereth unto the other nourishment
and life is in the bosom of the earth concealed; and if
there be at any time occasion to search into it, such
labour is then more necessary than pleasant, both to
them which undertake it and to the lookers-on."
The portion of his treatise for which Hooker offers
an apology is that which has especially given it a
permanent interest for minds which are other than
ecclesiastical.

Hooker's conception of the universe, and of the order
which presides throughout and over it, is theistic. For
him the word *law* means not a general statement of the
changes or uniformities of phenomena, but a manifestation
of the Divine will. The fountain of law is God Himself.
Hooker's attitude of reverence is that of one who gazes
upward and also bows the head. Neither can we comprehend the Most High, nor can we escape from His
presence though we fly to the uttermost ends of the
earth—" Whom, although to know be life, and joy to
make mention of His name, yet our soundest knowledge
is to know that we know Him not as indeed He is,
neither can know Him ; and our safest eloquence concerning Him is our silence, when we confess without
confession that His glory is inexplicable, His greatness
above our capacity and reach. He is above, and we
upon earth ; therefore it behoveth our words to be wary

and few." If, however, we are to think of God at all, we must represent the Unknowable to ourselves through our highest faculties. We must think of Him, not as an arbitrary tyrant, ruling His creatures by caprice, but as a Will freely accepting reason as its rule ; His wisdom has set bounds to the effects of His power. This reason, this wisdom—the rule of God's being—which Hooker terms " the first eternal law "—goes forth from God to become operative upon all His creatures visible and invisible, angels of heaven, moving worlds, stars and sun, wind and rain, the clods of the field and the waves of the sea, the beast of the field, and man as an individual and in societies ; constituting thus the " second law eternal." It cannot but be that " Nature hath some director of infinite knowledge to guide her in all her ways." In Him we live, and move, and are.

But what is the special character of this law as impressed upon the spirit of man? Hooker's answer is the same as that uttered with ardour for our own generation in many of Browning's most characteristic poems; the law of man's being is that it shall perpetually aspire to perfection, that it shall constantly tend upwards to God. Man's intellect aspires to knowledge ; man's will aspires to goodness. And these two tendencies are intimately connected, for in order that our will should seek after goodness, goodness must first be discerned by the reason. Should our attempt to identify what is best and highest by a study of its inmost nature and its essential causes only lead us into perplexity, we may yet recognise it by signs or tokens, of which the most trustworthy is the common consent of men at all times and under all conditions of life : " The general and perpetual voice of men is as the sentence of God Himself."

Reason is, then, our guide to the discovery of what is good ; and we support, supplement, control our private judgment by the collective reason of mankind. Thus may be ascertained those natural laws which should govern man's life as an individual. But merely as an individual no man can attain to the perfection of his nature. He is a sociable being, who stands in need of the aid of his fellows. Hence political communities are formed; hence governments are established upon a basis of common consent. The particular form of government, monarchy, oligarchy, democracy, Hooker regards as a matter of political expediency. He had not learnt, like the High Churchmen of the next generation, the doctrine of the Divine rights of kings ; rather he insists that under every form of government the consent of those who are governed is essential; otherwise what is called a government becomes in fact a tyranny. In the time of the Tudors he anticipated the political teaching of Locke.

So far as has been set forth man seeks his perfection by the light of reason. But his desire for good is infinite, a desire which can be completely satisfied by nothing less than the union of his own life with the life of God. We seek a threefold perfection—sensual in the necessaries and the ornaments of our material existence ; intellectual in the possession of truth ; and last, a spiritual perfection in the attainment of things only to be reached by ways which are above and beyond nature in the ordinary meaning of that word. The laws which regulate man's supernatural duties are de-livered by revealed religion. Reason, however, is not displaced by revelation; it is reason which warrants our admission of the claims of revealed truth; and, indeed, many natural laws are repromulgated by the revealed word, in order that what is obscure may be made clear, and that further sauctions may be added. Every *natural* law, whether it concerns man as an individual or men in society, is of permanent obligation. *Positive* laws, although imposed by Divine authority, are not of necessity invariable.

We are at length brought to the point at which the connection of all that had gone before with the Puritan controversy becomes apparent. Positive laws fall into two classes; laws, in the first place, which refer to men as men, without regard to time or circumstances, and these, although positive, having been once promulgated, remain of perpetual and universal authority; laws, in the second place, which refer to temporary conditions, circumstances, or affairs, and such laws, though of Divine imposition, have no more permanence than the matter with which they are concerned.

Thus, while his Puritan adversaries asserted that no law which is not found in Holy Scripture can be of permanent obligation, Hooker maintains that all those natural laws discovered to us by human reason are binding upon man as long as he is man. And again, while his Puritan adversaries asserted that every rule and regulation found in Scripture is therefore a law for all time, Hooker maintains that such regulations may indeed be valid for ever, but may also be temporary and variable ; their abiding validity depends not on the fact that they are declared and delivered by the voice of God, but on the character of the laws themselves ; if they deal with things that are unchanging, they are themselves unchanging ; if they deal with matter that is transitory, they also are transitory.

To degrade human reason and to set up Scripture as the sole and sufficient rule of life, though it may wear the appearance of humble piety, is in truth a disguised arrogance, which opposes its own wisdom to the Divine wisdom, manifested alike in human reason and in revelation. The sources of truth are many ; to discredit any one of these is to wrong our own nature and to wrong the Divine order. It may render hasty and violent revolution easier ; it is not the way of prudent and just reform.

IV

Such, in brief, is the substance of the first book of Hooker's great treatise ; such is Hooker's temper of liberal-conservatism. What is most remarkable throughout the whole argument is not any incisiveness or any originality of thought. Hooker's originality lies rather in his equable grasp of many truths, and in his power of co-ordinating and harmonising those truths. He does not effect a breach between what is natural and what is supernatural ; both proceed from the same source ; each is auxiliar to the other. He does not oppose reason to revelation ; both are of celestial origin. He does not discover a discordance between the inward spiritual life of man and the outward manifestations of that life ; he rather exhibits their harmonious action. He does not reduce religion to a mere affair of the individual soul; he has a feeling for the corporate life of society; each man as an individual has supernatural duties; but he is also a member of a great community which has supernatural duties. He conceives the whole universe as a vast harmonious system; and human creatures, who, on the one side, are akin to the beasts of the field, to the grass of the earth and to the clay from which it springs, are on the other side only a little lower than the angels, those glorious intelligences who, looking down upon the children of men, in their countenance "behold themselves beneath themselves." This conception of the cosmos, its wonder and its harmony, is at least a majestic vision, a piece of the poetry of theology not unworthy of the period which mirrored the moral world of man in Shakespeare's plays and attempted a method of exploring the laws of the material world in Bacon's "Novum Organum."

These great masters of strategy were also skilled in tactics; Bacon less skilled than either Shakespeare or Hooker, for the tactics of science were slow in their development. From his wide-orbing survey of the whole field, Hooker proceeds to capture the key of the position. The second Book is devoted to a refutation of the Puritan thesis that Scripture is the only rule of all things which in this life may be done by men. Hooker's contention is not against the authority of Scripture; it is against narrowing the bounds of that wisdom which comes to us through many and diverse channels: "Whatsoever either men on earth or the

angels in heaven do know, it is as a drop of that un-
emptiable fountain of wisdom ; which wisdom hath
diversely imparted her treasures unto the world. . . .
Some things she openeth by the sacred books of Scripture ; some things by the glorious works of nature ; with
some things she inspireth them from above by spiritual
influence ; in some things she leadeth and traineth
them only by worldly experience and practice. We
may not so in any one special kind admire her, that we
disgrace her in any other." The liberal spirit of the
Renaissance, which does honour to every human faculty,
reacts in Hooker against the narrower spirit of the
Reformation. The argument is pressed home that
Scripture, apart from reason, is incapable of verifying
itself as a rule of life. The elephant may rest upon
the tortoise, but can the tortoise rest upon the void ?
"For if one book of Scripture did give testimony unto
all, yet still that Scripture which giveth credit to the
rest would require another Scripture to give credit unto
it, neither could we ever come unto any pause whereon
to rest our assurance this way." The audacity of Hooker
as a rationalist is not the less remarkable because it is
tranquil and unaggressive.

Among the sources of wisdom which lie outside of
Scripture one in particular is justified by Hooker—that
of human authority, the collective good sense of many
minds ; " utterly to infringe the force and strength of
man's testimony were to shake the very fortress of God's
truth." There are degrees of certitude in knowledge ;
the first is that of the senses (a statement which in
another form gave much offence at the time, and in

later days startled Coleridge) and that of what Hooker terms "intuitive beholding"; the second is founded upon demonstrative reasoning. The authority not of four but of ten thousand general councils cannot, he declares, overthrow or resist a plain demonstration. But in many things probability is the rule of life, and as a guide to probable truth we constantly resort to authority. Do we seek to interpret the law found in Scripture? Good sense directs us to call in the aid of wise and learned men. God in delivering Scripture to His Church did not abrogate the methods of nature. But, while thus maintaining the place due to authority, Hooker asserts the superior rights of reason : " For men to be tried and led by authority, as it were, with a kind of captivity of judgment, and though there be reason to the contrary not to listen to it, but to follow like beasts the first in the herd, they know not nor care not whither, this were brutish. Again, that authority of men should prevail with men either against or above reason is no part of our belief. Companies of learned men, be they never so great and reverend, are to yield unto reason, the weight whereof is no whit prejudiced by the simplicity of the person which doth allege it." In such an utterance there may seem to be nothing very profound or very novel. But at a time when one angry array of disputants overbore all private judgment with authority, and another gave no place to authority in their assertion of the right of private judgment, such a temperate statement, bringing together the dismembered fragments of truth, had the high originality of good sense.

Richard Hooker

91

Hooker's plea that ecclesiastical government and order are in large part a matter of expediency was a plea for human liberty. At the outset of the third Book he confronts the Puritan conception of the Church as a congregation of elect souls with the opposite view arising from a recognition of the distinction between the invisible Church—the mystical body, a communion of saints on earth and of those departed from earth— and the visible Church comprising all those who acknowledge or profess one Lord, one faith, one baptism. According to the Puritan idea the Church is an *imperium in imperio*, a spiritual assembly existing within the State, and in theory detached from the State. But what if the saints should be prompted to make the will of God prevail in the gross world? What if they should resolve to rule the earth? With Hooker the visible Church and the State are a single society viewed from different sides : " We mean by the Commonwealth that society with relation unto all public affairs thereof, only the matter of true religion excepted ; by the Church, the same society, with only reference unto the matter of true religion, without any other affairs besides." Whether we accept such a theory or not, we cannot but admit that it tends to mediate between the dualism of spiritual and material interests, that by a process of levelling up and levelling down, it establishes a broad plateau, where the mundane temper may be elevated by a constant regard for interests that are not merely mundane, and the ecclesiastical temper may be held in check by worldly prudence and experience. It provides a basis for religious toleration.

" Is it possible," asks Hooker, " that the selfsame men
should belong both to the synagogue of Satan and
to the Church of Jesus Christ ? " And he replies :
" Unto that Church which is His mystical body, not
possible," but in the field of the visible Church " tares
manifestly known and seen by all men do grow inter-
mingled with good corn, and even so shall continue till
the final consummation of the world." Even heretics,
though a maimed part, are still, Hooker maintains, a
part of the visible Church. Excommunicated persons
are not shut out from the mystical Church, nor entirely
from the visible Church, but only from fellowship in
certain holy duties.

The faith once delivered to the saints is unaltered and
unalterable ; with ecclesiastical regiment and order it is
otherwise. One and the same polity may not be expedient for the several national churches. For episcopal
authority Hooker had a deep respect ; he looked upon
the government by bishops as primitive, and he regarded
it as an arrangement excellent in itself. But he did
not hold that this form of Church polity is necessary.
He lamented that certain reformed churches, in particular the Scottish and the French, had accepted what
seemed to him a less admirable form of government,
and one, as he believed, less in consonance with
Scripture ; but their unfortunate decision was in no
sense fatal—" men oftentimes without any fault of their
own may be driven to want that kind of polity or
regiment which is best, and to content themselves with
that which either the irremediable error of former times,
or the necessity of the present, hath cast upon them."

Having established the broad principle that Church polity—both government and order—is a matter of expediency, Hooker enters on his defence of the polity of his own church. One entire Book—the fourth—is occupied with meeting the general objection that the national Church is corrupted with Popish orders, rites, and ceremonies, which had been banished from other Reformed Churches. It is a vindication of the way of moderation and good sense, which is also the way of peace, as against extremes on either side. Having set forth his reasons of an argumentative kind, he closes by attempting to show, as a practical proof of the soundness of the English method of reformation, that it had worked well. Even if fault-finding should seem to be warrantable, it may be that suspense of judgment and the exercise of charity are safer and seemlier than the hot pursuit of controversy, in which the most fervent disputants are not always the persons best qualified to arrive at just conclusions.

The fifth Book proceeds to details. "In careful and exhaustive treatment it leads its readers"—the words of Bishop Barry's brief summary may here suffice—"from the consideration of the material fabric of our Churches, through the discussion of the various forms of teaching God's Word; the examination of the principle of a Liturgy; and then of all the various parts and accessories of our Prayer Book worship; the doctrine of the Sacraments and their forms of ministration; the principles of Fast and Festival; the details of our Occasional Services; the three Orders, and even the accidents of our ministry and parochial

system." [1] This is not the place in which such matters
of detail can be discussed.

Hooker's liberal spirit is tolerant of many diversities
of opinion. There is a point, however, at which his
tolerance disappears. Regarding true religion as not
only the root of the private virtues but also as the
support of all well-ordered commonwealths, he has no
feeling but indignation for that atheism which is bred
rather from intellectual conceit than from rude ignorance.
Towards the "forlorn creatures" who would sap the
foundations of all order in the world we are "too
patient." They profess to see a politic use in religion ;
godless themselves, they would as a piece of political
craft invent a God by art. For such an "execrable
creed," such a "wicked brood," such "wise malignants,"
Hooker would not shrink from making ready the faggot
and the stake. Towards the other chief enemy of true
religion, towards superstition, he is more tolerant than
many of his contemporaries. Its sources are zeal,
unguided by sobriety, and fear, which leads men to
employ every means suggested by fancy to propitiate
an angry Deity. From the East, with its subtleties of
the intellect, have come the ingenious creations of superstitious thought ; from the West have come the cruder
and grosser forms of error. Yet even in many super-
stitions that seem upon a first view gross or fantastical,
Hooker recognises a portion of truth, or, as Burke
would have called it, a certain latent wisdom. Thus
the doctrine of the transmigration of souls contained
within an envelope of falsehood, the truth of human

[1] "Masters in English Theology," edited by Alfred Barry, D.D., p. 36.

immortality; the belief in auguries drawn from the flight of birds or the entrails of beasts, contained within it a recognition of Divine power and providence. Hooker's respect for human intelligence had put him on the track of a modern way of regarding the religions of the world. He did not dismiss them in the manner of many of his own contemporaries, as the inventions of the fallen angels to delude mankind; he did not view them, in the manner of eighteenth-century philosophers, as the frauds of priestcraft. The false religions lived by that in them which was true—"no religion can wholly and only consist of untruths."

Before the revolutionist ventures on the redress of superstitious ceremonies in the Church, there are certain considerations which he would do well to bear in mind, and which may serve to temper his zeal. First, a particular rite or ordinance, though not better than some other which can be devised, may yet be fit and convenient; this may be the case although certain inconveniences should also be present. Secondly, the approval of past generations and the long-continued practice of the whole Church may indicate that some fitness resides in things, even should the fitness not be at once apparent. Thirdly, the Church is itself a living authority, having power to ordain new rites and ceremonies or to ratify those that are old; her sentence concerning fitness and expediency is surely weightier than any "bare and naked conceit to the contrary." Last, it must be remembered that there are evils which must needs be endured, lest, if they should be removed, greater evils might take their place.

Important as may be the results arrived at by Hooker's argument, his method and his temper are more important. His influence is at once to liberalise and to sober the mind of one who has submitted to his teaching. Possessed by a deep enthusiasm for order, he had nothing of the arbitrary temper of Laud, which without adequate regard to circumstances, and with a pitiful indifference to the proportion of things, would work from without inwards, and skin the ulcer of disunion with the superficial healing of an enforced uniformity. Yet Laud, who was far from intolerant in matters of dogma, however harsh he was in discipline, probably owed to Hooker some of his affinities to liberal thought. Hooker's vindication of the claims of reason prepared the way for Chillingworth and Hales. It is his high distinction that he cannot be identified with any party within the English Church; in his method and in his temper he represents nothing less than the better mind of England; its courage and its prudence; its audacity and its spirit of reverence; its regard for principles and its dislike of doctrinaire abstractions; its capacity for speculation controlled by its consideration of circumstances; its respect for the past and its readiness for new developments; its practical tendency; its lofty common sense.

ANGLO - CATHOLIC POETS:

HERBERT, VAUGHAN

I

THE poetry of the Anglican communion is most happily represented by two books— George Herbert's "The Temple" and Keble's "The Christian Year." Each was the fruit or the foretaste of an Anglican revival. But Keble's collection of poems—designed to exhibit "the soothing tendency in the Prayer Book"—had more of a deliberate purpose and plan than that of Herbert. Many of Keble's pieces are poetical studies of themes, delicately touched with personal feeling, but rather meditative than possessed by lyrical passion. Herbert's best poems are lyrical cries, taken up by the intelligence and daintily arranged as if for the viol or the lute. The vitality of what he wrote is attested by the witness of two centuries, the seventeenth and the nineteenth. During the eighteenth century—the *sæculum rationalisticum*—his light shone dimly through a cloud.

The great event of Herbert's life was undoubtedly his turning from a mundane career to the humble duties and the quiet gladness of a country parson's lot. As a child, Walton tells us, "the beauties of his pretty behaviour and wit shined and became so eminent and lovely . . . that he seemed to be marked out for piety, and to become the care of Heaven, and of a particular good angel to guide and guard him." His classical scholarship at the age of twenty-five justified his appointment as public orator at Cambridge ; he was skilled in Italian, Spanish, French, and hoped at one time that he might attain to the position of a Secretary of State. He kept himself at a distance from his inferiors, valued his parts and his distinguished parentage, and enjoyed his " gentle humour for clothes and court-like company." We learn with some satisfaction from his brother, Lord Herbert of Cherbury, that he was not exempt from passion and choler, the infirmities of his race ; meekness that is grafted on ardour of temperament is something far removed from tameness.

A time came when Herbert began to doubt of the world and its coloured gifts :

> I shake my head, and all the thoughts and ends,
> Which my fierce youth did bandy, fall and flow
> Like leaves about me.

In the poem named "The Pilgrim," he appears as a traveller whose eyes are set upon a distant hill ; passing the dangers of the way and its meadows of flowery temptation, he comes to the wild of passion, which some call the wold—

> A wasted place but sometimes rich.

At length the hill where lie his heart and hope is attained ; alas ! when the brow has been reached, all that the pilgrim finds is a brackish pool of tears ; his true goal lies yet onward, only to be come at by the way of death ; yet even so, weary but courageous, he resolves to pursue his brave adventure.

It is an allegory of Herbert's spiritual life. We may rest assured that the worst dangers of the wild of passion were unknown to his experience; his heart was never concentrated in one evil desire, but it had been scattered and squandered amid mundane attractions which afterwards seemed to him, in comparison with joys that he had found, mere dust or dross. He needed some coherence, some controlling unity, some centre of activity, some central rest in his spirit; and he found there, no overmastering evil perhaps, but a crowd of pestering idle wishes and shallow cares — " quarries of piled vanities," " thousands of toys," " bubbles of foam," " balls of wind," " balls of wild-fire " :

> Chases in arras, gilded emptiness,
> Shadows well mounted, dreams in a career.

How far is man, he exclaims, from power and from settled peace! He is " some twenty several men at least each several hour." Herbert did not feel like Bunyan's Christian that he was crushed by a burden, a doomed and terrified inhabitant of the City of Destruction; he resembled rather Bunyan's other pilgrim who quitted Vanity Fair to seek abiding joys in the Celestial city.

He longed for constancy—a confirmed will—and he longed for true rest. He, the friend of Bacon, had known the ways of learning—

> what the stars conspire,
> What willing nature speaks, what forced by fire,
> Both the old discoveries, and the new found seas,
> The stock and surplus, cause and history.

He, a courtier, high in the King's favour and not meanly valued by the most eminent and powerful of the great lords, had known the ways of honour :

> what maintains
> The quick returns of courtesy and wit,
> In vies of favours whether party gains,
> When glory swells the heart.

He had known the ways of pleasure :

> What mirth and music mean ; what love and wit
> Have done these twenty hundred years, and more.

And the distractions of knowledge and honour and pleasure seemed only to make an idle noise of thoughts within his heart. " Man," he cries, " is out of order hurled,

> Parcelled out to all the world."

He desired to escape from idle anarchy of the will, and to enter into the Divine order, which gives to all things their set forms, making sweet walks and bowers where the wild woods had been. He would fain be a link of God's great chain ; a piping reed, if no more, in God's great concert ; a flower, however lowly, in God's garden ; a tree giving either fruit or shade—

> at least some bird would trust
> Her household to me, and I should be just.

How should constancy be attained amid vicissitude ? And where is the dwelling-place of Peace ?

He felt the dignity as well as the poverty of man, and knew that such dignity is wronged by entering as an atom into a vain whirl of dust. Man is in truth a stately palace built for God ; a noble piece of symmetry; a harmony made to bear a part with the whole of the Divine creation—

> For head and foot hath private amity,
> And both with moons and tides.

Man is a master attended by the winds and the fountains, by stars and sun, by night and day. And yet he is a palace in decay; a tree that bears no fruit; a dissonance in nature; a master who wields no true authority, but squanders his wealth as a spendthrift. Since the world has grown old it seems as if life had become more difficult and the Divine Presence were less near. In the former days, when God lodged with Lot, struggled with Jacob, advised with Abraham, He might be encountered at any moment, suddenly on the right hand or the left:

> One might have sought and found Thee presently
> At some fair oak, or bush, or cave, or well :
> Is my God this way ? No, they would reply,
> He is to Sinai gone, as we heard tell :
> List, ye may hear great Aaron's bell.

Yet, with such a sigh as this for the primitive age of wonder and direct intercourse with heaven, Herbert felt or came to feel that the secluded Deity is not far from every one of us, that in Him we live, and move, and have our being :

> Thou art in small things great, nor small in any :
> Thy even praise can neither rise nor fall.
> Thou art in all things one, in each thing many :
> For Thou art infinite in one and all.

> Tempests are calm to Thee ; they know Thy hand,
> And hold it fast, as children do their father's,
> Which cry and follow. Thou hast made poor sand
> Check the proud sea, ev'n when it swells and gathers.

And thus the age of wonder is perpetually present.

In the City of Destruction by one who is oppressed beneath his awful burden God is thought of at first as the angry judge. Herbert thinks of God rather as a loving strategist, who lures His children to Himself by finer bribes than Vanity Fair can offer. He is like the mother who would not startle her infant when it was crawling on the edge of the precipice, but silently displayed her bosom and won the straggler back. We are beset by temptations to piety more than by temptations to sin. Dawn arises, and with it comes a sunbeam by which the soul may climb to heaven :

> I cannot ope mine eyes,
>> But thou art ready there to catch
> My morning soul and sacrifice ;
>> Then we must needs for that day make a match.

Evening descends, and night shows no less love than the day ; if day was the gale, evening is the harbour ; if day was the garden, evening is the grove. Joy should lead us Godwards, and if joy fail, then there is grief ; even weariness should toss us to God's breast. On every side our heart is enticed to its true happiness; millions of surprises waylay us ; and the sound of glory is for ever ringing in our ears. The springtide of gladness, when

> Our days were strawed with flowers and happiness,
> There was no month but May,

is followed by the mercies of affliction—

> Thus thin and lean without a fence or friend
> I was blown through by every storm and wind.

And gladness and sorrow are alike parts of the Divine art by which souls are captured for their own good.

But the way to constancy and to content is through humility and obedience. Wits may enter into contest, and inscribe their rival posies on the pane : let our posy be the words, "Less than the least of all thy mercies." More than the other enthroned Virtues, Humility, who sits the lowest, is wise ; let us till our own ground ; let us roost and nestle under God's tent, not gadding abroad at the call of wandering thoughts and passions :

> Who cannot on his own bed sweetly sleep
> Can on another's hardly rest.

Let us know how to possess our secret, and harbour the flame within us as safely as the fire is hidden in the flint. Whether the world rides by him or lags behind, the honest man will constantly ride his sure and even trot ; if trials come, he neither seeks nor shuns, but calmly abides them ; his words and works are all of a piece, and all are clear and straight ; if he has to deal with those who are governed by passion, he allows for that and keeps his steadfast course.

Constancy and content attained through humility and obedience—these substantial gains Herbert must needs choose rather than the various toys men chaffer for in the world's fair ; and so the courtier of King James was transformed into the rector of Bemerton. He viewed deliberately the two methods of life, the two regiments, God's and the world's—

> Thine clad with simpleness and sad events,
>   The other fine,
> Full of glory and gay weeds,
> Brave language, braver deeds—

and after certain scruples of conscience had been overcome with the aid of counsel from Laud, the issue was
decided. What it meant for Herbert we can but in-
adequately conceive. "When at his induction," writes
Walton, "he was shut into Bemerton church, being
left there alone to toll the bell, as the law requires
him, he stayed so much longer than an ordinary time
before he returned to his friends, that stayed expecting him at the church door, that his friend Mr
Woodnot looked in at the church window, and saw
him lie prostrate on the ground before the altar; at
which time and place, as he after told Mr Woodnot,
he set some rules to himself for the future manage
of his life, and then and there made a vow to labour
to keep them."

To become part of a great and Divine Order, to
regulate his life by rules, to perform a round of duties
exactly, reverently, gracefully, gladly, and at the same
time to express in song the tides, the fluctuations, the
incursions, the ebb and flow of the spirit, made up the
life of George Herbert. He could not wholly shape his
course by rule. Still the passionate temperament of his
race remained with him; but his ardour was in great
measure regulated, and served before all else to quicken
his fidelity in duty and to prevent his observance of
forms from sinking into formalism. Still he was subject
to swift alternations of mood:

> How should I praise Thee, Lord ! how should my rhymes
>   Gladly engrave Thy love in steel,
> If what my soul doth feel sometimes
>   My soul might ever feel !

> Although there were some forty heavens, or more,
> Sometimes I peer above them all ;
> Sometimes I hardly reach a score,
> Sometimes to hell I fall.
> O rack me not to such a vast extent.

In the poem entitled "Misery," Herbert reviews the infirmities and follies of the race of men ; at the close, by a sudden return upon himself, he gives the whole a personal application. What is man, wavering on the billows of the world and flung upon the sands or rocky shelves? What is he but "a sick tossed vessel"

> —dashing on each thing ;
> Nay, his own shelf :
> My God, I mean myself.

Yet beneath all fluctuations of mood now lay steadfastness ; beneath all restlessness of desire lay a deep content.

He knew that he was a tiny wheel or cog in the divine machinery, a machinery which had its pulse and movement in the spirit. A lover of beauty, he carried his sense of beauty into his realisation of a sacred order. He still could smell the dew and rain and relish versing. What are the songs that celebrate with ingenious praise a girdle or a glove but "dust blown by wit"? All his inventions he would seriously lay upon the altar. He had nobler beauties to sing than the red and white of a woman's cheek or the trammels of golden hair. He could wittily play with fancies and twist his metaphors, if the mood took him ; for God does not disdain the pretty, pious sports of His children. He could spread his Easter wings, or build his visible altar of verse, upon the page, or labour his devout anagram, or tangle his wreath of rhymes ; it was the fashion of the day, and why should

not fashion itself be sanctified?   But he could also be
plain and bid farewell to sweet phrases, curled metaphors,
trim inventions, honey of roses, winding stairs of subtle
meaning:—

> Shepherds are honest people ; let them sing :
> Riddle who list for me, and pull for prime :
> I envy no man's nightingale or spring.

And in truth Herbert's range as a poet was considerable.
He could wind himself into the daintiest conceits.   He
could be gravely majestic:—

> This heap of dust,
> To which the blast of death's incessant motion,
> Fed with the exhalation of our crimes,
> Drives all at last.

He could write in a strain of genuine simplicity:—

> Teach me, my God and King,
> In all things Thee to see,
> And what I do in any thing,
> To do it as for Thee.

And whatever was within him, ornament or simplicity,
seriousness or innocent play, belonged to God and to
God's Church.

To God's Church, for that was part of the Divine order,
through which he had been delivered from the anarchy
of the world, and it was a part beautiful to his heart's
desire.   In all visible things he was pleased by comeliness.   His gentle humour for clothes did not disappear
on the morning when, forsaking his sword and silk, he
summoned a tailor to come speedily from Salisbury to
Wilton to take measure and make him canonical garments against next day, " which," adds Walton, to satisfy
the reader's expectant sympathy, " the tailor did."   But

Herbert, we know, frail and graceful as he was, would not scruple to put off his canonical coat at need to help a poor man with a poorer horse that was fallen under his load, and never did the country parson, "which used to be so trim and clean," look happier than when he came soiled and discomposed into the company of his musical friends at Salisbury. He had now, however, a wider field than his own person on which to expend his decorative skill. He was already the re-edifier of the parish church at Layton Ecclesia, "being for the workmanship a costly mosaic, for the form an exact cross, and for the decency and beauty," his biographer assures us, "the most remarkable parish church that this nation affords." He proceeded forthwith to repair the chancel at Bemerton, and to rebuild in great part the parsonage, inscribing it to his successor in words which exhorted him to be good to the poor, that so the builder's labour should not be lost.

Herbert's feeling for order and beauty was satisfied by that middle way between splendour and plainness which he found in the Anglican Church :—

> The mean thy praise and glory is,
> And long may be.

The title given to his poems, perhaps by his friend Nicholas Ferrar, "The Temple," sounds somewhat too stately ; as far as they are concerned with the public ordinances of religion "The Parish Church" would have been sufficient. Herbert's imagination was not spacious or rich enough to move at ease amid the noble pomps of ritual ; these would have oppressed rather than borne upwards his spiritual aspirations. He needed grace and refinement as incentives, and he needed for repose some chastened order made sensible. The parish music of voices accompanied with viol and flute sufficed to lift him above all temporal cares :—

> Now I in you without a body move,
> Rising and falling with your wings :
> We both together sweetly live and love,
> Yet say sometimes *God help poor Kings.*

He loved to moralise the simple accessories of worship or of the place of prayer into dainty meanings—the checkered stones of the floor signify humility and patience, the stains of the marble are the stains of sin, the storied windows, in which colour and light combine to show forth sacred things, are the holy preachers; even the lock and key must yield a moral. The rites of the Church have for their character a spiritual power clothed in the beauty of simplicity. Baptism is the little gate and narrow way through which we enter into the realm of divine order; it reminds us that the childlike spirit should still be ours, for "childhood is health." In the Holy Communion Christ conveys Himself to the faithful "not in rich furniture or fine array" but by the way of nourishment and strength. The habit of the Christian priesthood is "a severe attire"; God makes vessels of lowly matter meet for high uses. The splendour of the true Aarons is now only for the inward eye :

> Holiness on the head,
> Light and perfections on the breast,
> Harmonious bells below raising the dead,
> To lead them unto life and rest.
> Thus are true Aarons drest.

From Walton's detailed account of the instruction given by Herbert to his parishioners we learn that the central thought of the teacher with respect to the whole service of the Church was that it is a reasonable service, and therefore acceptable to God.

A certain beautiful method and order is imparted to the religious emotions, which are too apt to run wild, by the progress of the Christian year. At Christmas the soul of the singer arrays itself in the garments of the shepherds, and leads its flock of thoughts to spiritual pastures. Lent is a "dear feast" rather than a season of fasting; if Christ fasted, we should follow and, though far behind His forty days of entire abstinence, we may meet Him in His own way:

> Perhaps my God, though He be far before
> May turn, and take me by the hand.

At Easter we taste the joy of the sun's early light and perfume, and are met by a deeper joy :

> I got me flowers to straw thy way ;
> I got me boughs off many a tree ;
> But thou wast up by break of day,
> And brought'st thy sweets along with thee.

On Whitsunday we pray that the Dove may spread his golden wings above our hearts. On Trinity Sunday we translate the mystery into renewed faith and hope and charity. There is no Sunday of all the year that does not pull and turn us round from worldly cares, to look on One whom if we were not very dull we should look on constantly :

> On Sunday heaven's gate stands ope ;
> Blessings are plentiful and rife,
> More plentiful than hope.

To the Virgin mother Herbert is dutifully reverent and presents her with the toy of an anagram on her name. To her and to all angels and saints he is very courteous ; reluctantly declining the dulia and hyper-dulia because these are not bidden, he dares not go beyond the divine command, which they also gladly observe—

> Where His pleasure no injunction lays,
> ('Tis your own case) ye never move a wing.

Such self-denying apology on her singer's part must surely gratify the blessed Maid more than any fervours of misdirected homage.

Curious questions, which create divisions in religion, are set aside by Herbert's piety. "Love God, and love your neighbour. Watch and pray. Do as ye would be done unto"—these are the Gordian knots of religion, and they need no severing nor untying. Astronomers invent their epicycles to save a theory of the spheres; in divinity we may burn the ingenious epicycles of the theologians. The Holy Scriptures are a book of stars that lights us to eternal bliss. After entire self-confession to God, how lucid all things have grown ! And there is the wisdom of prayer, concerning which Herbert has said perhaps his deepest word. The sonnet on Prayer is one of piled-up metaphors, as if no imagery were sufficient to express its sweetness and its strength ; prayer is God's breath in man, a plummet, an engine against the Almighty, a tower, a tune, a bird of paradise ; but in the last word of the sonnet all metaphor is dropped, and prayer is felt like the deep

and satisfying and inexpressible discovery of Saint John
as he lay on the divine comrade's breast; prayer is

> Church-bells beyond the stars heard, the soul's blood,
> The land of spices ; something understood.

" Something understood," which it is impossible to utter
in words, and to which no imagery corresponds.

The last word of Herbert is neither of death nor
doomsday, of judgment nor heaven ; it is the poem
named " Love." By Love the soul, " guilty of dust and
sin," is welcomed to the feast ; but the poor guest is
embarrassed by a sense of unworthiness—

> I, the unkind, ungrateful ? Ah, my dear,
> I cannot look on thee.
> Love took my hand, and smiling did reply,
> Who made the eyes but I.
>
> Truth, Lord, but I have marr'd them : let my shame
> Go where it doth deserve.
> And know you not, says Love, who bore the blame ?
> My dear, then I will serve.
> You must sit down, says Love, and taste my meat :
> So I did sit and eat.

Exquisite courtesy to the close, the courtesy of heaven
meeting the humble fears and affectionate desires of
earth. The last delicacy of Love, the strategist.

II

Herbert's " A Priest to the Temple, or the Country
Parson," is at once an expression of his own character
and a document which presents one aspect of the
religious life of the time. It exhibits, in a gracious
ideal, the life and practice of the rural priest of the
Anglican Church, who belonged rather to the school

of Andrewes and of Laud than to that of the doctrinal
Puritans. The ideal is one of piety, pure, peaceable,
balanced, amiable, which avoids the madness of extremes,
which has no vast ambitions, which has no passion for
reforming the Reformation by revolutionary methods,.
which rather seeks constantly to irrigate the garden
by the appointed channels, and yet attains originality
through the degree in which the beauty of holiness is
shown to be consistent with a reverent order.

The pastor is the deputy of Christ; even if he is
chaplain in a nobleman's house, it is right that he should
remember the dignity of his office, and be neither over-
submissive nor base towards his lord and lady. The
country parson is " holy, just, prudent, temperate, bold,
grave, in all his ways"; not greedy of worldly gain (for
country folk feel their own sweat, and know the price
of money); not luxurious in meats and drink; a strict
keeper of his word, one whose yea is yea, and nay nay;
plain in his apparel, but reverend and clean, " without
spots or dust or smell," the purity of his mind " breaking out and dilating itself even to his body, clothes, and
habitation." His knowledge may be of many things,
for all will serve his uses; but especially he studies in
the Book of Books, interpreting the Holy Scriptures with
the aids of a holy life, constant prayer, the diligent col-
lation of text with text, and the guidance of the Com-
menters and Fathers. For the Fathers, the Schoolmen,
and later writers are familiar to him, and have been
digested into a body of divinity, made by way of ex-
pounding the Church catechism. With simpler learners
he chooses a simpler manner of catechising; for all his

people he is skilled in resolving cases of conscience, since this is far from being the least important of the duties of Christ's deputy.

In public prayer the priest expresses his devotion by a serious and becoming aspect, by reverent gestures, by a " grave liveliness" of utterance, " pausing yet pressing." He exacts from his people the most dutiful behaviour ; when they stand up they must hold themselves erect ; when they kneel it must be no half-kneeling ; when they make their responses it must be with distinctness, not in a " huddling or slubbering" fashion, but " gently and pausably" ; the magnates of the parish must not be permitted to make a kind of state-entry when half the prayers are over; should they persist in such unseemly conduct, it must be made the subject of an official inquiry. As for the pulpit, it is the parson's " joy and throne" ; he procures attention for the sermon by all possible art ; he enlivens his discourse by anecdote and pithy saying ; but its essential character is holiness. He chooses some ravishing text, rather of devotion than of controversy ; he steeps his words in his own heart ; he breaks forth at times in apostrophes to God, as if he were alone in his Maker's presence—" such irradiations scatteringly in the sermon carry great holiness in them ; " he deals with his text as a whole, developing its meaning with natural expansions, not crumbling it into small fragments ; he is content with one hour of such edifying interpretation and appeal, and does not turn the glass. In the afternoon he chooses rather to catechise than to preach, requiring all, young and old, poor and rich, to be present, that they may either answer

H

or attend to the Catholic answers of those whom he questions with a Socratic skill, learnt in part from the examples in Plato's dialogues. Sermons may "inflame"; it is catechising that "informs." The rest of his Sunday is spent in goodly offices to those who are at variance with one another, to the sick, and to such as have been unavoidably hindered from church-going.

Virginity is held by the parson to be a higher state than matrimony; yet if his parish duties require him to converse with women, he must needs marry. If unmarried he keeps only men-servants, and sees that his linen is washed abroad. Never has he speech with any woman alone, and even in the presence of others he speaks seldom and seriously. A true virgin, he spends his days in fasting and prayer, and in frequent reading of the lives of the primitive monks, hermits, and virgins. Should he take to himself a wife, he chooses her rather by the ear than by the eye, with judgment rather than through the impulse of passion. To her he yields half the government of the house, while holding the reins in his own hand. It is her part to train up her children and maids in the fear of God, to be skilled in the lore of simple and petty surgery, and to see that provision be made for her household without contracting debts. His sons he "first makes Christians and then Commonwealth's men"; they are trained in little charities to other children, and in due time may be bound apprentices to respectable trades; but to serve in taverns is as unbecoming for a clergyman's son as the vain trade of lace-making is for his daughters. The parson's house is a school of religion; on the walls pious texts are seen;

his servants are given time for devout reading; every one is in his own way a preacher; every fault is confessed, every sin is rebuked; maids and men kneel by his side and are taught to pray; yet he governs his servants more by fear than by love. The furniture of the house is very plain, "but clean, whole, and sweet, as sweet as his garden can make"; the fare is plain— beef, mutton, veal—but all is very good; swine and poultry consume the refuse. When he fasts it is genuine fasting, with food not only small in quantity but unpleasant. If fish gratifies his palate, then let him fast on flesh.

Hospitality and charity are among the parson's duties. Those who conduct themselves well he distinguishes and rewards by an invitation to his table; he makes his alms a hook by which to capture those who require such a reward for dutiful observances; on occasions, indeed, he will run the risk of rash almsgiving, "since, of the two commands, we are more enjoined to be charitable than wise"; yet, before giving, he will require his supplicants to say their prayers, or the creed, or the ten commandments. When he is wronged in his tithes, he forgives the offender as a child, if there be hope of amendment. In visiting his parishioners, he enters the house with a blessing, he lends good books, he furnishes recipes for the cure of minor ailments, he reproves the idle and exhorts the industrious not to make riches the end of their labour; he comforts the sick, persuades them to private confession, and urges them to charitable works; he is particular in inquiring as to the regular religious observances of every household; while, to temper his inquisitorial duty, he indulges in innocent mundane discourse for conversation's sake. In everything he is the sentinel of God, or, rather, he is "in God's stead to his parish," the rewarder and the punisher of good and evil doers; the lawyer, the physician, the priest to his people.

In his church all things are decent, whole and clean ; at great festivals strawed and stuck with boughs and perfumed with incense ; he aims at keeping the middle way between superstition and slovenliness. At communion times, having "to break and administer God," he is in great awe of mind. At baptism he admits no vain or idle names (such, we may suppose, as a Puritan might choose), but those that are usual and accustomed ; he cheerfully crosses the child. Should any in his parish hold strange doctrines, he bears himself towards them lovingly and sweetly, places special courtesies on them and studies the particular grounds of their error, whether they be Papists or schismatics ; then, having prayed for them and for his own guidance, is the time to argue with them, avoiding all heat and needless contention. Serious as the parson habitually is, he sometimes condescends to human frailties by intermingling some mirth in his discourses. Yet, knowing the general ignominy cast on his profession, he is careful to maintain its dignity and authority. He himself honours the powers that be ; encourages every one to public spirit and usefulness ; recognises how brave an institution is that of justices of the peace ; commends the study of the civil laws ; esteems it wise that worthy men should aspire to a seat in the great council of the kingdom; exhorts young gallants to become skilled in military and naval affairs, to serve their mother country in the plantations, or if they travel into Germany and France, to endeavour to bring home profitable learning and not foreign vices. He loves the old customs of England, and helps to maintain them. When he blesses his people it is but a brief summary in words of that to which his whole life tends.

George Herbert's ideal of the country parson's life has the beauty which belongs to method and habit rendered quick and energetic by the presence of an animating spirit. Such an ideal was not without its uses for the Church of England at the time when Herbert himself became incumbent of Bemerton. At that date Richard Baxter was a boy of about fourteen or fifteen. The old incumbent of the Shropshire parish in which he was born never preached; the services of a thresher and of a tailor in reading the lessons on his behalf were replaced by those of the incumbent's kinsman, a stage-player turned parson. His skill on the stage and in the reading-desk was supplemented by skill in forging holy orders for the benefit of the pastor who guided the flock at High Ercall. " After him," writes Baxter, " another neighbour's son took orders who had been a while an attorney's clerk and a common drunkard, and tippled himself into so great poverty that he had no other way to live." The people in general were sunk in ignorance and irreligion. Only some two or three families in twenty spoke and lived as serious in the Christian faith ; these were no schismatics, but neither were they of the revived Anglo-Catholic way of thinking; "by the rest they were called *Puritans*, and derided as hypocrites and precisians," to merit which reproach it was enough that they read the Scriptures, prayed, and talked a few words of the life to come.

It must be said also that the leaders of that movement with which Herbert was in sympathy did not always present religion in the amiable aspect set forth in "The Country Parson." Laud, who sincerely desired a doctrinal comprehension within the Church, who was at once the patron of Chillingworth and Herbert, who regarded (or professed to regard) outward ceremonies as of less importance than the inward worship of the heart, yet by his action made those outward ceremonies the seeming essentials of the religion of England. A harsh Anglican intolerance was set over against a harsh Puritan intolerance. The words of a writer so temperate and so well-informed as Professor Gardiner are of more weight than any words of any partisan on either side of the great controversy: "Under Charles especially," he writes, "all the forces of the Crown were placed at Laud's service, and it was not merely the stricter Puritans, but all who cherished the Protestant spirit, who were revolted by the effort made, with the full support of the King, to enforce certain ecclesiastical forms upon the whole people of England. They naturally forgot that, in 1629, their champions in the House of Commons had attempted to silence every preacher who did not chime in with their own doctrinal scheme. The full tide of Puritanism dashed itself against Charles, strengthened and rendered more stubborn by the obstacles which he had raised to check its course. If those obstacles had not been there, we should have had no revolutionary fervour, no revival of thoughts and beliefs which had originally come into existence in the struggle of the sixteenth century." The measures taken against the Puritan party were strong enough and weak enough to produce the maximum of evil which unwisdom can attain; they were strong enough to cause deep and just indignation; weak enough to fail of genuine success.

The country parson of Herbert, devoted to the spiritual good of his people, mildly ascetic, amiably inquisitorial, benevolently despotic, the saintly "Deputy of God," might train a school of docile children in the ways of pious order; he could hardly lead them to attain the fulness of the stature of men. He is the governor, gentle yet severe, of a people in tutelage. The years that were coming tested the virility of Englishmen. From the city and from the fields came forth a bold and resolute race of thinkers and of actors, who, whatever may have been their errors, proved that they were adult, men whose virtues and whose crimes had alike the quality of masculine force and independence. In the same year in which Herbert's volume of poems was published the Star-chamber took measures to suppress the "faithful preaching ministry" of Puritan lecturers. William Prynne, for his censure of plays, which was regarded as reflecting on the Queen, was imprisoned, and by and by was pilloried, with the loss of his ears, which were sewed on, only to be effectually eradicated in 1637, in presence of a great crowd, "silent mainly and looking pale." "Sundays," sang Herbert—

> "the pillars are
> On which heaven's palace arched lies ;
> The other days fill up the spare
> And hollow room with vanities."

And while his words were in the air, the grave Puritan temper of England was outraged, for good or for ill, by the republication with royal authority of King James's "Book of Sports."

III

George Herbert was not only a poet himself, he was the father of poets. Henry Vaughan, a convert from earthly to divine love, was Herbert's spiritual son. The thoughts and phrases of Herbert which he transfers to his own verse seem less an appropriation than an inheritance. Yet the two poets not only differed in the character of their gifts, but may be said to have moved on different poetical planes. "The unthrift sun," wrote Vaughan, "shot vital gold"; of such vital gold there is far more in his poetry than can be found in that of his master and model. But Herbert was better skilled in coining his metal in the mint, and so he gave it a more extended currency.

The essential difference, however, between the poet of "The Temple" and the poet of "Silex Scintillans" lies deeper. The one is the interpreter of an ideal of beauty in order, an ideal of the spiritual life which accepts and is assisted by rule and habit; the regularity, indeed, is far from being merely formal or mechanical ;

the flowers which grow in the garden are living flowers; but Herbert thinks that they flourish best and show most comely when they are bedded in definite patterns and are watered through nicely directed channels. He is the poet of the Anglican communion, and has benefited by all the advantage of harmony with an established system. Vaughan was an excellent churchman; he sincerely deplored the religious dissonance of his time; he could join Herbert in a reverent delight in "the British Church": "O rosa campi! O lilium convallium! quomodo nunc facta es pabulum aprorum!" If questioned, he would doubtless have declared that his position was identical with that of the teacher to whose words and example he owed the awakening of his spiritual life. But Vaughan's best and most characteristic work came from a region below his conscious intelligence. When he set himself a theme and wrote deliberately, his inspiration too often deserted him. On Church festivals and incidents of Scripture history he could compose verses, in which, as Mr Beeching observes, commonplaces are strung together without the advantage of such delicate rhetoric as Herbert practised. He is the poet of what cannot be methodised—the incalculable beams and irradiation of the soul, the incalculable wind that blows where it listeth; his garden is watered by the sudden shower and the invisible dew.

The word "mystic" suggests some initiation into a secret tradition of wisdom. Vaughan is rather one of the *illuminés* whose eyes are opened to a light which shines, if they will but accept it, for all men. His desire is not so much for order in conduct as for unity in the soul. The spirit of man, as he conceives it, is a beam emanating from the original source of light, and holding commerce with that radiant fountain of things. Nature itself is permeated, as a cloud might be, by the divine streams of luminosity, or is shot through by sudden pencils or single rays. The senses, though they may be abused, are properly inlets for the sacred actinism. The ascetic temper of Herbert is therefore absent from the best poems of Vaughan. The colour, the flush, the glow of life, indeed, do not speak to his soul ; he rather fears their distracting influence. It is light in its unity—whiteness of illumination—towards which he aspires, and with which he would unite himself ; a light having no intemperate heat, coming not in torrid waves, but abiding clear and serene.

But here, in our mortal life, the apparition of such light is intermittent; it comes and suddenly disappears ; it is here this moment, and the next it is gone ; we cannot capture and hold it in a noose ; we cannot fix it in forms ; the door opens and shuts ; the brightness flashes and fades. We may prepare for its arrival by inward clearness and quietness ; we cannot in our present state possess it in equal measure from day to day. Such is the prerogative of light; such is our infirmity, but such also is our blessedness. What is most precious in life is not subject to our wills ; it cannot be reduced to a method of piety ; it flows from a well-head in the far-off hills.

We are exiles, but exiles who receive messages from our native land. Hence we suffer, and may rejoice because we suffer, an incurable nostalgia. We are islanded between two seas of light—the bright eternity from which we came, the bright eternity of the future towards which we progress. Each new-born infant is like the mysterious child of old romance, who is borne to shore in a little ark, and brings with him tokens of his royal origin, tokens of that palace whence he came. Hence the radiance of our early years. "My striving eye," Vaughan writes 'of childhood, " dazzles at it, as at eternity."

> O how I long to travel back,
> And tread again that ancient track !
> That I might once more reach that plain,
> Where first I left my glorious train ;
> From whence the enlighten'd spirit sees
> That shady city of palm trees.

And beyond the other term of earthly life there are the happy dead who,

> wing'd and free,
> Rove in that mighty and eternal light.

The triumph of their brightness makes this life of ours seem a mere glimmering:

> I see them walking in an air of glory,
> Whose light doth trample on my days.

Yet they are themselves our pillar-fires—the white dead ; and such guides are needful, for he who stays long on earth must pursue his course

> O'er dark hills, swift streams, and steep ways
> As smooth as glass.

Little wonder is it that such a traveller should pine for his relinquished home and his home that is still unreached.

But unless we clothe ourselves in cloud and mist, we

are not left in the power of darkness. Heaven and
" close eternity " abide within us :

> Should poor souls fear a shade or night
> Who came—sure—from a sea of light ?

We can " think on our dream " ; we can fill our breast
with home ; through thick pangs and high agonies faith
can break into life. Or if we should but be silent and
attend, inward voices and mysterious reverberations grow
audible :

> I came at last
> To search myself, where I did find
> Traces and sounds of a strange kind ;
> Here of this mighty spring I found some drills,[1]
> With echoes beaten from th' eternal hills.

Scattered fragments inscribed with ancient hieroglyphics
lie about our feet ; if only we could bring them together
aright, many things would grow intelligible. Even in
the masques and shadows of life the discerning soul
may see God's sacred way—

> And by those hid ascents climb to that day
> Which breaks from Thee
> Who art in all things though invisibly.

The world, with all that it possesses, is circled by the
great sphere of everlasting light :

> I saw Eternity the other night,
> Like a great sphere of pure and endless light,
> All calm, as it was bright ;
> And round beneath it, Time in hours, days, years,
> Driven by the spheres,
> Like a great shadow moved ; in which the world
> And all her train was hurl'd.

---

[1] *Drill*, a small trickling stream.

Universal nature acknowledges its commerce with the heavens; its forms are "shadows of eternity." The bird, through whose lodging the busy wind blew all night, rejoices in the dawn :

> And now as fresh and cheerful as the light
> Thy little heart in early hymns doth sing.

Even the speechless rocks and stones, struck by the morning gleam, are "deep in admiration." Much more may the heart of man possess and enjoy the divine brightness :

> For each enclosèd spirit is a star
> Enlight'ning his own little sphere ;
> Whose light, though fetch'd and borrowed from far,
> Both mornings makes and evenings there.

However long the night, however dim the way, an hour will arrive when the cry, "The Bridegroom cometh," will fill the heavens, and what hour should that be but the dawn ? The seed grows secretly ; the dew silently descends ; let us cherish the green and growing blade ; the rule of life is a plain and simple one :

> Then bless thy secret growth, nor catch
> At noise, but thrive unseen and dumb,
> Keep clean, bear fruit, earn life, and watch
> Till the white-wingèd reapers come !

And even if at the last there is in God, as some say, "a deep but dazzling darkness," in that darkness, which means excess of light, we may rejoice to live invisible.

Such is the vision which came to the seventeenth-century *illuminé*. It is set forth, when Vaughan writes at his best, with a large utterance and a recognition of the spiritual presences in external nature, which have more kinship with the earlier poetry of the nineteenth century than with that of his own day. It anticipates something of the visionary power of Wordsworth's art; but in Wordsworth the idealist was supported by the strong north-country dalesman; his wandering lights and shadows played over granite cliff and scaur. Vaughan lacked such support; the framework of rites and ordinances, which served the genius of Herbert, may have given strength to Vaughan's life as a man; it aided him little or not at all as a poet; the light within him would not submit to a rule or measure; the breeze of the spirit would not be taken in the meshes of a net. His " Eastern traffic " dealt in " bright and boundless empyrean themes "; Herbert's themes recognised willingly and to their own advantage a bounding line.

Each of the two poets has compiled a poem of precepts. Herbert's " The Church-porch " is designed as a kind of sprinkling with holy water before the entrant of the Temple bows his head in presence of the altar. Its tone is therefore designedly subdued—no exaltations of piety are as yet becoming. Keep clean in conduct, do not get drunk, avoid profane swearing, do not tell lies, be active, steadfast, manly, live by rule, be thrifty, be charitable, do not run into debt, do not gamble, dress well but inexpensively, be pleasant in company, seek no quarrels, laugh moderately, argue temperately, be decent in speech, be neither over-bold nor servile, envy no man, go regularly to church, but do not, like the Puritans, set preaching above prayers, each night cast up the account of the day's spiritual gains and losses —all this is

a wholesome sprinkling, and the priest manipulates his
aspergillum with a neat hand. Vaughan's " Rules and
Lessons," written in discipleship rather than in rivalry
to the " Church-porch," and, identical in the form of its
stanza, gives counsel for the conduct of a single day
from dawn to nightfall. With the best intentions to
be didactic, Vaughan is unable to constrain his pen to
the task of mere edification, and he loses himself ever
and anon in pure delight and wonder. On waking, it
is right that the soul as well as the body should open
its eyes :

> True hearts spread and heave
> Unto their God as flowers do to the sun.

Prayer should dawn with the day ; " they are set, awful
hours 'twixt heaven and us." Then, for mornings are
mysteries, the purged spirit may taste the pureness of
the air and observe the goings-on of the fields and
woods :

> Walk with thy fellow-creatures : note the hush
> And whispers amongst them.   There's not a spring
> Or leaf but hath his morning-hymn.   Each bush
> And oak doth know *I am.*

And not only in the prime but at all hours the influences of the visible world may serve to heighten
devotion or to cool the fever of the blood and brain :

> Here fountains flow,
> Birds sing, beasts feed, fish leap, and the Earth stands fast ;
> Above are restless motions, running lights,
> Vast circling azure, giddy clouds, days, nights.

And so the hours pass by in duties and in delights,
until the glorious evening fades, and we can say that

one more sun is strung on our bead of days. The moralising and even the piety of the "Church-porch" read somewhat like copy-book headlines for the good children of Bemerton parish. Vaughan's rules imply a larger spirit of duty—duty in whose footing treads fragrance, and through whom the ancient heavens are fresh and strong.

Richard Crashaw passed from the Anglican Communion to the Catholicism of Rome. His body lies in the Chapel of Loretto, where for a few weeks he was a sub-canon, and where he died in 1650. But before he left the Church of England his religious passion had been heightened and inflamed by the writings of the great Spanish mystics. At Cambridge it was "in the temple of God, under His wing, he led his life, in St Mary's Church, near St Peter's College; there he lodged under Tertullian's roof of angels; there he made his nest more gladly than David's swallow near the house of God, where like a primitive saint, he offered more prayers in the night than others usually offer in the day."[1] Perhaps he made acquaintance with Herbert's poems under the guidance of Herbert's editor, Nicholas Ferrar, in the devout community of Gidding. The description of a religious house which he found in Barclay's "Argenis," and rendered into English verse, aptly applies itself to the life of those pious recluses who kept the lamp of prayer burning the whole night through, who translated Valdesso, compiled their Concordances of the Scriptures, and knew how to bind a precious

[1] "Steps to the Temple": the Preface to the Reader. The word "nest" can never be resisted by Crashaw; it nestles in nearly every poem.

volume in purple velvet stamped with acorn, sprigs of oak, and fleurs-de-lis:

> A hasty portion of prescribed sleep,
> Obedient slumbers that can wake and weep.
>
> .   .   .   .   .   .
>
> [For] reverent discipline, and religious fear,
> And soft obedience find sweet biding here,
> Silence and sacred rest, peace and pure joys,
> Kind loves keep house, lie close, make no noise.

The hands of Mary Collett may have helped to bind the little prayer book given to a young gentlewoman, " M. R.," and enhanced in its value by the ode which Crashaw prefixed:

> A nest of new-born sweets ;
> Whose native fires disdaining
> To lie thus folded, and complaining
> Of these ignoble sheets,
> Affect more comely bands,
> Fair one, from thy kind hands,
>   And confidently look
>   To find the rest
> Of a rich binding in your breast.[1]

It was not "the soothing tendency of the Prayer Book" that attracted Crashaw ; he found in the end that its " native fires" were too little ebullient to satisfy a " flaming heart."

The "pious orgies" of Crashaw's muse belong to a world remote from the "decent prayers" of Herbert. He commends the poems of Herbert in a copy sent to another gentlewoman than M. R. (in the Dionysiac mysteries gentlewomen may toss the thyrsus) but his commendation would hardly have been to the taste of

[1] See "Nicholas Ferrar, his Household and his Friends," edited by the Rev. T. T. Carter, pp. 235, 236.

the parish priest of Bemerton ; the lady's eyes are to
kindle Herbert's sacrifice ; when her white hands open
the volume she will hold an angel by the wings—an
angel who would gladly

> flutter in the balmy air
> Of your well-perfumèd prayer.

The country parson, who in a state of virginity would
never have spoken to a woman alone, might have chosen
rather to take flight than to flutter in the cell of
Crashaw's " fairest."

Crashaw is as far removed from Vaughan. Vaughan
is the mystic (if we must use that inappropriate term)
of light; Crashaw is the mystic of flame. It is not
strange that Herbert should have innocently played
with pious fancies, or should have fitted his metaphors
to his ideas, tooth by tooth, and have given the pretty
cog-wheel a twist. But we may wonder that the fire of
Crashaw's ardour did not burn away the tinsel ornament
of the school of Marino. It is to be feared that the
language of mysticism may, when the mood cools, itself
degenerate into a trick. Neither Vaughan nor Herbert
equalled Crashaw in his greatest lines; all the eagle, all
the dove were for a moment in his genius; his face
might well have appeared in some Italian painting
among those of the " bright youth of heaven," who in
his own poem bear our Blessed Lady through the clouds
on golden wings, and sing " under so sweet a burden";
he alone among poets of his time was capable of receiving
the full "dower of lights and fires" from that Britomart
of Spanish piety, Saint Teresa. But the live coal may

fade, the altar-flame may sink, and still it may be possible to manipulate the conventional terms—"love's delicious fires," " sweet pains," " intolerable joys," "amorous languishments," "luminous trances," "dear and divine annihilations." And so we may come to respect such modest pieties and edifying counsel as the country parson, even in the porch of the temple, commends to our hearts and conscience. The irradiation in Vaughan's best poems is too pure and various ever to pall upon the spirit of sense within us. The " amorous languishments" of Crashaw may for a time melt our will in a divine voluptuousness; and then it comes to our recollection that the great saints often found more spiritual gain in aridity than in sweetness. Saint Teresa's eulogist might well have remembered her strong good-sense, her power of wise organisation, her genuine feeling of humour.

Crashaw's flame is full of changing colour; at its purest, the flame is varied with beautiful surprises ; but if coloured lights fail him, the poet is well pleased with what Bacon calls the "oes and spangs" of tinsel. Calculated hyperboles, neat extravagances, the ineffable set forth by a fanciful identity of contradictories— flaming fountains, weeping fires, gold hair that is a wandering mine, eyes that are walking baths, and whatever else can unhinge the sanity of imagination, are after all poor temptations to draw a true poet into sin. To criticise Crashaw's poetry as Johnson criticised Cowley's, from the standpoint of common-sense, is legitimate and is useful; to criticise it as showing a defect not of judgment but of true passion is more important. There is something to admire in almost every poem by Crashaw; and there is hardly a single poem that we can admire with a good conscience, for his lyrical ardour was too intermittent to enable him often to achieve a beautiful whole. True love should lead to quiet, or at least to confidence in its theme; Crashaw is always alert for dazzling legerdemain of pious fancy, and so little trusts his theme that he must bedizen it with every paltry bead and spangle of cheap religious merchandize. He praises austerity; and his converted muse still loves the earrings, the crisping-pins, and the pots of rouge. Where Herbert could be content with a field daisy for an offering, Crashaw must fasten with wire to his Magdalen or his Virgin a brilliant basketful of roses in coloured muslin.

V

MILTON: CIVIL LIBERTY

I

MILTON'S prose works form the true complement of his poems. Two words may be said to express in brief the tendency of his total effort as a poet and as a combatant in prose—the words liberty and obedience. All his greater writings in verse revolve around the idea of obedience; all his writings in prose are concerned with liberty, with deliverance from a lower rule as the condition of obedience to a higher rule. He wages war against custom, tradition, tyranny in Church and in State, for the sake of what seems to him a nobler order and a stricter allegiance. Loyalty to the Divine order, a free obedience to that law which is supremely righteous is Milton's dominant idea.

His writings in prose, taken as a whole, are commonly represented as of temporary and transitory interest, claiming attention in their own day but with little significance for ours. The political historian notices them in passing as incidents of a period of civil and religious strife. The biographer is tempted to regard them as an unhappy episode which diverted the poet from his true line of development; he points to them, with Mark Pattison, as examples of " the prostitution of genius to political party." The historian of literature rescues from them certain shining passages, in which Milton vindicates his past or utters his lofty aspirations for the future ; the rest, heavy with the dross of circumstance, is allowed to sink under the waters of oblivion. This is to misconceive the real worth of what Milton wrote. It is true that his pamphlets are encumbered with much matter which concerned the seventeenth century, and which has long since ceased to interest England and Englishmen. But behind all that is occasional lies what gives these writings an enduring value—a series of ideals, more lofty, complete, and in a high sense reasonable, than can readily be found elsewhere among his contemporaries, ideals for the domestic and the corporate life of England, which form a lasting contribution to the higher thought of our country. The refulgent passages may be presented in a collection of extracts ; but that which is of highest virtue, that which shines with the steadiest illumination lives through the gross body of these huge pamphlets — ideals of obedient freedom and of free obedience in the duties of private and public life. To deliver these elements of enduring worth from the wood, hay, stubble of seventeenth-century controversy is not only of some service in rendering justice to the memory of a great poet, but may be an aid to those who seek in the past for living powers to enrich and invigorate the life of our own time.

His ideals for the family, the education of youth, the freedom of the individual in the expression of opinions may in a logical order take precedence of his ideals of corporate life, civil and religious.

II

Milton's discussion of the principles which should regulate the relations of husband and wife affords a striking illustration of the passionate impulsiveness of his temper, and of the way in which his reason was ready to sustain and reinforce his passions. Mr Masson has shown that the first pamphlet on divorce was written during that brief period, immediately following his first marriage,— a few weeks — which preceded his wife's departure from the unhappy house in Aldersgate Street. In June 1643 Milton's married life began; on August 1 of the same year his "Doctrine and Discipline of Divorce, Restored" was in the hands of the public. On a sudden Milton accepted the bond of wedlock; as suddenly he desired to cast the bond away. Did any other illustrious bridegroom, known to history, beguile the honeymoon with the composition of a treatise on the benefits of divorce? It is like the violent swing-round of a great ship, forging swiftly forward, upon the cry of "Breakers ahead." Shelley, even while a boy, never acted in a way so strange, so precipitate, so alien from the ordinary standards of men and women. But Milton could not permit himself to suppose that he yielded to a mere impulse of passion. He was the servant of God, the champion of freedom, the spokesman for a people; he must preserve his dignity, and cherish his self - reverence; he must therefore justify the passion to his own reason and to the reason of mankind; he must, above all, prove that the law of God was on his side; he must argue out the whole question of divorce. Accordingly in the vehemence of his perturbation, but alleging to his own consciousness that thus he might become a great public Reformer, a heroic Deliverer, removing from men's shoulders a burden which they are not able to bear, he rushed into print.

The Divorce pamphlets form part of his pleading on behalf of domestic liberty, liberty, that is to say, for God's vicegerent in domestic life—the man; as for the woman, she, according to the Hebraic doctrine of Milton, exists not as an independent unit, exists not for any direct relation to God, but for God in and through her husband.[1] What is more essential for a life of heroic energy than light and joy in the home? If these are unattainable, the sacred freedom of wedded union is converted into the most grievous of servitudes—a servitude to sorrow. Milton's ideal of marriage is a lofty one; wholly unchivalric, but perhaps higher than the chivalric ideal which reserved its songs and sighs and adorations for lovers who could not be wife and husband. In proportion to the loftiness of his demands and expectations was the passionate scorn which he felt for his timid bride of seventeen years. He had not tired of her as the average sensual man might, after a time, have

[1] In one passage Milton admits that if a wife be wiser than her husband, she may rule, the law of sex being in such an exceptional case superseded by the superior law that power should belong to wisdom.

tired; he saw, or believed he saw, that the spiritual
incorporation, which is the essential part of marriage,
was in this case impossible. He pleaded not for
license, but, as he held, for a stricter and nobler
marriage rule, in which rule alone, and not in im-
moral custom, could just liberty be found; he pleaded
for this in the name of reason, of the soul, of a
purer life, of the Divine order as declared in Scripture.
Honest liberty, he assures us, is the greatest foe of
dishonest license : " He who wisely would restrain the
reasonable soul of man within due bounds must first
himself know perfectly how far the territory extends
of just and honest liberty." It seemed to him that
he, a private man, might suggest a way of bettering
the internal life of a thousand homes, and of emanci-
pating a multitude of sufferers from " a drooping
and disconsolate household captivity." A courageous
individual might lead the way; England should then
remember her precedence in teaching nations how to
live; Parliament might remove the chains which were
eating into the flesh of many victims who now concealed their misery; the whole civilised world might
follow the glorious example of England; man might
again resume his freedom as God's noblest creature.
And thus, instructed by a private calamity, he himself might play the part of a great deliverer. It
was an amazing development from his discovery of
a week or two that Mary Powell had proved an un-
satisfactory companion. Looked at from the point
of view here indicated the first Divorce pamphlet is
a prose-poem in honour of marriage written by an

uncompromising idealist. The sufferings of Milton's young bride disappear in his vision of a great nation exulting in its deliverance from a yoke which checked the motions of joy and vigour and sacred gratitude. Never before or since was such an Epithalamium sung.

The proposition which Milton aimed at establishing on the evidence of reason and of Scripture is this— " that indisposition, unfitness, or contrariety of mind, arising from a cause unchangeable, hindering and ever likely to hinder the main benefits of conjugal society, which are solace and peace " is a just ground for a dissolution of marriage to be pronounced by God's vicegerent, the husband. It seems to follow as a direct consequence, that an idealist like Milton, in search of the perfect wife, might repeat his experiment until Aldersgate Street was strewed with Mrs Miltons *emeritœ*, and the not-impossible She was at last found. Mutual consent, he admits, is desirable in effecting a final separation ; it is not absolutely necessary. Milton's thesis is general, but he scarcely attempts to veil his personal interest in the matter : " A discreet man may be mistaken in his choice. . . . The soberest and best-governed men are least practised in these affairs ; and who knows not that the bashful muteness of a virgin may ofttimes hide all the unliveliness and natural sloth which is really unfit for conversation." Obviously we have a picture of the shy Royalist girl in presence of a Puritan admirer, discreet, sober and well-governed, of more than twice her age.

Love, Milton tells us, was the son of Loneliness,

begot in Paradise. When this original penury or
loneliness of soul is not removed by marriage, "then
enters Hate," not the hate that sins, but an inevitable, ineradicable dissatisfaction; and surely, if
the woman be of a gentle spirit, not to be beloved,
and yet to be retained as a domestic appendage,
would be the highest injury. "To profane that
mystery of joy and union"—true wedlock—"with a
polluting sadness and perpetual distemper," were the
greatest wrong against marriage. When he touches
on the opinion of Beza that divorce was divinely
permitted for the release of afflicted wives, we get
a glimpse into his domestic interior, and can perceive
some of the causes which made the overawed girl
so speedily desirous to return to her kinsfolk. Divorce
permitted only for the relief of wives! "Palpably
uxorious!" cries Milton; "who can be ignorant that
woman was created for man, not man for woman,
and that a husband may be injured as insufferably
in marriage as a wife? What an injury it is after
wedlock not to be beloved! What to be slighted!
What to be contended with, in point of house-rule,
which is the head; not for any parity of wisdom,
for that were something reasonable, but out of a
female pride." So quickly can the bride of a haughty
idealist accumulate on her girlish head every disquali-
fication for wifehood; so remorseless is the passion
for the unattainable perfection. "No man knows
hell," writes Milton, "like him who converses most
in heaven; so there is none that can estimate the
evil and the affliction of a natural hatred in matri-

mony, unless he have a soul gentle enough and
spacious enough to contemplate what is true love."

The art of creating happiness, the most beautiful
and most difficult of the fine arts, Milton had not
studied. His genius was not fired by the ambition
of evoking smiles from sadness. But his pamphlet,
futile as are its practical suggestions, is still of worth
as a plea for a noble joy and energy in domestic
life as against faintness and timidity of heart, the
lethargy of sadness and the indolence of despair.
The Puritan home, as he conceived it, would have
been one of heroic gladness, of comradeship in aspir-
ing thoughts and generous deeds. The first of wifely
duties is that of inward and spiritual help; he did
not reflect how difficult is the part which he assigns
to the woman—that of confessed inferiority without
inadequacy. If through fault of nature or irremediable failure of heart and soul, she deserts her chief
duty, she forfeits thereby all right to wedded happiness, and her fate is placed in her husband's hands.
The union, as he conceived it, is no sacrament; it
is no more than a civil contract terminable if the
purposes of the contract cannot be fulfilled. The
modern divorce court Milton would have looked on
as causing a needless injury to the weaker party.
Why bandy up and down a wife's unpleasingness, he
asks, and aggravate it in open court by hired
masters of tongue-fence ? Far better is it that the
doom should be pronounced in private ; to the husband God has given power over his wife ; let him
declare that the contract is dissolved.

Milton's writings on the subject of divorce are four in number. Two of these may be disregarded. Some months after the second edition of his " Doctrine and Discipline of Divorce" had been published, Milton discovered that he had been anticipated in an expression of the same opinions by an eminent divine of the Reformation, Martin Bucer. He was glad to have the support of an authority in high credit among Protestants; accordingly he collected from Bucer such passages as seemed to confirm his own views. The book is devoid of interest. But the dedication to the Parliament of England is written in Milton's lofty manner. If anything generous, noble, and above the multitude were left in the spirit of his country, he felt confident that it might be found in the great council of the nation. As for himself it seemed as though he were the agent of some superintending Providence, prompting him to labour for the general good, or rather no agent, but a " passive instrument" under a power and direction higher than human. He reverenced himself as God's envoy to his people of England. As a poet he uttered only what it was given him to say by the Spirit; when fallen on evil days he was an afflicted champion, like Samson, possessed of a divine gift of invincible strength, which one day perhaps might overwhelm the Philistines. Even as a pamphleteer on the subject of divorce, although Milton was aware that the immediate occasion of his writing was a personal grief, he was still " no other than a passive instrument under some power and counsel higher and better than can be human, working to a general good in the whole course of the matter." Perhaps we should

reverence Milton more if he could for a moment have
been a mere mortal, aware of human infirmities, and
capable of manly protectiveness to one whose infirmities
were more excusable than his own. But it was his way
to drive haughtily from error into error.

On the same day, March 4, 1644-45, were published
" Colasterion," Milton's answer to an anonymous critic,
and his " Tetrachordon."   The former of these was
written in a rage of scorn.   Milton follows his adversary
through his several arguments, the seventh, the eighth,
the ninth ; he denies the major ; he denies the minor ;
he dashes rock and stone and mud of abuse and objur-
gation on the foeman's head ; a serving-man, a trivial
fellow, a dolt, a pork, a phlegmy clod, an idiot by breeding,
a nameless hangman, a groom, a hoyden, a hobby-horse
jesting and frisking in the luxury of his nonsense—such
are some of the swashing blows of the controversialist
who wrote as " a passive instrument under some power
and counsel higher and better than can be human."
The rapier of satire was not in fashion among learned
combatants ; the club was still a favourite weapon.   Yet
some fifty years earlier, Hooker had conducted his controversy not only with human dignity but with Christian
charity.   Milton followed the common way of contention
with a Berserker fury which has in it almost a touch of
genius ; it is impossible to be more insulting than he
succeeded in being.   If we compare such an urbane
swordsman as Newman, the antagonist of Kingsley, with
the mammoths and megatheria of the sixteenth and
seventeenth centuries, who tore each other in their learned
slime, we shall see reason to believe in the evolution

of warfare, with all its decencies and tactics, from the epoch of the antediluvian combats of monsters. The capacity for rage and scorn is admirable ; it was possessed in abundant measure by the Hebrew prophets ; but their rage and scorn were purified and elevated. It is assuredly a trial to the admirers of the author of " Paradise Lost " and " Paradise Regained " to encounter such a pamphlet as " Colasterion." How could the great idealist, who reverenced himself and reverenced what was above him, lose all sense of dignity and decency ? The answer lies partly in the fact that the man who lives in ideas is often the man who has learnt least a fitting behaviour towards persons ; the individual becomes in his eyes the symbol of a hated cause ; he flings himself into the mêlée with a cry of " I do well to be angry." Milton could soar on the steady wings of an albatross ; but the albatross on deck is an ungainly creature.

In " Tetrachordon " Milton enters upon an exposition of the four chief passages of Scripture which treat of marriage and the grounds of its dissolution. Whether we agree with the drift of his argument or not, we cannot but admire the courageous spirit of the writer and the genuine literary feeling which, now and again, he brings to bear upon the interpretation of the Bible. Aspiration towards a life of active righteousness and generous pursuit of wisdom breathes through Milton's words a life strong, joyous, free, yet obedient to the highest law. Christ in cancelling the handwriting of ordinances has " set us in the free custody of His love, and left us victorious under the guidance of His living Spirit, not under the dead letter, to follow that which most edifies, most aids and furthers, a religious life, makes us holiest and likest to His immortal image, not that which makes us most conformable and captive to civil and subordinate precepts." And as he has this ideal of a life strong in the pursuit of what is highest, so he has his ideal of the blessedness of rest and refreshment after toil in the sunshine of the home : "No mortal nature can endure, either in the actions of religion or study of wisdom, without some time slackening the cord of intense thought and labour, which, lest we should think faulty, God Himself conceals us not His own recreations before the world was built. 'I was,' saith the Eternal Wisdom, ' daily His delight, playing always before Him.' And to Him, indeed, wisdom is as a high tower of pleasure, but to us a steep hill, and we toiling ever about the bottom. He executes with ease the exploits of His omnipotence, as easy as with us it is to will ; but no worthy enterprise can be done by us without continual plodding, and wearisomeness to our faint and sensitive abilities. We cannot therefore always be contemplative, or pragmatical abroad, but have need of some delightful intermission, wherein the enlarged soul may leave off awhile her severe schooling, and like a glad youth in wandering vacancy, may keep her holidays in joy and harmless pastime." Such support in labour, and such refreshment after toil Milton had not found in the company of his girl-wife. The "Tetrachordon," indeed, is on fire with pain. Milton describes the wedded life of those who are not united in spirit as the life of "deadly enemies in a cage together" ; it is a shipwreck without haven or shore ; it is the mere carcase of a marriage ;

to endeavour to establish harmony between such wedded adversaries is " to weave a garment of dry sand." The only effectual remedy for such inward disruption is complete release. Such an unhappy couple could not desire to be unhappy parents ; they are disqualified for true fatherhood and motherhood. If children are already born, let them follow either parent, as shall be agreed or judged, quitting the house of hatred and discord for a place of more holy and peaceable education.

Passion with such a mind as Milton naturally tends to generalisation. His private grief led him to an enquiry into first principles. Our reward for wading through the sandy wastes of controversy is that Milton conducts us, as almost always is the case, to an altitude from which a noble prospect may be viewed. Although he accepts the Hebraic teaching that

> God's universal law
> Gave to the man despotic power
> Over his female in due awe,
> Not from that right to part an hour
> Smile she or lour—-

although he asserts the inferiority of woman, his conception of marriage is more honourable to woman than the chivalric conception. Wedded happiness resides in a union of hand and heart for spiritual service, for joyous energy, and for delighted refreshment after toil :

> Favoured of Heaven who finds
> One virtuous, rarely found,
> That in domestic good combines !
> Happy that house ! his way to peace is smooth.

The condemnation of Dalila is Milton's homage to

K

her sex as truly as is the celebration of virginal strength
and purity in " Comus."

In his classification of the prose writings which treat
of domestic liberty Milton places after the pamphlets on
divorce his letter to Hartlib on Education.   After the
wife he considers the child.   He demanded freedom in
the training of the youth of England, but only such
freedom as comes through obedience to a higher and
stricter law than that of custom and tradition.   As the
divorce pamphlets are not merely destructive of what
Milton regarded as the tyranny of civil and canon law,
a servitude fatal to vigorous joy, but are also constructive,
presenting his ideal of the true union of husband and
wife, so his Letter on Education aims at destroying a
system which he held to be obsolete and enfeebling only
with a view to replace it by a more exacting as well
as a more enlightened discipline.   He had himself
known the methods of the University; he had himself
practical experience as a teacher of youth.   Nothing is
more obvious than that he makes extreme demands on
the energy of young scholars, and expects more than an
average student can attain ; but by one who has the
passion for perfection much may be accomplished before
one-and-twenty.   Milton would relieve the student
from many idle burdens and preposterous exactions ; he
would gradate studies so that what is easy should
precede what is difficult ; and he had a modern sense
of the importance of vigorous recreation.   It would be
a grave mistake to suppose that he wrote as a phantast,

enamoured of the impossible. His scheme of education may be regarded as ideal, as a guiding light by which to steer. A prudent mariner, whose course is determined by the observation of the heavens, will know how to make allowance, with hand on helm, for veering flaws and cross and counter currents.

The tyranny of the traditional system, against which Milton contends, started from the idea of making scholars ; scholarship was taken to consist of a knowledge of the classical languages ; yet even with this limited object in view, the methods adopted could end only in failure : methods, in themselves vicious, were languidly pursued, and much of the inestimable season of youth was squandered in sheer idleness ; during long " vacancies " what had been learnt was more than half-forgotten. No enthusiasm for knowledge could be aroused by such a system ; the student, invited to " an asinine feast of sow-thistles and brambles," lost all zeal for learning.

Milton starts with the idea not of making scholars, admirable scholar though he was, but of making men. A religious conception lies at the basis of his proposed system ; man has fallen from his original high estate ; his nature has shrunk and dwindled in the absence of the light and warmth needful to a complete and vigorous humanity ; the end of all learning is not to instruct us in words or to qualify us for turning out an elegant copy of Latin verses ; its end is religious—that we may know God aright, and out of that knowledge may love Him, imitate Him, and be like Him. To be a complete man is to be God's image on earth ; education should aim

not at the accomplishment of scholarship, but at the
formation of manhood, in its plenitude of intellect, its
energy of passions, its strength of will : " I call a complete and generous education that which fits a man to
perform justly, skilfully, and magnanimously all the
offices both private and public of peace and war."

If " to know God aright " be the first end of education, the Puritan Milton does not suppose that this
knowledge is to be gained solely or chiefly from churches
and creeds and catechisms, or even from Holy Scripture.
Through the visible world, through the nature of man,
through the laws of human society we make acquaintance with what is divine.   Through sense we ascend
to spirit.   To spell our lesson aright we must begin
with easy and simple things.   The external world lies
spread around us, and it is God's world ; let us try to
understand it, and thus the senses may become inlets
for the soul.   Man is God's image not through any
special faculty, but as a complete creature.   Reason,
the passions, the feeling for beauty, the energies which
tend to action, strength and skill of hand, the principles
of public conduct, statesmanship, law, art, war—all are
sacred, because all are portions of the fully developed
life of man.   The whole of education is religious ; no
fragment of it can be called profane.   Such special
instruction in religion as is given in the seminary of
Milton's devising is built into the general body of
culture.

The uses of an ideal are related to ends rather than
to means.   Milton's proposed means may be at times ill-
chosen, impracticable, or unsuited to the present day ;

his ends are the worthiest and the highest that can be conceived. At the outset he would above all else arouse the honest pride of knowledge, the ardour of hope in his pupils ; they are to be " enflamed with the study of learning and the admiration of virtue ; stirred up with high hopes of living to be "—what? masters of erudition? patterns of pedantry? ascetic saints? No : but " brave men, and worthy patriots, dear to God, and famous to all ages." Such a high ambition might well enter into the heart of a spirited boy, inspired by the words and example of such a teacher as Milton desired to see.

Then, while the young scholars are acquiring the elementary principles of science and receiving their first lessons in language, let them look around and learn a manly reverence for their mother Earth. Let it be part of their ambition to leave some piece of England better than they found it for the needs of their fellows who till the soil and cast the seed ; such a task is worthy of heroes ; " this was one of Hercules' praises." The old books which tell of agriculture and country life will not seem idle or dull to them if they consort with professors not bred in the library but smelling of the fields, true and honest enchanters to a vigorous boy —hunters and fowlers, fishermen and shepherds and gardeners, themselves the brave children of Earth. Let them extend their view beyond the hills and fields of England, and through maps and globes embrace the prospect of this world which is our appointed home and habitation ; let them look upwards on a starry night and read the meaning of the heavens. And as they progress in their knowledge of mathematical and physical science, let them learn how needful are these to the life of human society, receiving the lesson not from the lecturer's chair but from engineers and architects and mariners and anatomists.   Let their studies in literature go hand in hand with their studies in science and in the arts of life.   The poetry which treats of nature, of the ways of rural toil, and of the crafts of primitive society, will be for them no weary exercises in syntax and prosody, but will insensibly add an ideal charm to what they have come to know as part of the glad realities of earth.

Having observed the outer world, Milton's pupils have reached that moment of culture when they may look within ; having surveyed the life of man in relation to external nature, they may advance to the study of man in relation to his fellows.   The laws of personal conduct may be read in the ancient moralists, and before the serious close of each day's task, by lamplight, in the pages of Hebrew singer, evangelist, or apostle.   From the principles of individual duty, the student of the moral world advances to the laws of the household ; and as these are investigated, he may see them put into action, and pregnant with laughter and with tears, in the comedies, classical or Italian, and the great tragedies that present the characters and fortunes of parent and child, and lover and wife and husband.   One further stage, and he passes on to politics—the life of man in the commonwealth—to the principles of public justice, to the history of ecclesiastical organisations, and, in connection with this, to the highest matter of theology. And this is surely the moment when he can feel the life that pulses in those supreme works of art which are concerned with national events, with the good of a people, the glory or the shame of dynasties or races—"heroic poems, and Attic tragedies of stateliest import and most regal argument, with all the famous political orations."

It remains, when these have been felt and enjoyed, to investigate their principles and method in logic, rhetoric, and poetics.[1] He only who has studied the laws and possibilities of art can fully know "what religious, what glorious and magnificent use might be made of poetry both in divine and human things." When nature and man as an individual and in society have thus been explored, when the laws of reasoning, of persuasion, and of fine art have been ascertained, when in truth "an universal insight into things" has been attained, then, and not until then, may Milton's pupils aspire to become orators or writers. They will have something to say; they will have learnt by example and by precept how to say it. A rational sequence and an enlightened co-ordination of studies is attempted throughout Milton's entire scheme; he endeavours to make it from first to last coherent, so that the learners, as he says in his magnificent way, may at length "have confirmed and solidly united the whole body of their perfected knowledge, like the last embatteling of a Roman legion."

---

[1] The often-quoted sentence, attributed to Milton, that poetry should be simple, sensuous, and passionate is not to be found in his writings. What he says is that Poetry, by which he means Poetics, being "less subtle and fine, but more simple, sensuous, and passionate" than Logic or Rhetoric, should on this account precede them in the order of studies.

But the ideal man, God's image on earth, is not yet complete, nor as yet is he qualified for the full duties of citizenship. Milton honours the body, and regards its energy as a tributary which broadens and deepens the energy of the soul. The athletics which he commends are not sports but heroic duties, yet duties which are also delights. They are of two orders—individual and social; some are designed for the uses of war, some for the uses of peace. The exact practice of the sword, the locks and grips of wrestling, concerted military evolutions on foot and on horseback, training, if it can be had, on shipboard, will prepare the youths to be " renowned and perfect commanders" at their country's need. But they must also learn through active pleasure, without toil, riding abroad, " in those vernal seasons of the year when the air is calm and pleasant," when indeed " it were an injury and sullenness against nature not to go out and see her riches, and partake in her rejoicing with heaven and earth." All the more strenuous exercises and recreations are designed by Milton not merely to strengthen the muscle and invigorate the lungs, but to promote true fortitude and patience, so laying the basis on which to build up a heroic valour and a hatred of wrong-doing as a form of cowardice.

His young athletes are at the same time to be educated by the delights of fine art. Milton, himself a lover of music, the son of an accomplished composer, accepts the doctrine of Plato that melody and harmony have a true formative effect upon character. His earlier poems possess something of the quality of the lute ; his later poems are breathed, as it were, from the stops of an organ ; he names these two instruments, which had a certain kinship with his genius, as of refining and calming, or arousing and elevating, influence. Sweet concords of voices are also to play upon the spirit in sense of the youths in his ideal academy, telling of religious joy or martial enthusiasm, or the delights of peaceful life.

Religion, science, literature, art, manly exercises of the body—all of these enter into Milton's scheme ; each is kept in close communion or interaction with the rest, and one and all are directed towards, not learning merely, but life. Science ceases to be abstract, and is viewed in connection with the arts and crafts which give application to its principles. The study of literature in all its forms, up to the highest, remains ; but real things (as they are called) serve to quicken and vitalise the feeling for literature. Great poems are seen and felt in relation to human life—the life of the individual, of the household, of the commonwealth. It may have been an error to suppose that a young reader can fully acquire such a power of interpreting art ; but Milton's method would at least put him on the way to acquire it. If his scheme have no other value, it is assuredly significant as to Milton's manner of regarding literature and its function in society. But in truth no more majestic ideal of education is elsewhere to be found ; it is the ideal of the Christianised Renaissance, of Hebraism and Hellenism brought into harmony. The Letter to Hartlib is a soul-animating strain, which, if we cannot literally translate it into a method or an

institution, may serve as a guiding-light, or as a heroic
call—*Sursum corda*—to those who undertake the sacred
charge of youth.

IV

A great and courageous faith in human nature and its
possibilities underlies what Milton has written on education. The same faith animates the "Speech for the
Liberty of Unlicensed Printing," which completes the
cycle of writings on what he has termed Domestic
Liberty. He knows that the nature of man is fallen,
and that we move in the midst of temptations; it is
our part to accept these conditions with a righteous
boldness, and to work out all possible good from things
as they are. He would have us grapple with evil
as heroic combatants, not fly from its presence : "I
cannot praise a fugitive and cloistered virtue, unexercised
and unbreathed, that never sees her adversary, but
slinks out of the race, where that immortal garland is
to be run for, not without dust and heat. Assuredly we
bring not innocence into the world, we bring impurity
much rather ; that which purifies us is trial." He
chooses " a dram of well-doing before many times as
much of the forcible hindrance of evil-doing." He
desires freedom in the utterance of opinions, as in all
other matters, not because he loves laxity or insubordina-
tion, but in order that the minds of individual inquirers
and the mind of the whole nation may come under
a stricter and a higher rule than that of the licenser.
The higher rule is that of perpetual progress in the
never-ending research for truth. To press forward

to that which is before is the one true safeguard against wanderings into the illicit by-paths of literature. Such a conjoint effort may not result in an outward uniformity of belief, but it ensures an union of spirit, internal, free, vital, and energetic, the only union which is to be attained on earth. The body of truth for us exists in fragments ; our task is to gather these fragments and to bring them together, until, as far as may be, the original and glorious form of truth reappear living and moving among men. "The light which we have gained," Milton writes, " was given us, not to be ever staring on, but by it to discover onward things more remote from our knowledge." This is our law, but it is a law of liberty.

Milton's faith in human nature is reinforced by his enthusiastic confidence in his own nation and his own time. Great experiments in the affairs of Church and State were being made ; a new epoch of reformation seemed to have begun ; God was revealing Himself more fully to His servants, and, "as His manner is, first to His Englishmen." Milton looked around him, and saw in his country an universal zeal for freedom, knowledge, and valiant enterprise. London rose before his vision as a huge factory in which were being forged the weapons of truth : " Behold, now, this vast city ; a city of refuge, the mansion house of liberty, encompast and surrounded with God's protection ; the shop of war hath not there more anvils and hammers working, to fashion out the plates and instruments of armed Justice in defence of beleaguered Truth, than there be pens and heads there, sitting by their studious lamps,

musing, searching, revolving new notions and ideas
wherewith to present, as with their homage and their
fealty, the approaching Reformation ; others as fast reading, trying all things, assenting to the force of reason
and convincement. . . . What wants there to such
a towardly and pregnant soil but wise and faithful
labourers, to make a knowing people, a nation of prophets, of sages, and of worthies ? " This trumpet-call
of hope and confidence is touched with pathos when
we contrast it with the sad, yet courageous tone of
autobiographical passages of " Paradise Lost," written
when Milton had fallen on evil days, or with the
poem of the blind Samson, for whose strength no other
noble use remained than that of drawing down the
roof-tree in a common ruin of his enemies and himself.

V

Milton's writings in defence of public liberty in
England have for their centre that act which he regarded
as a solemn vindication of justice and the rights of an
injured and insulted people—the execution of the King.
A fortnight after the death of Charles he came forward
to identify himself by the publication of " The Tenure
of Kings and Magistrates " with those who had given
a great example of tyrannicide. The pamphlet may
be styled the *Contrat Social* of Milton, but his social
contract is a divine, and not merely a human ordinance.
For those who hesitated to take the responsibility and
the praise of assisting at the sentence of the Court,
those who " coming in the course of these affairs to have
their share in great actions, above the form of law or

custom, begin to swerve and almost shiver at the grandeur and majesty of some noble deed, as if they were newly entered into a great sin," he feels only a commiserating shame. His fierce examination of that book which Royalists regarded as the precious testament and legacy of the royal martyr—the " Eikon Basilike "—drew Milton into a controversy which resounded over Europe. There is much in these political writings of merely temporary and transitory interest, much that is truculent in temper ; but while the writer often appears as a man in armour clambering, sword in hand, heavily, and with ungainly postures, among rocks, of a sudden he puts forth wings, and, soaring in upper air, looks like one of the mailed combatants of his own angelic warfare.

The late Professor of History at Cambridge, Sir John Seeley, in a luminous study of Milton's political opinions,[1] repels with some indignation the notion that the great poet was in public affairs an impracticable dreamer. The place which he assigns to Milton is in a special group of thinkers, including among those of the nineteenth century, Coleridge, Ruskin, and Carlyle, men of genius who apply to politics one or two intense convictions. With a comprehensive view of the national well-being rare among his contemporaries, Milton was equally interested in the political and the religious revolutions of his day, and from his high point of vision could regard these movements as essentially one. His large concern for the life of his people included other elements of public good—literature and education—of

[1] " Lectures and Essays," 1895, pp. 97-130.

which politicians and ecclesiastical reformers thought
but little. The central idea to which he gives various
applications, is that of liberty, liberty, however, not
for its own sake, but as increasing vigour. His zeal
on behalf of strong and joyous living was derived partly
from his own sanguine temperament, and partly from
the spirit of courageous hope and energy which animated the reforming party to which he belonged. They
were not impatient of restraint : " their tendency was
rather to strictness than to laxity, their excess was
on the side of over-government." What they opposed
was not severity but inefficiency of government. The
same idea of liberty as increasing vigour which Milton
applied to Church and State he applied equally to
education and to literature.

The criticism is just and goes to the roots of the
whole matter ; it may be extended so as to include
Milton's writings on divorce. Among his political
pamphlets one in a special degree gives an interpretation of that conception which is central in all. On the
eve of the Restoration, when Monk had been confirmed
in · his dictatorship and appointed Captain - General,
Milton put forth his scheme of republican government
in " The Ready and Easy Way to Establish a Free
Commonwealth." The moment was one of the utmost
doubt and anxiety. Milton's sanguine temper was at
last troubled by a secret despondency. Yet he would,
as far as was possible, hold up his head bravely, bate
no jot of heart or hope, and steer right onward through
the waters of strife. He would make a last effort on
behalf of liberty ; he would show how order might be

educed from chaos, readily and easily if only reason and courage remained with Englishmen ; but it is evident that Milton's hopes for his country were more than equipoised by his fears.

His position is not that of any of the contending parties or fragments of parties. He declares himself in favour of a free commonwealth, without "Single Person," whether named King or Protector, and without a chamber of peers. Yet he is no democrat of the modern type. A mere majority, whether in Parliament or of the people, did not suffice, in Milton's view, to settle anything. A majority may be corrupt; "there is little virtue," he says, " in number." A licentious and unbridled democracy he abhorred ; he honoured what Burke afterwards called a natural aristocracy, and he would distinguish them not by trappings or titles, but by grave duties and laborious tasks performed for the public welfare. "What government," he asks, "comes nearer to the precept of Christ than a free commonwealth, wherein they who are the greatest are perpetual servants and drudges to the public at their own cost and charges; neglect their own affairs, yet are not elevated above their brethren ; live soberly in their families, walk the street as other men, may be spoken to freely, familiarly, friendly, without adoration ? "

But how was a free commonwealth to be established and maintained ? How was a vigorous government to arise out of anarchy and the liberty of England to be preserved ? Milton distrusted Parliaments, which with every new election might change their policy. He desired, after so many vicissitudes of divided rule, a

continuity of order and a continuity of progress ; this,
he believed, could be attained only in one way—by an
oligarchy of wisdom and virtue resting upon a popular
basis.   He would have the supreme central authority
entrusted not to a Protector, not to a shifting crowd of
delegates elected on a cry of the hour or of the day, but
to a perpetual Grand Council of the nation.   " The ship
of the Commonwealth," he writes, "is always under sail;
they sit at the stern ; and if they steer well what need
is there to change them, it being rather dangerous ? "

The choice of these rulers of the people could not be
entrusted to " the noise and shouting of a rude multitude."   Duly qualified electors might nominate a body
of men, from whom by their own votes a smaller body
might be selected, until perhaps " by a third or fourth
sifting and refining of exactest choice they only be left
chosen who are the due number and seem by most
voices the worthiest."   Thus, through a series of ex-
clusions, a band of true patriots might be found, just
guardians of the liberty of England.   Should it appear
that the permanence of this Council created a danger
of power too nearly absolute, or excited distrust and
jealousy, or excluded other deserving persons from
authority, an arrangement might be made for partial
rotation, by which a third part of the Senators should
annually retire and a like number be elected in their
place.   Such a concession might prove to be necessary
or expedient, but it was reluctantly admitted by Milton.
What he regarded as essential was a strong central
government, placed above the risks of accident and
popular passions.

Here, then, was a supreme authority chosen, but wisely chosen, by the nation, and having power to deal with all imperial affairs. At the same time Milton desired to quicken the vigilance and zeal of the whole people ; this, he believed, could be accomplished by the delegation of power in local matters to local authorities. He aimed at the establishment all over the commonwealth of a system of vigorous provincial governments. In every chief town of every county should meet a County Council, with power to enact such laws and regulations for the county as might seem fit. If province should conflict with province, formulating such rules as might tend to disintegrate the Empire, the several County Councils should meet together and determine the issue by a vote of the majority. Thus Milton's scheme was devised with a view to secure the advantages of centralisation together with those of decentralisation ; its object was to establish freedom, but freedom for the sake of vigour. Many minor commonwealths were to flourish under the supreme authority of one imperial commonwealth. Among the subjects which should engage the attention of the local bodies, Milton insists strongly on the importance of a liberal system of education : " They should have here also schools and academies at their own choice, wherein the children should be bred up in their own sight to all learning and noble education ; not in grammar only, but in all liberal arts and exercises." By which generous discipline the entire people of England might in due time become " flourishing, virtuous, noble, and high-spirited." The question of religion should create no difficulty : "As for spiritual liberty, who can be at rest, who can enjoy anything in this world with contentment, who hath not liberty to serve God, and to save his soul, according to the best light which God hath planted in him to that purpose, by the reading of His revealed will and the teaching of His Holy Spirit ? " Unfettered freedom of conscience was the only law which should be observed in things spiritual.

The whole scheme is of peculiar interest as exhibiting the statesmanship of a great poet, who was not without some training in public affairs. It attracted immediate attention, and was fiercely assailed. In the state of England on the eve of the Restoration Milton's pamphlet could not of course effect its immediate purpose ; but its underlying principles have in large measure been justified by time. In recent years and at the present moment the need of a supreme imperial authority working in harmony with a subordinate system of decentralisation — such a system as can enter into no rivalry with the central power — has been and is recognised as in no previous period. Throughout the pamphlet Milton appears as a political thinker whose ends are in a high sense reasonable, if the means proposed for attaining those ends were impracticable ; at its close he gathers his singing garments about him and rises into the prophet. A prophet not, indeed, altogether of hopeful cheer, but of hope mingled with fears, and of dauntless courage showing through both : "What I have spoken is the language of that which is not called amiss 'The good old Cause.' . . . Thus much I should perhaps have said, though I was sure I should have spoken only to trees and stones; and had none to cry to but with the prophet, ' O earth, earth, earth ! ' to tell the very soil itself what her perverse inhabitants are deaf to. Nay, though what I have spoken should happen (which Thou suffer not who didst create mankind free ! nor Thou next who didst redeem us from being servants of men !) to be the last words of our expiring liberty. But I trust I have spoken persuasion to abundance of sensible and ingenuous men ; to some perhaps whom God may raise from these stones to become children of reviving liberty . . . to exhort this torrent also of the people not to be so impetuous, but to keep their due channel; and at length recovering and uniting their better resolutions, now that they see already how open and unbounded the insolence and rage is of our common enemies, to stay these ruinous proceedings, justly and timely fearing to what a precipice of destruction the deluge of this epidemic madness would hurry us, through the general defection of a misguided and abused multitude." The last stand of one of the company of Ironsides, maintaining the good old cause against overwhelming odds, is a spectacle to animate the courage of Milton's countrymen in every great crisis of events.

VI

MILTON II.—ECCLESIASTICAL AND
THEOLOGICAL LIBERTY : POEMS

I

MILTON'S first entrance into controversy was as an
ecclesiastical reformer. He would fain have been a
messenger of gladness and contentment to his countrymen, the poet that he was born to be : "but when
God commands to take a trumpet, and blow a dolorous
or a jarring blast, it lies not in man's will what he
shall say, or what he shall conceal." His quarrel
with the Church of England arose from his conviction that, under the rule of Laud, it had become
destructive of spiritual liberty and yet did not gain
in spiritual vigour. His conception of a Christian
commonwealth assuredly could not err on the side
of laxity. "Alas, sir !" he writes, "a commonwealth
ought to be but as one huge Christian personage,
one mighty growth and stature of an honest man,
as big and compact in virtue as in body." Wisdom,
virtue, magnanimity, likeness to God, enjoin and
require national as well as individual self-government.
The invisible divine life must be made external, not
in ornament but in something that more fitly expresses it—in conduct. Is there to be discipline in

164

the home, discipline in the State, and no discipline, or an infirm and servile one, in the Church ? " There is not that thing in the world of more grave and urgent importance throughout the whole life of man than is discipline ; . . . she is that which with her musical cords preserves and holds all the parts thereof together." Its function is not so much to repress as to strengthen and develop : " Certainly discipline is not only the removal of disorder, but if any visible shape can be given to divine things, the very visible shape and image of Virtue, whereby she is not only seen in the regular gestures and motions of her heavenly paces as she walks, but also makes the harmony of her voice audible to mortal ears."

But sound discipline in things spiritual must itself be spiritual. Fines, exactions, nose - slittings, ear-croppings were not regarded by Milton as the methods of Christ or of His apostles ; the extreme punishment of the Church, or of its instigating, can be no more than the withdrawal of spiritual communion. Its officers are to be distinguished not by worldly titles and carnal pomp but by brotherly love, matchless temperance, frequent fasting, incessant prayer and preaching, continual watchings and labours, truly apostolical distinctions. To one who sees with purged and lucid vision, the grandeur of religion is degraded, not enhanced, by mundane power and splendour : " So long as the Church, in true imitation of Christ, can be content to ride upon an ass, carrying herself and her government along in a mean and simple guise, she may be, as he is, a lion of the tribe of Judah ; and in her humility all men with loud hosannas will confess her greatness. But when, despising the mighty operation of the Spirit by the weak things of the world, she thinks to make herself bigger and more considerable by using the way of civil force and jurisdiction, as she sits upon this lion she changes into an ass, and instead of hosannas every man pelts her with stones and dirt."

A part of the policy of Laud was to work from without inwards ; through uniformity, enforced by pains and penalties, he trusted that unity might in the end be attained or at the least promoted. As regards dogma, he was more liberal than many of his Puritan adversaries ; as regards ceremonial order, he would tolerate no irregularity. Milton desired to work from within outwards ; religion should indeed incarnate itself in visible acts, it should obtain expression and externality, not in ornament or symbol, but in deeds and lives of righteousness. With a profound sense of the majesty of religion, all glorious within, he believed that its dignity is heightened by the fact that its external habit is plain and homespun. The beauty of holiness is seen aright only in the living temple ; shall altars, and cloths, and vessels, be profaned by the touch of a lay Christian, who is himself the adopted child of the Divine Father ? If the feet of him that bringeth good tidings are beautiful, how shall the "spinstry" of ceremonies add to their decency ? Milton, a poet and a lover of comely things, is ready to sacrifice the lower beauty of ornament in order that the invisible beauty may shine forth with intenser radiance. The

" chaste and modest veil " of Christ's Gospel "surrounded with celestial beams " loses something of its brightness if it be overlaid with a "flaring tire."

Milton thought of the intercourse between God and the soul as, on the part of man, an indefatigable soaring upward. There are two humilities—that which bows and that which soars, the humility of a servant who looks down, the humility of a son who gazes up. Milton's humility invigorates itself in the effort to ascend. He would not prostrate himself in the presence of material symbols, but would enter as a glad child into the courts of heaven. He suspects a rich ceremonial because it seems to him a specious mode of easing the stress of devout effort; the soul, with flagging pinions, "shifts off from herself the labour of high soaring." He honours the senses; but he finds within himself a faculty—not the intellect, but the religious faculty—which cleaves its way past things of sense, and communes with the unseen. " Our understanding," he writes in the Letter on Education, " cannot in this body found itself but on sensible things, nor arrive so clearly to the knowledge of God and things invisible as by orderly conning over the visible and inferior creature." That is God's way of utilising the senses for religious purposes ; but to manufacture an artificial body of material symbols, neither found in nature nor authorised by the Divine word, seemed to him the way to check or hamper the soul in its upward flight. Voluntary humility before material objects styled sacred belongs, as Milton conceives, rather to a religion of mingled fear and self-will than of love and genuine self-abandonment.

The true attitude of the soul is filial, cheerful, and courageous; son and Father may meet face to face, without servile crouchings or the veils of piebald frippery.

Such was the Puritan position; but it is enlarged and strengthened by the genius of its defender. He was no enemy of art, as were some of those who stood upon his side; he was no enemy of pleasure. But, although his approved polity in state and church was in theory democratic, Milton was deficient in popular sympathies. He found in the sacred writings magnificent examples of lyric poetry, as well as of tragedy (the Apocalypse of St John) and of pastoral. But in the Sunday afternoon dance of villagers upon the green, permitted by the Declaration of Sports, he saw only a provocation to drunkenness and lust. Instead of desiring that recreations should be suppressed by authority, he desired that the pleasures of England might be regarded by the government as part of a public schooling, and might be studied and superintended with a view to their just honour and stateliness: "It were happy for the commonwealth if our magistrates, as in those famous governments of old, would take into their care, not only the deciding of our contentious law-cases and brawls, but the managing of our public sports and festival pastimes; that they might be . . . such as may inure and harden our bodies by martial exercises to all war-like skill and performance, and may civilise, adorn, and make discreet our minds by the learned and affable meeting of frequent academies, and the procurement of wise and artful recitations, sweetened with

elegant and graceful encitements to the love and practice
of justice, temperance, and fortitude, instructing and
bettering the nation at all opportunities, that the call of
wisdom and virtue may be heard everywhere, as Solomon
saith: 'She crieth without, she uttereth her voice in
the streets, in the top of high places, in the chief
concourse, and in the opening of the gates.' Whether
this may not be, not only in pulpits, but after another
persuasive method, at set and solemn paneguries, in
theatres, porches, or what other place or way may
win most upon the people to receive at once both
recreation and instruction, let them in authority consult." The proposal for the organisation of pleasure,
its recognition and development with government aid,
came not from courtier or cavalier but from the Puritan
Milton.

In his liberality towards differences of opinion in
matters of religion Milton had more in common with
the prelates whom he so passionately attacked than with
the Presbyterian party on whose side for a time he
ranged himself. There was something which seemed
to him a greater evil than a conflict of sects—the
insensibility of spiritual palsy, the uniformity of intellectual death. Weeds do not flourish in a December frost;
but neither do wholesome herbs and flowers. He had
little fear of the "fond errors" and "fanatic opinions"
which arise at a time when truth and error engage
in fierce encounter. The English people is at bottom "a
right pious, right honest, and right hardy nation"; with
wise nurture the uncouth opinions of a period of excited
conflict will gradually pass away. Before long Milton

discovered that his friends of the Westminster Assembly
were themselves the chief forcers of conscience :

> "Men, whose life, learning, faith, and pure intent,
> Would have been held in high esteem with Paul,
> Must now be named and printed heretics
> By shallow Edwards and Scotch What-d'ye-call."

Unquestionably Milton's progress to broad principles
of toleration was accelerated by the fact that he himself,
the advocate of divorce, was among the heretics ; but
his personal indignation only brought more vividly into
the light of consciousness what had lain within him
from the first.

In the same year in which Milton proposed his ready
and easy way to establish a free commonwealth he turned
away from his great epic to address the Parliament, or such
members of it as Vane, who might support his views
on the subject of the relations of Church and State.
He was now assured that their respective provinces were
of right distinct and separate.   The civil magistrate
shall not lift a finger against any form of religious belief
as such.   Popery, indeed, cannot be tolerated, but this
is because Popery involves allegiance to a foreign
sovereign.   For the rest, the law of Christian liberty
requires that every man be free to search the Scriptures
and to hold fast that which he deems good.   The word
heresy, even the word *blasphemy* had no terrors for
Milton ; let truth and error grapple, and there need be
no fear as to the issue.   A commonwealth is not Christian
because it establishes one form of religion, but because,
establishing none, it recognises the freedom of Christ,

whose kingdom is not of this world, and of all those communities which make up the Church universal.

Opinion, however, though not forced may be bribed. Against this danger also Milton would guard. Let a free ministry be supported by free gifts or, like Paul the tent-maker, by the labour of their own hands. He thought with indignation of that form of persecution, as it appeared to him, which consists of exactions made for the benefit of spiritual hirelings bound to teach some authorised system of religious belief. Birth, marriage, death—why should each of these be made the occasion of taxing the poor? Did John the Forerunner demand fees for baptising or Christ for His christenings? What scriptural ground is there for the meddling of priests with the contract of wedlock, which is but a civil ordinance? What have ministers of religion to do with the interment of a corpse?

If villages and rural districts are unable to maintain a minister without a system of ecclesiastical taxation, the state of things is not desperate. Have they not the Scriptures and God's assisting spirit? "It is not necessary to the attainment of Christian knowledge that men should sit all their life long at the feet of a pulpited divine." The wealthier congregations may of their good will aid the poorer by sending some of their members on circuit as itinerary preachers ; let these appoint duly qualified elders who may teach and govern the rest. Let the English Scriptures be published with sufficient notes; let a body of divinity be issued unencumbered with scholastic terms and metaphysical notions. Thus instructed the poor folk may meet for mutual edification in house or barn, needing neither incumbent, incumbrance, nor incubus.

That the whole people of England should be educated, spiritually alive, and eager for things of the mind, was Milton's aspiration and his ideal. He was a prophet of the movement for free national education, and, holding that a collection of books is the true university, a prophet of the movement for free libraries of public endowment. The writer of a good book, the teacher of youth, the guardian of a library, he viewed as members of the true clerisy of a nation, more diligent for the general welfare than the hired parson, pledged to a particular set of opinions and droning out his dole on one day in seven to earn his state wages. " So all the land would be soon better civilised," and those who receive the free gift of education might reasonably be required not " to gad far out of their own country," but continue there, thankful for what they had received, bestowing it on others as need arose, without soaring above the rank in which they were born. Education, as Milton conceived it, should be not merely literary ; it should be also technical ; every boy should be taught an honest trade. And why should not worthy teachers of religion arise from among such cultivated craftsmen ? Let Christians but know their own dignity, their liberty, their adoption, their spiritual priesthood, "whereby they have all equally access to any ministerial function, whenever called by their own abilities and the Church, though they never came near commencement or university," let them but know their true prerogatives, and with liberty a new and noble vigour will be infused throughout the whole

spiritual life of the country. If Milton's ideal was half
a dream, it was also half a prophecy. Schools and
libraries at the close of the nineteenth century in some
measure realise what he anticipated in his vision. And
of the spiritual teachers of our century not a few of
the most influential have been unsalaried by the State,
sprung from the people, and claiming their function
by no other title than their ability. "Hirelings," as
Milton named them, have not been removed from the
Church; but the sense of responsibility and duty has
been quickened; side by side with the national church,
the free churches of England may grow unharried and
unharassed, and the unorganised clerisy of letters has
asserted its dignity and widened its sphere of influence.

II

Milton's prose writings are not a mirror held by the
artist to reflect the forms of his own time; they are a
sword or some fiercer two-handed engine wielded on
behalf of civil and religious liberty; they are themselves a portion of the strife. The illustrations which
they afford of his poems are found in occasional
passages, in autobiographical episodes or outbreaks,
and to some extent in their general spirit. But
among the prose works there is one which was not
written in a combative mood, one which sets forth in
great detail the results of prolonged research after
religious truth, a work begun early, but probably, in
the main, of Milton's elder years, and this constitutes
an undesigned commentary upon the poems, and a
commentary as valuable as it is authoritative. The

Treatise on Christian Doctrine, a Latin manuscript, lay forgotten in the old State Paper Office until the year 1823. Milton seems to have entrusted the manuscript to the care of young Daniel Skinner, a Fellow of Trinity College, Cambridge, in 1674, nephew of his friend, Cyriac Skinner, with a view to its publication. Troubles caused by the appearance of Milton's " State Letters " led to the suppression of the daring Treatise on Theology ; the manuscript was forwarded by the publisher, Elzevir, to the English Secretary of State, and it waited for nearly a century and a half before it found an editor in the chaplain of King George IV., Sumner, afterwards a successor of Bishop Andrewes in the See of Winchester.

The general idea around which Milton grouped the cycle of his prose writings is that of *liberty* ; in his earliest series of pamphlets he pleaded for ecclesiastical liberty ; in others he presented his ideal of domestic liberty ; and in yet others he vindicated the civil liberties of his country. The treatise on Christian Doctrine—including both faith and morals—exhibits in an example the importance of theological liberty— " the liberty," as Milton declares, " not only of winnowing and sifting every doctrine, but also of thinking and even of writing respecting it, according to our individual faith and persuasion." It is the attempt of one man, and that man the most cultivated of his time, to determine for himself, and, as far as may be for others, the truth concerning religion as it is found in Scripture. Of all its author's prose works it is the most ambitious ; it is also the most modest. He will construct a complete theology ; but no article of that theology shall be of human invention. The Holy Scriptures are accepted without discussion as the rule of faith and as the law of conduct ; by human reason, with the enlightenment of the Divine Spirit, the Scriptures are to be interpreted. Milton's audacity is founded in obedience ; he aspires because he submits. Propositions deduced from the Bible are supported by an array of texts. Much of the book—to be frank—is unreadable ; but many of its conclusions are of interest, as throwing light upon the body of dogma which lies behind the imaginative work of his elder years ; " Paradise Lost " is built upon a creed ; in the Treatise on Christian Doctrine we can study the lines of its foundation.

Milton's intellect supports his imagination. He would build no cloud-palaces of a fancy *in nubibus*. His art was not like Bunyan's, the outcome, almost involuntary, of a personal experience. He never knew Bunyan's agonies of hope and fear ; he saw hell, but he did not feel its terrors ; he explored heaven, but he was not smitten senseless by its radiancy of joy. From his earliest years Milton toiled steadily, as under a great task-master's eye ; his higher life was not like Bunyan's, the outcome of a conversion ; it was rather a going-on towards perfection. He worked as an artist, consciously and deliberately, not without a deep inspiration, but with all the powers of intelligence and will, hammering on the anvil his material—doctrine, emotion, and image—until they were (as he conceived) inseparably welded together. It may be confidently said that every idea of importance which lies within or behind

Milton's poetry was held by him not merely as service-able for his art, but as warranted by his reason on scriptural authority. His fancy might body forth de-tails, as where modern artillery is employed in the angelic warfare ; but every cardinal thought of his poems was an article of belief. He regarded the poetic function as that of a prophet ; he could not toy or trifle with the sacred truth ; he must deliver it as he found it, or as it was revealed to him. His theological convic-tions were, accordingly, formative influences with his poetry. These, in the " Treatise on Christian Doctrine," are nakedly stated, with their appended proofs from Scripture. In " Paradise Lost " and " Paradise Regained " they are clothed with a body of the imagination.

We shall understand Milton aright only when we follow the track of his mind from ideas to imagery. " How strange an inconsistency," wrote Sir John Seeley, " lies in the construction of ' Paradise Lost.' A Puritan has rebelled against sensuous worship. He has risen in indignation against a scheme of religion which was too material, too sensuous, which degraded invisible and awful realities by too near an association with what was visible and familiar. But in the meanwhile a poet, who is the same person, having a mind in-veterately plastic and creative, is quite unable to think, even on religious subjects, without forms distinctly conceived. And, therefore, while with one hand he throws down forms, with the other he raises them up. The iconoclast is at the same time an idolater. For one of the most striking features of ' Paradise Lost ' is the daring materialism that runs through it, the

boldness with which the Divine Persons are introduced, the distinctness with which theological doctrines are pragmatised." And the critic goes on to
affirm that Milton, the Puritan, is as mythological as
Dante, the Catholic, but that the mythology of Dante
is Christian, and sprang up naturally, whereas the
mythology of Milton is Greek.

Now the answer to such criticism as this—the
answer, at all events, which Milton would have given
—is supplied by the Treatise on Christian Doctrine.
He was an iconoclast of those sensuous forms which
were the growth of human tradition. He reverenced
those forms which were authorised by God Himself.
His mythology, if we must use that word, was not
Greek, but exclusively and strictly scriptural ; or, rather,
it was no mythology, but the divinely approved way of
representing God to ourselves, with faculties which are
incapable of comprehending Him as He essentially is.
In His revelation God has condescended to our capacities ;
to accept His representation of Himself is safe ; to take
flights of our own above the reach of human understanding is dangerous mysticism ; to conceive God in
other than the authorised forms is idolatry. When
the Scripture says "it repented God," let us believe
that He indeed repented ; when the Scripture says
that God was grieved, let us believe that He was in
truth grieved. If God habitually assigns to Himself
the members and form of a man, why, asks Milton,
should we be afraid of attributing to Him what He
attributes to Himself ? God may not actually be in
form like a man ; but, in as far as He can be known

M

to us, that is the truest way of conceiving Him, for it is the way prescribed to us by God Himself.

The materialism of " Paradise Lost " has surprised and offended many of its readers. How could the Puritan Milton, so ardent in his spirituality, present a material heaven, angels who fling rocks and fire off heavy batteries of artillery, angels who dine and digest, a Messiah, who, seated in His chariot, bears upon His side a bow and quiver, as though he were some far-shooting Apollo ? Are we reading a Pagan or a Christian poem ? Christian and scriptural, Milton would reply. If to think scorn of visible things was a Puritan habit of mind, if the party with which Milton was most closely connected strove to make a breach and division between the spiritual and the material, then he had assuredly transcended the Puritan modes of conception, and in so doing he held that he was following the guidance, not of his own imagination, not of classical literature, but of the Divine Word. Milton, the theologian, and Milton, the poet, were in entire agreement. He looked on the earth, indeed, as suffering from the consequences of the fall of man ; but he was the reverse of a Manichean; he honoured the material universe ; he did not suppose that there is any opposition between soul and body, or between God and His effluence in sun and stars and earth.

God the Father is the primary and efficient cause of all things. What, then, is the origin of matter ? That matter should have existed of itself from all eternity is inconceivable. Some original it must have had ; and no other source was in existence from whence

material substance could have proceeded save the substance of the Divine Being.   Matter—so Milton held—
was not created out of nothing ; it was an efflux from
God's own nature ; nor was matter evil or worthless ;
it was essentially good, as the bodying forth of Himself
by God must needs be.   How, it may be asked, can
that which is corruptible proceed from the incorruptible?
With a touch of indignation, Milton answers that matter
came forth incorruptible from God, and, even though
Adam fell, incorruptible it remains, as far as concerns
its essence.   The sin of Adam lay in his will and
was spiritual ; matter has never sinned ; at the utmost
it may have contracted some taint or contamination
from the evil spirits who during so many ages have
possessed the earth and the air.   As a corollary of the
belief that God drew all things out of Himself, Milton
adds that no created substance can ever be annihilated,
for that were to destroy a portion of God's own being.
Matter and spirit are alike indestructible.

Surely the Puritan Milton must regard the nature
of man as twofold—material and spiritual, the flesh
warring against the spirit and the spirit warring against
the flesh ?   This warfare is indeed real, but it is
a spiritual warfare, a warfare within the human will.
On grounds which he believed to be in harmony with
Scripture Milton rejected the bi-partite conception of
man's nature.   Man, he maintained, is a living being
intrinsically " one and individual, not compounded and
separable, not, according to the common opinion, made
up and framed of two distinct and different natures,
as of soul and body."   The whole man is soul, and the

soul man, " that is to say, a body or substance individual, animated, sensitive, and rational." Body and spirit, according to Milton, are not two separate things; they are different aspects of one and the same thing; "That the spirit of man should be separate from the body, so as to have a perfect and intelligent existence independently of it, is nowhere said in Scripture," and the doctrine is evidently at variance both with nature and reason. Into the organic clay God at first breathed some vital and rational virtue, and the clay became a living soul, or, as perhaps we should rather render the words, a living animal; there is nothing spiritual in a human creature which is not also material, and nothing material which is not also spiritual. Milton does not imagine that at some unascertained moment of an unborn infant's existence God creates a soul, and, as it were, inserts it in the body; he held, on the contrary, that the complete human being is the natural offspring of its parents. Refusing to sever our manhood into two parts, a superior part and an inferior, the Puritan poet never casts contempt upon the body. He honours the entire spiritual animal Adam, and the entire spiritual animal Eve; he regards every natural appetite and passion, the craving for food, the joys of wedlock, as sacred :

> Whatever hypocrites austerely talk
> Of purity, and place, and innocence,
> Defaming as impure what God declares
> Pure.

Only when these appetites and passions transgress the Divine rule and order does sin come into existence.

Even the angels of God are material creatures, though of finer substance than man. They are not pure spirit, the existence of which Milton cannot conceive, and does not feel authorised to attempt conceiving, since such an attempt seems forbidden by God's revelation. Like human beings, the angels possess five senses; they require food; they feel hunger; they digest and assimilate, turning corporeal to incorporeal, that is to say, turning the gross matter of food to a finer and more tenuous consistence; they sleep, for heaven has alternations of evening and of morning. Whatever pure delight of love man and woman know, that in nobler ways the angels eminently enjoy. If in Milton's account of the warfare with the rebel angels there is a certain condescension to the powers of human imagination, and things of heaven are shadowed forth by things of earth, in this he follows the Divine method, which is the best and truest method of instructing our faculties to apprehend what in its own nature is beyond the scope of those faculties.

Man being one, indivisible, spiritual animal, what is the meaning of that punishment pronounced against Adam and his descendants for the sin of disobedience? What is death? The common notion that it signifies the separation of soul and body is of course inadmissible. If man dies, he dies not in part, but altogether; the whole man ceases from activity and conscious existence. But no created thing—the efflux of Deity—is destructible; man dies to be restored as a complete being, spiritually material, on the morning of resurrection. But death in a true sense entered into the world before Abel fell under the stroke of Cain; the guilt of Adam was a mortal blow directed against his own moral nature ; the obscuration of his reason by the mists of sin was intellectual death ; that which we commonly name death is only the third stage in a sequence of dreadful consequences, moral, intellectual, and physical.

If we may speak of a central point in the nature of man, we may call his will that central point. In the " Treatise on Christian Doctrine " as strongly as in " Paradise Lost," Milton insists on the freedom of the human will. It was a faith difficult to reconcile with the Calvinistic dogma of the Divine decrees. But Milton was not a Calvinist. By a long array of passages from Scripture he shows that nothing which God has left in the power of free agents is the subject of an absolute decree. Such decrees are contingent ; and thus man's liberty is in no sense controlled by God ; or, as the Father Himself declares it, in one of His scholastic dissertations to the inhabitants of heaven :

> Without least impulse or shadow of fate,
> Or aught by Me immutably foreseen,
> They trespass, authors to themselves in all
> Both what they judge and what they choose ; for so
> I formed them free ; and free they must remain
> Till they enthrall themselves ; I else must change
> Their nature, and revoke the high decree,
> Unchangeable, eternal, which ordained
> Their freedom ; they themselves ordained their fall.

" God," says Milton in his prose, " has Himself decreed that some things should be left to our free-will."

The publication of the "Treatise on Christian Doctrine" in the third decade of this century gave somewhat of a blow to Milton's popularity with many excellent people, who then for the first time discovered that the greatest religious poet of England was far from theological orthodoxy. "Paradise Lost" could no longer be considered a safe soporific for Sunday afternoons. Not only did the Puritan Milton declare that the entire decalogue was abrogated by a law of love, not only did he come forward as a pronounced anti-Sabbatarian, not only did he degrade marriage to a civil contract, advocate divorce for other causes than adultery, justify polygamy as lawful for Christians, but he deliberately rejected the orthodox doctrine of the Trinity. In "Paradise Lost" the unique position of dignity assigned by the Almighty to the Son arouses the jealousy of the revolting angels; it is not God who, in the second person of the Blessed Trinity, is made to rule over them; supreme honours have been granted to one who, like themselves, is less than Deity. In his digest of Christian doctrine Milton expresses himself without the slightest ambiguity; the Son is not coeval or equal with the Father; He is not of the same numerical essence; it was in God's power to have dwelt alone without bringing the Son into existence; by the Father's will was the Son begotten; by His will did the Son receive a portion of the Divine nature. The essential attributes of Deity—omniscience, omnipotence, supreme goodness, supreme glory—belong to the Father to the exclusion of the Son. The Holy Spirit is evidently—so Milton declares—far inferior to the Father and to the only-begotten Son of God; He is a minister and creature of the Almighty, produced probably before the foundations of the world were laid, but certainly not until after the Son had come into existence.

Thus with a patient and serene audacity Milton compiles his theology from the words of Scripture. In estimating the intellectual effort which went to the creation of his epic poems, we must bear in mind that Milton does not merely handle imaginatively an accepted body of thought on religious questions ; on the contrary, as a daring thinker he constructed on a scriptural basis, or what seemed to him to be such, his own theology. In Scripture he found authority for his method of treatment ; the imaginative medium by which he shadowed forth the abstractions of his creed was provided for him by the Old and the New Testaments. The creation of these poems was a far bolder and vaster undertaking than is commonly supposed. A theology and a philosophy of his own, akin in some respects to the Puritanism of his time, yet independent, and identical with no current doctrine, a theology and a philosophy original and extraordinary form the foundation of his amazing poetic structures. Few feats of the human mind have equalled that of collecting a complete faith and of transporting such a faith into art.

III

When Milton in his prose writings considered man in relation to his fellows, his central thought was that of freedom tending to a higher obedience ; he would cast away injurious human bonds that he might enter into the liberty of a stricter service under the divine order. When he wrote as a poet he stood in the immediate presence of God, and his central thought was that of obedience as the condition of true freedom. Let man falter for a moment from loyalty to his supreme Ruler, and he passes into the servitude of sin. The Lady of his Masque is set in the enchanted chair ; at the waving of a wand her nerves can be chained up in alabaster. But what of that ? While she maintains the inward law of chastity, she is freer than the air :

> Fool, do not boast.
> Thou canst not touch the freedom of my mind
> With all thy charms, although this corporal rind
> Thou hast immanacled while Heaven sees good.

It is the ugly-headed rabble, rolling with pleasure in a sensual sty, who are slaves. The Spirit who acts as the envoy and representative of Providence is but an attendant Spirit ; yet on his happy missions he can run to the green earth's end or soar to the corners of the moon. In his farewell words he expounds the meaning of this trial of the brothers' and sister's patience, faith and truth :

> Mortals that would follow me,
> Love Virtue ; she alone is free.
> She can teach ye how to climb
> Higher than the sphery chime.

With all the opulence of Nature spread abroad, it must be refused or wisely used, for loyalty alone is highest liberty. The test of virtue is not merely negative ; the commandment of prohibition " Thou shall not " is accompanied by a higher commandment of rapturous freedom—" Thou shalt." The doctrine of virginity is no fragment of frigid ethics ; chastity is dear and beautiful and saintly ; a thousand angels wait upon it ; clear dream and solemn vision are open to it

alone ; it illuminates with a sacred ray the outward
shape of loveliness ; it turns by some divine process the
very temple of the mind to the soul's essence, " till all be
made immortal." To exchange such light and freedom
for liquorish baits, fit to ensnare a brute, were treason,
inevitably followed by the degradation of serfdom.

In " Paradise Lost " earth and hell and heaven are
conjoined in most solemn interest about what great
affair ? The eating of ai apple. But that crude apple
which diverted Eve serves as a sufficient test of the
supreme duty of obedience. All the joys of Paradise
were on one side, the blessedness of labour and the
blessedness of rest, lordship over the docile and innocent
tribes, the fountain of pure love, communion with God
and angel guests, the freedom of glad allegiance to the
divine law-giver ; on the other side were "foul distrust"
and " breach disloyal," revolt and disobedience, with
servitude to an evil master. To Milton's imagination
the contest around the apple seemed a more heroic
argument for song than any warfare of fabled knights
on behalf of honour or of love. The most eventful
act in the world's history is an inward decision of the
will. All tyrannies, civil and ecclesiastical, against
which Milton fought lay involved in that first disloyalty
to true authority. Adam beholds in vision one of his
sons, a mighty hunter of men, who arrogates dominion
over his brethren, and Adam execrates his own offspring ; but such external domination of brute force
is only the natural development of his own disloyal
deed. The angel Michael interprets the significance of
the vision :

Since thy original lapse, true liberty
Is lost, which always with right reason dwells
Twinned, and from her hath no dividual being.

. . . .

. . . Tyranny must be,
Though to the tyrant thereby no excuse.
Yet sometimes nations will decline so low
From virtue, which is reason, that no wrong,
But justice, and some fatal curse annexed,
Deprives them of their outward liberty,
Their inward lost.

The spectacle of the Church oppressed by spiritual despots, employing secular power, follows, to be commented upon in like manner by that Independent Ironside of the angelic host :

What will they then
But force the Spirit of Grace itself, and bind
His consort, Liberty ? what but unbuild
His living temples, built by faith to stand—
Their own faith, not another's ? for on Earth
Who against faith and conscience can be heard
Infallible ? Yet many will presume.

And Adam, having seen the evils that were coming upon his successors and had his fill of knowledge, is ready to descend from the speculative mount, taking to heart the lesson : " Henceforth I learn that to obey is best." The highest heroism possible to man, he perceives, is loyalty in meekness of spirit :

Suffering for Truth's sake
Is fortitude to highest victory.

To know this is to possess one's soul " in peace of thought " ; to have learnt this much is " the sum of wisdom."

IV

It pleased Milton little to hear "Paradise Lost" commended to the disadvantage of his later and briefer epic. "Paradise Regained" bears to "Paradise Lost" somewhat of the relation which a lady-chapel bears to a cathedral ; it is less vast, but not less sacred ; it is an extension of the whole, yet an unity in itself; it harmonises with the general design, while it possesses a special grace and dignity of its own. The lesson which Adam had been taught before he was dismissed to wander abroad on earth is here enforced by a great example. The scene is not the happy garden but the austere landscape of the desert. An ideal man, beautiful in youth's full flower, ardent in patriotism and the passion of humanity, at a most critical moment, when he has just received the highest assurance of his public mission, is to be exposed to the temptation of greatness, and to remain victor through meekness, patience, fortitude, and entire obedience. He, like Adam, is the representative of our race ; his victory is ours, and as by disobedience Paradise was lost, so "by one man's firm obedience fully tried," Paradise is to be regained.

The moment was one of peculiar danger. Assured of his high destiny, the young leader of men might be eager to start on his career, to take his own way, to choose his own time. Satan, no longer the proud archangel, majestic though ruined, but a crafty counsellor with the experience of half a myriad of years, a Satan-Machiavel, a grey dissimulation, knows that his last chance has come, and he will put forth all his wiles. In deep agitation of mind, which begets a swarm of thoughts, the divine man is led into the wilderness. From childhood his aspiration has been for the public good ; he had boldly appeared as a boy among the doctors of the Temple; as a youth he had aspired to patriotic achievements:

> Victorious deeds
> Flamed in my heart, heroic acts—one while
> To rescue Israel from the Roman yoke ;
> Then to subdue and quell o'er all the earth
> Brute violence and proud tyrannic power,
> Till truth were freed, and equity restored.

Satan's best hopes are founded on the liability of a heroic leader, bent upon disinterested ends, to overlook the legitimacy of the means by which such ends may be attained, and on the impatience of that zeal which would hasten to the tasks of love.

After the salutation of combatants in the great duel, the first thrust, aimed at the common humanity of Christ, which knows the need of bread, and at his fears that he may perish in the wilderness with all his tasks unaccomplished, is instantly met and foiled. Few passages in either epic have more of the Miltonic grandeur than that in which the " aged man in rural weeds," detected and repulsed, declares himself with a majestic melancholy :

> 'Tis true, I am that Spirit unfortunate,

and like some dark bird of prey wheels in mournful flight above the thought of his eternal loss, only to recover his poise and watch his opportunity :

> Though I have lost
> Much lustre of my native brightness, lost
> To be beloved of God, I have not lost
> To love, at least contemplate and admire,
> What I see excellent in good, or fair,
> Or virtuous : I should so have lost all sense.

The old peasant has been suddenly transformed into the most dignified of sophists.

A pause and resting-place is afforded by the interlude of Andrew and Simon on the bank of Jordan in converse concerning the lost Messiah and that of Mary pondering motherly cares and fears in her heart. Then the duel is renewed. Charles Lamb was of opinion that the banquet spread by Satan's command in a scene, though in the wilderness, of visionary beauty, was wanting in poetic decorum—a temptation for a Heliogabalus rather than for the meek Saviour. But Milton's Saviour is a man, and a man whose brain has been disturbed by long abstinence from food. He had rejected food as a necessity ; now he is an-hungered, perhaps light-headed, and food may be accepted as a delight. The art of gastronomy is conceived by Milton as a species of poetry ; stripling youths and fairest nymphs are the attendants ; harmonious airs are heard from pipe and string ; the scent of vernal blossoms floats on the breeze ; it is not a civic feast, nor the luxury of a gaudy day at Cambridge, but an enchantment of the senses and the imagination. And Satan, though he will make his experiment, accepts his failure without surprise. It is at least an exhibition of his power— power which if worthless to gratify the appetite may be serviceable in other ways to one whose heart is set on high designs.

But the seduction of riches as a means to beneficent ends is met by a like tranquil yet unsubdueable resistance. True kingship begins by self - mastery, and more kingly than temporal power is the influence of truth which governs the inner man, the nobler part. True glory lies not in popular applause, but in God's approbation won by patience, temperance, genuine wisdom, deeds of peace. Climbing from the senses to the higher passions, and thence to the last infirmity of noble mind, Satan, inly racked yet maintaining a mastery under his successive defeats, appeals to Christ's sense of duty and his religious zeal. If he will not choose his own means of enterprise, has he a right to linger on his beneficent way? He is a heroic youth, unversed in the world's affairs. Should he not understand the situation, and learn, even from an old Satan-Machiavel, how a Jewish alliance against Rome may be cemented with the Parthian? But regal mysteries and politic maxims are a cumbrous learning little needed by the prophetic Son of God; he who best can suffer best can reign; all things are to be fulfilled in their due time.

The wisdom of Greece moves the spirit of Jesus no more than does the imperial power of Rome. Under the Roman magnificence he detects servility of soul :

> What wise and valiant man would seek to free
> These, thus degenerate, by themselves enslaved,
> Or could of inward slaves make outward free ?

The alleged kingship over self of the Greek stoical philosophy he regards as a vain boast. The fear of the Lord, taught by the Hebrew prophets and singers, that is wisdom. Milton, says Sir John Seeley, draws in the person of Christ " a more gifted and energetic Marcus Aurelius." Classical virtue, he tells us, " is self-dependence, love of country, contempt for pleasure in comparison with great deeds, love of fame "; the

Christian ideal is founded not on self-respect, but on self-sacrifice. In "Paradise Regained" we find the Renaissance through Milton's adoption of " the classical conception of virtue." Surely the criticism flies wide of the mark. Whatever Milton may have built into his structure from classical sources, the foundation is essentially Hebraic. The classical ideal of virtue is presented by Satan and is rejected by Jesus. His might is derived from dependence upon God. By "humiliation and strong sufferance" his weakness overcomes Satanic strength. His victories are those of entire obedience. But his obedience is filial. Self-respect, self-veneration Milton conceived as part of the Christian ideal of virtue, and such in truth it is. "Ye are," wrote St Paul, "the temple of the living God." True worship, as Milton understood it, is no servile crouching, but the happy boldness of a son, rejoicing in his Father's presence. The humility of Christ is the humility that soars and gladly obeys.

Satan's devices and sophistries are all but exhausted. The night of rage and tempest passes away; it is radiant morning again, and the Son of Man, after the dismal hours, is no worse than wet. The great gambler's last stake alone remains ; his despair reduces him to the effrontery of the last temptation. Jesus is challenged to substitute a demonstration of His Divine Sonship for filial faith in the meaning of the Father's testimony ; and no elaborate reasonings are needed to foil the antagonist ; a single word suffices :

Also it is written,
" Tempt not the Lord thy God."

And at the word the event is ended—" But Satan smitten with amazement fell."

The decorum which Lamb found wanting in the banquet scene is at least fully observed in the close of Milton's poem. Had " Paradise Regained " ended with the vast *coup de théâtre* of Satan's fall, or with the oratorio chorus of the angelic choir we should have felt that the humanity of Jesus was somewhat obscured. A classical triumph must not celebrate this great series of victories ; no chariots and horsemen and captive slaves must accompany this greatest of conquerors to the Capitol. We need something more truly human, more truly divine :

> He, unobserved
> Home to his mother's house private returned.

Nothing more : other tasks await the Son of God, which will be accomplished with the quietude and the dignity of humiliation and strong sufferance.

V

Though the forms of Attic tragedy are observed in "Samson Agonistes," its inner spirit, like that of " Paradise Regained," is essentially Hebraic. The central idea is still that of obedience and loyalty to a divine ruler in the great contention between good and evil ; the human actors of the drama stand forth from a background of providential disposal. No poem perhaps leaves a more single or a more inexhaustible impression—that of commiseration lost in victory, that of victory subdued

N

by the solemnity of death, that of divine purpose controlling both life and death. The protagonist is in truth not Samson but Jehovah. The great combatant, pre-eminent in strength and valour, the champion of his people, chosen of God for a high purpose, has fallen. Through no merit of his own but as an act of free grace the divine gift of strength had been conferred upon him; all that was demanded was that he should keep a secret entrusted to him ; in that test he had failed. He had forgotten his loyalty to God in a woman's lap, when nothing was required save the passive obedience of silence. As the consequence of that dereliction the Hebrew patriot and hero is reduced to blind servitude at the mill in Gaza, oppressed above all by the sense of his own unfaithfulness and of heaven's desertion, a man who is not "in the list of them that hope." Old Manoa with his uninspired reason and good-will, hoping to obtain his son's ransom and vainly dreaming that his eyesight may be restored, can bring him no true help. Dalila, a mist of frauds, Harapha, a storm of brute force, serve him only by rousing his spirit from supine despair to indignant passion.

Yet help there is for Samson, but his help can be from God alone. He has failed in the test of passive obedience; there is also obedience of an active kind: will he fail in this? Pleasure he was unable to resist; will he be able to confront pain and death? A second test of obedience is proposed to determine the issue of his life. When he is summoned to appear before the Philistine lords at their profane festival, Samson at first refuses—"I will not come." But presently sudden promptings stir within his mind, and he is aware that these promptings are from God:

> I begin to feel
> Some rousing motions in me, which dispose
> To something extraordinary my thoughts.
> I with this messenger will go along—
> Nothing to do, be sure, that may dishonour
> Our Law, or stain my vow of Nazarite.
> If there be aught of presage in the mind,
> This day will be remarkable in my life
> By some great act, or of my days the last.

In this final test Samson will not fail; even to his own destruction he follows out the divine promptings. And therefore after the hideous noise, the shouting, the universal groan, destruction and ruin at the utmost point, there follows deep peace of mind, a peace as pure as it is profound. Samson lies a ruin of manhood, but at the last the will of God has been loyally fulfilled, and through obedience he has obtained God's enfranchisement of death:

> Nothing is here for tears, nothing to wail
> Or knock the breast; no weakness, no contempt,
> Dispraise or blame; nothing but well and fair,
> And what may quiet us in a death so noble.

Not through Manoa's prudent diplomacy but through one act of heroic obedience, the blind and dejected captive has passed from servitude to freedom.

Critics have lamented that Milton did not embody his political experience in epic or in drama; "the epic of liberty, virtue, and religion, which he had it in him to write, remained unwritten." It seems at first sight as if his prose writings, devoted to the cause of freedom, and his poems were separated by a gulf that is wide and deep. But is this really the case? Or were not the prose pamphlets an attempt to give an application in detail to the one great principle which inspires masque and epic and drama? When Milton was a poet he could soar with no middle flight; he could occupy himself with none of the secondary truths which regulate conduct private or public. One primary truth filled all his mind—acceptance of the divine rule, submission to the divine mandate; heroic patience in accepting the will of God, heroic energy in making the will of God prevail; entire obedience, and, through obedience, freedom.

VII

AN ANGLICAN AND A PURITAN EIRENICON
JEREMY TAYLOR: BAXTER

I

A FUNERAL panegyric is not and cannot be a complete criticism; but true sorrow may be keen-sighted for the characteristic virtue of a mind and life. No better word, when allowance has been made for the occasion, has been spoken of Jeremy Taylor than that found in the sermon preached a few days after his death by his friend and follower Dean Rust, himself a writer of some distinction, whose affinities were with the school of the Cambridge Platonists. Taylor was not a great or original thinker; he was not always as wise as he was learned; the spirit of authority sometimes overbore with him the spirit of conciliation. "He was not unseen," says Rust, "in the subtleties and spinosities of the schools, and upon occasion could make them serve his purpose." It was not always an advantage to Taylor that he delayed among these subtleties and spinosities, and the panegyrist adds with a half apologetic touch : " Yet, I believe, he thought many of them very near akin to the famous knight of La Mancha, and would make sport sometimes with the romantic sophistry, and fantastic adventures of school-

errantry." We may remain unconvinced when Rust
ascribes to his friend "the profoundness of a philosopher, the sagacity of a prophet, the reason of an
angel." But when he speaks of the natural ardour of
Taylor's temperament, the opulence of his endowment,
the harmonious richness of his genius, and when he
adds that this ardour and these great gifts were
directed towards piety, we feel that he has found
the centre, and said a final word : "Nature had
befriended him much in his constitution ; for he was
a person of a most sweet and obliging humour, of
great candour and ingenuousness ; . . . his soul was
made up of harmony ; . . . all his words and his
very tone and cadences were unusually musical. But
that which most of all captivated and ravished his
hearers was the gaiety and richness of his fancy ; for
he had much in him of that natural enthusiasm which
inspires all great poets and orators ; and there was
a generous ferment in his blood and spirits, that
forcibly excited his imagination, and raised it to
such a degree of luxuriancy as nothing but the greatness of his wit and judgment could have kept within
due bounds." The truth could hardly be better told.
And Rust adds elsewhere in his *éloge* : "His humility
was coupled with extraordinary piety ; and, I believe,
he spent the greatest part of his time in heaven ; his
solemn hours of prayer took up a considerable portion
of his life ; and we are not to doubt but he had learned
of St Paul to pray continually ; and that occasional
ejaculations, and frequent aspirations, and emigrations
of his soul after God, made up the best part of his

devotions." There we have the whole man, his ardour, his rich endowments, his various learning, (of which Rust tells us also) and the zeal of his piety.

The restraint of Taylor's affluence, that which saved it from expanding into a luxuriant marsh, came less from his judgment than from his zeal. At his best he flows forward with a harmonious impetuosity, like a river that is wide, and is swifter than it seems, exultant, with many a refluent eddy which cannot check, but rather is part of, the sweep and progress of the stream. Nowhere perhaps does the natural ardour of Taylor's heart appear more attractively than in the discourse addressed to Mrs Katherine Philips—the matchless Orinda—on the nature, offices, and measures of Friendship. Orinda, whom Mr Gosse calls the first English sentimentalist, had erected friendship in her Arcady of the sweet shire of Cardigan into a kind of fine art. "The noble Palæmon," Jeremy Taylor, in his letter to her is passionate, with wise and sacred passion, but certainly is untouched by any effeminate sentimentality. He tells us how every common sorrow of the world, if brought home to the imagination, wounds the spirit of charity within him, yet he reserves his best affections for those whom kinship or circumstances have brought near : "I pray for all mankind; I am grieved at every sad story I hear; I am troubled when I hear of a pretty bride murdered in her bride-chamber by an ambitious and enraged rival; I shed a tear when I am told that a brave king was misunderstood, then slandered, then imprisoned, and then put to death by evil men;[1] and I can never read the story of the Parisian Massacre, or the Sicilian vespers, but my blood curdles, and I am disordered by two or three affections. . . . But though we must pray for all men, yet we say special litanies for brave kings and holy prelates, and the wise guides of souls; for our brethren and relations, our wives and children."

Not even the poet of " Leaves of Grass " has sung more enthusiastically of comradeship than Taylor in this Discourse. Friendship is like the sun, the eye of the world ; but men, according to their worth, differ in their capacity to receive its showers of warmth and light. The emanation of the beams of the sun is for all the world ; for the scalded Indian and the poor boy that shakes at the foot of the Riphæean hills ; but men receive of friendship only what they can ; " and some have only a dark day and a long night, snows and white cattle, a miserable life, and a perpetual harvest of catarrhs and consumptions, apoplexies and dead palsies ; but some have splendid fires and aromatic spices, rich wines and well-digested fruits, great wit and great courage ; because they dwell in his eye, and look in his face, and are the courtiers of the sun, and wait upon him in his chambers of the East." Such splendid fires and aromatic spices were the gifts of the sun to Taylor in his best creations. Addressing in this Discourse a woman celebrated for her genius in friendship, he must needs touch upon the subject of friendships in which a woman

---

[1] The reference seems to be to Charles I. ; the discourse was published in 1657.

bears a part, and he does so with a noble enthusiasm. Marriage in its ideal he conceives as friendship brought to perfection; and beyond this passage we have little to lead us to any inference as to the happiness which Taylor found in his first or his second wife:[1] "You may see how much I differ from the morosity of those Cynics who would not admit your sex into the communities of a noble friendship . . . I cannot say that women are capable of all those excellencies by which men can oblige the world; and therefore a female friend in some cases is not so good a counsellor as a wise man, and cannot so well defend my honour, nor dispose of reliefs and assistances, if she be under the power of another; but a woman can love as passionately, and converse as pleasantly, and retain a secret as faithfully, and be useful in her proper ministries; and she can die for her friend as well as the bravest Roman knight." Over which fine outbreak Orinda may well have given a sigh of satisfaction.

It is unfortunate for Taylor that he should be known chiefly by ornaments detached from his larger compositions. The lark rising from his bed of grass, and beaten back with the loud sighings of an eastern wind, the rose newly springing from the clefts of its hood, and dismantled of its too youthful and unripe retirements— these and the like are beautiful and memorable, but if read as elegant extracts they leave an impression that Taylor's excellence lay in filigree work, and that sweet-

[1] His second wife is believed to have been a natural daughter of Charles I.

ness with him was not united with severity or strength.
Nor, indeed, was it always. But Taylor's happiness of
temper and his florid graces, growing freely like the little
rings of the vine, were not inconsistent with habits of
almost ascetic discipline and with an energy of imagination which shows itself in greatness of composition. The
large ordonnance of some of his discourses will surely
strike any reader of those which treat of Christ's advent
to Judgment. There is in them a magnificence of
terror, but of terror relieved by a solemn joy, which
reminds one, if not of the splendid mastery of Tintoretto,
yet, at least, of the constructive power of Poussin.
The sweep and grandeur of the whole are the true
evidence of the preacher's imaginative passion. He
puts the trumpet to his lips, and it is a

> Tuba mirum spargens sonum
> Per sepulchra regionum,

such as might penetrate the ears, let us not say of
the watchful dead, but rather of Hogarth's sleeping
congregation.

Fervour in the pursuit of devout ends is what Taylor
above all desires to breathe into his hearers. If we
pray, let our prayers be as flames of fire ascending from
the heart's altar. When you reckon up your prayers,
"you must reckon, not by the number of the collects,
but by your sighs and passions, by the vehemence of
your desires, and the fervour of your spirit, the apprehension of your need, and the consequent prosecution
of your supply." For cold prayers are not put into
the account, but are laid aside "like the buds of roses,
which a cold wind hath nipped into death, and the

discoloured tawny face of an Indian slave." And again, without elaborated metaphor, yet in words no less characteristic of Taylor than the last : " He that is cold and tame in his prayers hath not tasted of the deliciousness of religion and the goodness of God ; he is a stranger to the secrets of the Kingdom, and therefore he does not know what it is either to have hunger or satiety ; and therefore neither are they hungry for God nor satisfied with the world ; but remain stupid and inapprehensive, without resolution and determination, never choosing clearly, nor pursuing earnestly, and therefore never enter into possession, but always stand at the gates of weariness, unnecessary caution, and perpetual irresolution."

Three sermons are specially devoted to the subject of " Lukewarmness and Zeal; or Spiritual Fervour." Taylor's own fervour makes him courageous in his teaching. Contrasting the spirit of Christian worship with that of the Mosaic ritual, he utters words which we might rather have expected to hear from the lips of a Puritan divine. By the shadow of the ceremony, under the law of Moses, God did indeed require the substantial worship ; "yet because they were to mind the outward action, it took much off from the intention and activity of the spirit; man could not do both busily." Milton has used the same argument against elaborate ceremony. The preacher again dares to declare boldly, though under the shadow of St Augustine's authority, that sin may be the cloudy porch which leads to sanctity ; the loss of chastity by one—virgin or widow—who is chaste and proud, may be, in a true sense, a means to grace ; to fall into offence is sometimes a remedy.

He asserts that a lukewarm religion, if it be not in progress to a better state, is "much worse" than no religion at all. He does not scruple to say, that to give to the poor is better than to give to a church. And for one whose preaching, no doubt, was hung upon by many enraptured auditors of the sex that most looks up to a gracious pulpiteer, it needed, perhaps, yet higher courage to announce pretty plainly that certain of them had better be at home attending to their household duties. "Martha was troubled with much serving; that was 'more than needs,' and therefore she was to blame; and sometimes hearing in some circumstances may be 'more than needs'; and some women are 'troubled with over much hearing,' and then they had better have been serving the necessities of their house." It would be base to conjecture that a popular Puritan lecturer was holding forth in the neighbourhood of Golden Grove.

Easy ways to salvation were viewed by Taylor with distrust; strait is the gate; the Kingdom of Heaven suffereth violence, and the violent take it by force. In the second sermon on "Godly Fear" he had ventured to say that our sins are not pardoned easily and quickly; pardon fluctuates like the wave when the tide has turned, and only gradually invades the shore; we are to expect it upon such terms as are revealed, which include time, and labour, and uncertainty, and fear, and holy living. How shall we know that we have received the grace of forgiveness? Not by some sudden inward light, which may be a false phosphorescence sprung from our own heart. There is a surer way of knowledge : " If I have sinned against God in the shameful crime of lust, then God hath pardoned my sins, when, upon repentance and prayers, He hath given me the grace of chastity. My drunkenness is forgiven when I have acquired the grace of temperance and a sober spirit. My covetousness shall no more be a damning sin, when I have a loving and charitable spirit ; loving to do good, and despising the world." In all things let us base our confidence on grounds that are solid and stable. " Let us proceed," says Taylor in one of his noblest words, " from causes to effects, . . . and believe felicity not to be a chance but a choice." And it is in such words as these rather than in the well-known decorative passages that we reach to the strength of the great preacher's spirit.

All the highest spiritual teachers have declared that a state of aridity is sometimes as profitable to the soul as a state of refreshment. Taylor exhorts his hearers to fill the dry places at least with duties well done : " This delight is not to be understood as if it were always required that we should always feel an actual cheerfulness and sensible joy ; such as was that of Jonathan, when he had newly tasted honey, and the light came into his eyes, and he was refreshed and pleasant. This happens sometimes, when God pleases to entice, or reward a man's spirit, with little antepasts of heaven ; but such a delight only is necessary, and a duty, that we always choose our duty regularly, and undervalue the pleasures of temptation, and proceed in the work of grace with a firm choice and unabated election." If we elect to go still forward under our load of difficulty and pain it is enough; what we choose, that we delight in.[1]

Out of the strong came forth sweetness; and here the strength is that of an eager, ardent nature. Let us see Taylor aright, and we shall perceive that his sweetness grows out of an inward severity, and that the blossoming passages of his writings mean often that the passion of his heart must break forth in beauty. The following, from the second sermon " Of Lukewarmness and Zeal," may serve as an example, which is highly characteristic of the writer; it is no ornament attached externally, but the flowering of sap ascending from roots that strike deep in earth : " You may observe it, that so long as the light shines bright, and the fires of devotion and desires flame out, so long the mind of a man stands close to the altar, and waits upon the sacrifice; but as the fires die, and desires decay, so the mind steals away, and walks abroad to see the little images of beauty and pleasure, which it beholds in the falling stars and little glow-worms of the world. The river that runs slow and creeps by the banks, and begs leave of every turf to let it pass, is drawn into little hollownesses, and spends itself in smaller portions, and dies with diversion; but when it runs with vigorousness and a full stream, and breaks down every obstacle, making it even as its own brow, it stays not to be tempted by little avocations, and to creep into holes, but runs into the sea through full and useful channels; so is a man's prayer, if it moves upon the feet of an abated appetite; it wanders into the society of every

[1] "Of Lukewarmness and Zeal," Part II.

trifling accident, and stays at the corners of the fancy, and talks with every object it meets, and cannot arrive at heaven; but when it is carried upon the wings of passion and strong desires, a swift motion and a hungry appetite, it passes on through all the intermediate region of clouds, and stays not till it dwells at the foot of the throne where mercy sits, and thence sends holy showers of refreshment." The sermons on Lukewarmness and Zeal close with certain warnings, for Taylor's religious prudence was great and taught him that true zeal has its measures, and intemperate zeal its dangers. His age seemed to him an age of violent passions tending to strife, but of much lukewarmness towards what is sincerely good. He pleads therefore for a zeal according to knowledge, not for a *via media* of tameness, but for a pure ardour in the pursuit of what he terms a persevering, a great, a passionate religion.

In days of trouble and division Taylor put forth an Eirenicon in his " Liberty of Prophesying." To reduce the essential articles of Christian belief to those of the Apostles' Creed, to maintain the prerogative of human reason, to exhibit the uncertainty of theological opinions, and to write in the temper of charity was certainly to serve the cause of toleration. But a man may widen the bounds of toleration, yet draw the line with a rigid pen. He may shrink from giving his fundamental principles their complete application. As an Irish bishop Taylor's action certainly did not result in peace; but it would be unjust not to bear in mind the difficulties of his position. He insisted on order and obedience within his own communion; and his opponents were not of a compliant temper. "We find," he writes in the dedication of his sermon preached at the opening of the Irish Parliament, "that all Christian churches kept this rule; they kept themselves and others close to the rule of faith, and peaceably suffered one another to differ in ceremonies, but suffered no difference amongst their own; they gave liberty to other churches, and gave laws, and no liberty, to their own subjects: and at this day the churches of Geneva, France, Switzerland, Germany, Low Countries, tie all their people to their own laws, but tie up no man's conscience; if he be not persuaded as they are, let him charitably dissent, and leave that government, and adhere to his own communion." Taylor's principles of conformity were rather defensive than designedly aggressive, yet in its result his action savours too much of Black Bartholomew day, and those who should celebrate his memory with most applause are the Presbyterians of the north of Ireland, who were gainers by his over-strained spirit of legality.

Yet to his Irish days belongs a second and a very admirable Eirenicon—the sermon which he named "Via Intelligentiæ," preached before "the little but excellent University of Dublin," and published in 1662. It is addressed to such earnest seekers for truth as a sanguine person might suppose would specially gather around a university, and the text is the conciliating one "If any man will do his will, he shall know of the doctrine." Such a text is indeed two-edged, and may lend itself to uncharitable handling. We, of this communion or of that, do God's will and know of the doctrine; those who maintain another doctrine have erred because of evil affections and unrighteous lives, and cannot be among the doers of God's will. There is something *naïve* in such sophistry as this; but Taylor in the sermon sophisticates his text with most sincere conviction. Kings and bishops are of divine ordinance; to submit to them is to be loyal to the will of God. What criminals therefore are they who oppose bishops and a king, men who "rise up against their fathers, and are cruel to their brethren, and stir up the people to sedition; and all this with a cold stomach and a hot liver, with a hard heart and a tender conscience, with humble carriage and a proud spirit." And in like manner consider, he cries, the "infinite unreasonableness" that is in the Popish religion, how against common sense their doctrine of transubstantiation is, how against the common experience of human nature is the doctrine of the Pope's infallibility, how against Scripture is the doctrine of indulgences and purgatory. How is belief in these absurdities possible? Simply enough; the devisers of the doctrines were not among those who did God's will; the doctrines were imposed upon the credulous for the sake of temporal ends. Every proposition of the Popish religion which differs from those held by us is meant "to serve the end of money or of power." Taylor does not raise the question whether a like argument could have been effectively used by a nonconformist against the Anglican establishment.

But putting aside matter of controversy, there is much that is of high excellence in the "Via Intelli-

o

gentiæ." It admirably describes the temper in which truth should be sought; it admirably distinguishes between a notional assent to propositions and the real and vital apprehension of truth ; it justly rebukes some of the trifling or over-curious learning of the schools. The drift of the whole is that "theology is rather a divine life than a divine knowledge."

Men of his time, says Taylor, had been wrangling about peace, and seeking the ascertainment of some common body of truth as the ground of religious unity. Each rival communion was prepared to exhibit a system of belief, and tell you that is the true religion, and they are the Church, and the peculiar people of God. Of this, says Taylor, there will be no end—"for divide the Church into twenty parts, and, in whatsoever part your lot falls, you and your party are damned by the other nineteen." Another imagined way to reconcile the differences of Christendom is that of moderation, a way favoured by Erasmus, Grotius, and others. Let each sect abate its asperities, and pare away something of its distinctive doctrine, and let all join in common terms and phrases of accommodation. "From hence"— such is Taylor's remorseless statement of his conviction —"can succeed nothing but folly and a fantastic peace : this is but the skinning of an old sore ; it will break out upon all occasions." Something, he thinks, may be gained by clearness of definition in questions of controversy ; but, after all, this is nothing else but "a drawing up the armies in battalia with great skill and discipline"; it brings the combat to a precise issue, and the next thing the combatants do is to thrust their swords into one another's sides. What remedy, Taylor asks, after all this? Is it to be found in the complete toleration of all opinions? This is a way of peace rather than of truth. It is indeed a highly reasonable way; yet how can the intolerant, who seek not equality but absolute rule, be themselves tolerated? Complete toleration—Taylor spoke of his own time, and the words were spoken in Ireland—" is better in contemplation than in practice." Mere opinions certainly are not to be persecuted; but it is equally certain that opinions which lead to violence in states ought not to be made public and permitted.

The human ways towards truth and peace have failed and must fail. What is God's way? "If any man do His will he shall know of the doctrine. . . . The way to judge of religion is by doing of our duty: and theology is rather a divine life than a divine knowledge. In heaven, indeed, we shall first see, and then love; but here on earth, we must first love, and love will open our eyes as well as our hearts; and we shall then see, and perceive, and understand."

Taylor does not mean that one who does the duty that lies nearest to him will be enlightened by new revelations, and be conducted by ecstasy, and pray in a transfiguration, and live upon raptures. The spirit of God does not spend its holy influences "in disguises and convulsions of the understanding." It does not destroy but rather heightens reason. The process is simple; good men see what is good, and they lay hold of it; "half a word is enough to make them understand; a nod is a sufficient reproof; the crowing of a cock, the singing of a lark, the dawning of the day, and the washing their hands, are to them competent memorials of religion and warnings of their duty." Human learning, indeed, brings excellent aids to the true knowledge of religion ; but by arguing and dispute we see no more than the shadow of God, in which are many dark appearances, little certainty, and much conjecture. If by human learning we have attained to the meaning of a divine word, there is still "a meaning of the meaning" (for the leaves of the book are written within and without), a living secret, which can only be made real for us through practice—"this is to be felt, and not to be talked of; and they that never touched it with their finger may secretly perhaps laugh at it in their heart, and be never the wiser." Taylor himself was a man of multifarious learning, a theologian and a casuist, but it seemed to him that scholars too often lived upon air and empty notions, troubling themselves, as he admirably puts it, with tying and untying knots, like hypochondriacs in a fit of melancholy, raising foolish questions, spending zeal in things unprofitable, making religion to consist of outsides. "No, no"; he cries, "the man that is wise, he that is conducted by the Spirit of God, knows better in what Christ's kingdom does consist than to throw away his time, and interest, and peace and safety—for what ? for religion ? no : for the body of religion ? not so much : for the garment of the body of religion?" no, not for so much: but for the fringes of the garment of the body of religion. A word that has meanings for the nineteenth century as truly as for Taylor's own day.

Stated in a word, Taylor's teaching is that truth

resides implicitly in goodness; it may never attain to an explicit statement in words or propositions, but it abides in the heart as a hidden wisdom, which regulates conduct and contains all that is needful for life and godliness. He does not shrink from illustrating his central thought by a striking example. Who is he that best knows, as far as it can be known to man, the unintelligible mystery of the Divine nature? Not he who can do no more than recite the "Quicunque vult," and brandish his sword in honour of the credenda. We may amuse ourselves, says Taylor, with essences and hypostasies and personalities, distinctions without difference, priority in coequalities, and unity in pluralities, and may be none the wiser; we may build three tabernacles for the Trinity in our head, and may talk something, and know not what. But the good man, who feels " the power of the Father," he to whom " the Son " is become " wisdom, righteousness, sanctification and redemption," he in " whose heart the love of the Spirit of God is spread "; he—though he understands nothing of what is unintelligible—alone understands the mystery of the holy Trinity, for, vigorous in holy actions, he sees with his heart what his tongue can never express, and his metaphysics can never prove.

Such is Jeremy Taylor's "Eirenicon"; one which settled nothing, and could settle nothing immediately; one which could not on the instant avert grave errors of judgment or stay unhappy courses of action; but one which, if taken to heart, and made real to the conscience and to conduct, must in the end form a temper favourable both to truth and peace.

II

This was an Eirenicon which came from the victorious side, from the party in power, and in the hour of triumph. A still more remarkable and beautiful utterance of that spirit which is peaceable and pure came from the party that suffered persecution. Baxter's autobiography, one of the most interesting books of nonconformist literature, was not published until after the author's death, but the first part, which is not, as are the later parts, encumbered with a chaos of documents, was written about two years after the disaster of Black Bartholomew day. Baxter was not then an old man ; he was not quite fifty ; but in experience he was old ; and bodily infirmities, incessant labours, 'and the intensity of his zeal on behalf of others had worn him and brought on what he terms a *prœmatura senectus.* No matter lay nearer to his heart, except the salvation of souls, than conciliation in the religion of Protestants ; he gave his best endeavours, not always perhaps with wisdom in details, but always with entire and disinterested sincerity, towards attaining a " comprehension," which should reconcile and unite the moderate " Episcopal men " with the moderates among the Presbyterians and the Independents ; and, though he succeeded for a time and in a measure in his own neighbourhood of Kidderminster, we know how completely his larger hopes and purposes were wrecked. These efforts towards a comprehension form a well - known piece of English ecclesiastical history, and cannot be considered here. But there is a passage at the close of the first part of the autobiography—" Reliquiæ Baxterianæ," as it was named by his colleague and editor, Matthew Sylvester—which tells of the changes that came over his mind and temper and opinions with advancing years, and it is in these memorable pages that Baxter's best "Eirenicon" may be found.[1]

Baxter's autobiography has one quality which is among the rarest in books of its kind, and which gives it a value almost unique—it is written with absolute sincerity. He dresses up nothing; he does not project before his imagination any ideal self, and fit things to correspond with that ideal; he aims simply at telling what he knew or what he believed to be true. We can see that he often viewed public affairs too much from what we may call the ministerial stand-point, but that was natural, and the fact is neither obtruded nor disguised. We perceive how his scrupulosity of conscience, his habit of balancing all the reasons for and against a course of conduct in some degree disqualified him for doing justice to men of action, who grasped truth largely and roughly, and who knew that lack of promptitude might be a greater evil than many errors committed on the way to a great end. The animal basis for audacity which lies in a vigorous body and hearty spirits was with him wholly absent; he was almost constantly a sufferer from physical infirmities,

[1] While preparing this chapter I noticed that admirable use was made of this passage from Baxter's autobiography in Jowett's " Sermons Biographical and Miscellaneous," pp. 73-78, and that he added a nineteenth-century application and extension. Sir James Stephen, " Essays in Ecclesiastical Biography," II., 60, spoke of the passage as " familiar to most students of English literature," which, I fear, was an amiable form of politeness to his readers.

with his acrimonious blood, his excoriated finger-ends,
his rheumatic head, his flatulent stomach, his extreme
chilliness without, his bleedings at the nose, his pearls
in the eyes, his latent stones in the reins, and all else
of which he has to tell his readers, because "the
case of his body had a great operation on his soul."
But he found that the best palliative for his ailments
was incessant activity; there was much to be done;
death stood always, as he thought, at hand; the spirit
lodged in this crazy tenement of clay was aflame with
love for the souls of men; and he toiled as if with the
strength of ten.   The union in Baxter of the indefatigable pastor and the inquisitive and restless schoolman
of Protestant theology is perhaps his distinguishing
characteristic.   His intellect pursued logical distinctions
and subtleties with an almost morbid curiosity; his
heart was quick with a passion of charity, which did
not expend itself in mere contemplation, but animated
a life made up of methodical and industrious habits.

He belonged to no party; in each he saw some things
to applaud and some things to condemn.[1]   He was
neither Episcopal (in what he calls the diocesan sense)
nor strictly a Presbyterian; he was too Arminian for
the high Calvinists and too Calvinistic for the
Arminians.   He thought kneeling at the Communion
lawful, and made no scruple about the ring in marriage;
he doubted of the surplice, and never could bring himself to use the Cross in baptism; he admitted that a
form of prayer and liturgy is not in itself forbidden, but
held that the English liturgy has much disorder and

[1] See the opening of Part II. of "Reliquiæ Baxterianæ."

defectiveness in it. He had duly subscribed to the thirty-nine articles, but, in his maturer days, came to judge subscription unlawful. In each matter of conscience he tried, with the aids of Scripture and much study and prayer, to puzzle out for himself the right or the wrong.

"How beautiful upon the mountains are the feet of him that publisheth peace." Baxter's feet were often upon those Delectable mountains of which Bunyan speaks, from whose heights the celestial city can be seen, but his work lay among the weavers of the streets of Kidderminster. Sermons, catechisings, visitings, the resolution of doubts, meetings for parish discipline, conferences and discussions with ministers, works of charity, the unpaid practice of physic, and, with all this, the incessant exercise of his pen, filled up fourteen years with what he calls sweet employment. "For ever blessed be the God of mercies," he cries, "that in times of usurpation I had all this mercy and happy freedom, when under our rightful king and governor I and many hundreds more are silenced, and laid by as broken vessels, and vilified as scarce to be tolerated to live privately and quietly in the land !" Preaching to a people who had not been made sermon-proof—the word is Baxter's own—by an awakening ministry, he lit up a spirit of piety hitherto unknown in the town. Five galleries were added to the church ; on the Lord's day there was no disorder to be seen, "but you might hear an hundred families singing psalms and repeating sermons as you passed through the streets." When Baxter preached at Worcester the poor nailers and other labourers would not only crowd the church, but would hang upon the windows and the leads without. The preacher was not of an over sanguine temper—a man, indeed, "of a discouraged spirit"—but he believed that were it not for the faction of the prelatists on the one side, and the factions of the giddy and turbulent sectaries on the other, "England had been like, in a quarter of an age, to have become a land of saints and a pattern of holiness to all the world." He admits that new and strange sects, some of which he has described in a passage of great interest, arose ; but though he was a lover of religious harmony, he called to remembrance "that sects have most abounded when the Gospel hath most prospered." It is better, he thinks, that men should be purblind, and make the mistakes of the purblind, than that they should make no mistakes, being blind : "He that never regardeth the word of God is not like to err much about it ; men will sooner fall out about gold or pearls than swine or asses will."

His books and pamphlets, most of which had some immediate work to do, and having done their work might well fall on sleep, were the outpourings of an eager intellect and a fervid heart. "Indeed, for the 'Saints' Rest,' I had four months' vacancy to write it (but in the midst of continual languishing and medicine) ; but for the rest I wrote them in the crowd of all my other employments, which would allow me no great leisure for polishing and exactness, or any ornament ; so that I scarce ever wrote one sheet twice over, nor stayed to make any blots or interlinings, but was fain to let it go as it was first conceived ; and when my own desire was rather to stay upon one thing long than run over many, some sudden occasion or other extorted almost all my writings from me ; and the apprehensions of present usefulness or necessity prevailed against all other motives." He tells us that in little more than a year twenty thousand copies of " A Call to the Unconverted " were printed in authorised editions, while many thousand copies appeared in surreptitious impressions which poor men stole for lucre's sake. His wife was of opinion that he " had done better to have written fewer books, and to have done those few better"; he maintained that while he wrote none needlessly, the imperfection of two was a less evil than the total omission of one. But in the end he came round to his wife's point of view, and confesses that fewer well studied and polished had been a real gain.

A notice of Baxter, however slight, would do him wrong, if it failed to make some mention of the noble and tender woman who devoted her life to him and to his work. The two figures, that of the zealous pastor, the great divine, touched with premature old age and worn with bodily infirmities, and the young wife once "glittering in costly apparel and delighting in her romances," who was stronger and weaker than he, and who for nineteen years supported him with her wisdom and her faithful affection, live in our imagination side by side ; and each leans upon the other. The minister's love story was never fully told ; some passages of it were too wonderful and too intimate for public record. Margaret Baxter, with her tender, over-passionate nature, had still " a concealing temper " ; she could not often

speak of her deepest inward experiences, erring, her
husband thought, through her morbid dread of hypocrisy,
loving deeds more than words; confessions of the soul,
written by her at various times and printed by Baxter,
were first seen by him after her death among the
papers which she left ; and in that most beautiful and
touching memorial of her life, the outpouring of his age,
weakness and grief, he respected her temper of reserve
as to the full opening of her case and his, and the many
strange occurrences which brought it to pass.

Margaret Charlton was of the same county as
Baxter, but of a higher social station; she had wealth
and he was poor; she had youth, and he had infirmity
and advanced years; and she saw that she could bring
him help. He insisted that he should have nothing of
her wealth, and that she should expect none of the
time which his ministerial duties might require; she
consented, and they lived together "in inviolated love
and mutual complacency."   When he was carried to the
common jail she cheerfully went with him, and, he
thinks, had scarce ever a pleasanter time in her life.
All worldly affairs were left in her hands with perfect
confidence; she busied herself to find or create spheres for
her husband's usefulness, and spent her money in establishing him as far as was possible, under great difficulties
and restrictions, in his work; she was especially proud,
with a noble kind of pride, that he should not be
dependent on the liberality of patrons or of his people.
She had an incredibly quick and penetrating wit, an
incredibly ardent heart, and the finest and most delicate
self-control. Her mind, says Baxter, was " like the

treble strings of a lute, strained up to the highest, sweet, but in continual danger." The troubles and calamities of the time preyed upon her sensitive spirit, and at length the lute-strings snapped. "Perhaps love and grief," writes her husband, "may make me speak more than many will think fit"; and again; "I am waiting to be next: the door is open. Death will quickly draw the veil, and make us see how near we were to God and one another, and did not sufficiently know it." Assuredly through the past, carried on into the present, she was always near him as an impulse and a control, as the most loving of helpers, the most faithful of monitors. It was no posthumous remorse for things ill said or done that quickened Baxter's sorrow when he wrote the Breviate of her life. He had little to remember with sorrow except a certain "impatience with her impatiency," when the wranglings of divines, or other things which she could not approve, wounded her charitable spirit. But he must always have had a touch of grief in feeling that he could not give as much as he received. "Dear heart," he wrote to her, "the time of our mutual help is short; O let us use it accordingly; but the time of our reaping the fruit of this and all holy endeavours and preparatory mercies will be endless. . . . . The Lord forgive my great unprofitableness, and the sin that brought me under any disabilities to answer your earnest and honest desire of greater help than I afford you, and help me yet to amend it towards you. But though my soul be faulty and dull, and my strength of nature fail, be sure that He will be a thousand-fold better to thee, even here, than such crooked, feeble, useless things as is thy R.B." She died in the summer of 1681, at the age of forty-two. Her knife, say Baxter, was too keen, and cut the sheath.

And now let us turn to that passage in the autobiography in which Baxter reviews his former self and notes the alterations which time and experience and perhaps also the decline of youthful vigour had brought to him. There were losses, but there were also gains; and he balanced the one against the other. He felt that he had now less energy, affection, and fervency in preaching than in earlier years, yet his discourses then, though more moving to his hearers, had both less substance and less judgment than of late. His understanding was formerly quicker; now it is better furnished and better balanced. On reperusing some of his earlier writings he was struck in certain places by their emptiness and insufficiency. Where he had thoroughly studied a subject even in those early years his judgment was not deficient; but many things he had studied only slightly and by halves, yet he would then write confidently, and many things he took wholly upon trust from others, so that he scarcely knew what he seemed to know. "And this token of my weakness accompanied those my younger studies, that I was very apt to start up controversies in the way of my practical writings, and also more desirous to acquaint the world with all that I took to be the truth, and to assault those books by name which I thought did tend to deceive them, and did contain unsound and dangerous doctrine." This was partly, he believes, because he was then in the vigour of his youthful apprehension of truth, but also partly because he "did not discern how much in most of our controversies is verbal, and upon mutual mistakes." Now he knows how seldom men are convinced against their will, and that nothing so much hinders the reception of the truth as urging it with harsh importunity and falling too heavily on the errors of others; "for hereby you engage their honour in the business, and they defend their errors as themselves, . . . and to confess the truth, I am lately much prone to the contrary extreme, to be too indifferent what men hold, and to keep my judgment to myself." He felt impatient, faultily impatient, he admits, with the frowardness and self-conceit of some, from discussion with whom he was tempted to take refuge in silence ; he did not perhaps so sensibly bring home to himself—and this was a loss —the worth of truths which had long found a dwelling-place in his mind. But on the other hand there was a gain in his increased feeling that a holy life, founded upon the principles of religion which we are all agreed in, and fusing these in practice, was of more importance than many opinions. In his youth he was " quickly past his fundamentals," and ran up into a multitude of controversies and was greatly delighted with metaphysical and scholastic writings; "but the elder I grew the smaller stress I laid upon these controversies and curiosities (though still my intellect abhorreth confusion), as finding far greater uncertainties in them than I at first discerned, and finding less usefulness comparatively, even where there is the greatest certainty." The creed, the Lord's prayer, and the ten commandments seemed now to Baxter to contain all that is essential, and in these he found themes of meditation less easy to exhaust than those suggested by the school niceties. A like change of mind he had observed, he tells us, in his friend "old Bishop Ussher" and in others; and he would ascribe it partly to a certain decay of vitality, the inward life quitting as in autumn the leaves and branches and drawing down into the root; and partly to a better cause—the fact that experience leads us to value things according to their use and ends. No portion of true learning can be called useless; but the best learning is that which makes men better and tends to make them happier.

These are simple things, easy to understand; but they are often forgotten, and they come from Baxter not as abstract statements, but as realities learnt through experience. He goes on to tell us of other changes. In his younger days he was never tempted to doubt the truth of Scripture or of Christianity; all his doubts and fears were concerning his own salvation. But since then his sorest assaults were on the other side, and he had certainly apostatised, he says, to infidelity had he been void of inward experience and the adhesion of love. Now he feels and sees that the great witness to the world for Christ is the Spirit as known through the hearts and the lives of good men. He recognises that there are degrees of belief, and even with respect to the mysteries of the gospel, whatever men may pretend, the subjective certainty cannot go beyond the objective evidence. Nor is he ashamed to acknowledge his want of complete assurance as to many things—"I am not so foolish as to pretend my certainty to be greater than it is, merely because it is a dishonour to be less certain." He does not lump all matters of belief together, and swallow them by a single act of faith: "My certainty that I am a man is before my certainty that there is a God. My certainty that there is a God is greater than my certainty that he requireth love and holiness of his creature. My certainty of *this* is greater than my certainty of the life of reward and punishment hereafter. My certainty of that is greater than my certainty of the endless duration of it, and of the immortality of individuate souls. My certainty of the Deity is greater than my certainty of the Christian faith. My certainty of the Christian faith in its essentials is greater than my certainty of the perfection and infallibility of all the Holy Scriptures. My certainty of that is greater than my certainty of the meaning of many particular texts, and so of the truth of many particular doctrines, or the canonicalness of some certain books." And accordingly as Baxter held that the truths of natural religion are better established than those of revealed, the work of an evidential writer should base itself, he maintains, on what is most clearly ascertained.

"O God, forgive my sins," murmured the indefatigable Ussher on his death-bed, "especially my sins of omission." In his earlier years Baxter's trouble for sin was chiefly for actual faults of thought, or word, or deed; but now he is much more troubled for inward defects, and omission or want of the vital duties or graces in the soul. It seems to him that some immoralities are less grievous evils than such defects as these. Yet he does not set so much store as he once did on

sorrow for sin or penitential tears; love of what is best
and highest, joy and praise, he reckons as more profitable
parts of spiritual life than any lamentation over the
stains upon our sorry selves. For his mind has greatly
turned away from self and striven to fix itself upon outward objects which alter and elevate the mind that lives
in communion with them. He is much more sensible
than formerly of the breadth and length and depth of
the radical sin of selfishness, and of the excellency of a
public spirit, and of loving our neighbours as ourselves ;
and he is much more concerned than formerly about his
duty to God, and less solicitous about God's dealings
with him, dealings which may indeed be trusted to
the Father of our spirits. . He finds great mutability
in his own moods, and places small confidence in
them ; but if anything gives him assurance of his
own sincerity, it is constant action and duty that
can do this.

Again, Baxter contrasts his early state of mind, when
he knew much less than now, but was much less aware
of his ignorance—daily delighted by new discoveries
of truth—with his present state when he has far meaner
thoughts of his own understanding, and finds far greater
darkness upon all things. Formerly, he had an exalted
opinion of learned persons and of books that professed
much wisdom or scholarship ; now experience has con-
strained him against his will to recognise that reverend,
learned men are imperfect : "and the better I am
acquainted with them, the more I perceive that we
are all yet in the dark ; and the more I am acquainted
with holy men, that are all for heaven and pretend not

much to subtleties, the more I value and honour them."
As to books, he takes them less on credit than formerly;
he is less captivated by the style, attends more to the
matter, and does not, as once, accept the whole, but can
accept and reject in the same author. He is himself
less influenced than in earlier years by applause, partly
perhaps from having been glutted and surfeited with it.
He loves solitude more than formerly, and could be
willing to fly from the press of men ; yet, while he
finds it easy to despise earth, it is not easy to be conversant in heaven. He sees the dangers and temptations to which the great ones of the world are exposed,
and laments their unhappiness ; he values more the life
of poor labouring men, and especially the life of one that
has neither poverty nor riches.

In brief, he perceives more good and more evil in all
men than heretofore : " I see that good men are not so
good as I once thought they were, but have more imperfections. . . . And I find that few are so bad as
either their malicious enemies or censorious separating
professors do imagine." Accordingly, his sympathies
have widened ; he cannot limit his Christian charity to
any one communion ; he thinks of his brother men in
remote parts of the world : " Could we but go among
Tartarians, Turks, and Heathens, and speak their language, I should be but little troubled for the silencing
of eighteen hundred ministers at once in England."
And yet, he adds, " I am not so much inclined to pass
a peremptory sentence of damnation upon all that never
heard of Christ ; having some more reason than I knew
of before to think that God's dealings with such is much

unknown to us." As for nearer neighbours, the "Papists," his judgment has greatly altered; formerly he thought that their errors in the doctrine of faith were their most dangerous mistakes: "but now I am assured that their mis-expressions and misunderstanding us, with our mistakings of them, and inconvenient expressing our own opinions, hath made the difference in these points to appear much greater than they are; and that in some of them it is next to none at all. But the great and unreconcilable difficulties lie in their Church tyranny and usurpations, and in their great corruptions and abasement of God's worship, together with their befriending of ignorance and vice." Yet he does not now doubt that God has "many sanctified ones among them," and that the errors of such are like a conquerable dose of poison which nature can overcome.

Baxter would still labour for a comprehension among Protestants; but he is less sanguine of its attainment than formerly. He no longer lays that stress upon the external modes and forms of worship which many young and ardent spirits do. "I have suspected," he says with his characteristic sincerity, "as perhaps the reader may do, that this is from a cooling and declining from my former zeal (though the truth is, I never much complied with men of that mind); but I find that judgment and charity are the causes of it, as far as I am able to discover." He cannot be so narrow in his principles as to refuse communion with a Church on the ground of ceremonial differences, and were he among the Greeks, the Lutherans, the Independents, or the Anabaptists, he would hold occasional communion with them as Christians, if they would give him leave. But he is farther than ever from expecting great matters of unity, splendour, or prosperity to the Church on earth.

One other change in his mind, which indeed makes much for charity, Baxter notices : " I am much more cautious," he says, " in my belief of history than heretofore." The prodigious lies published as matters of fact in his own age, and that with unblushing confidence, made him incredulous of the statements of past ages, unless there were freedom at the time to challenge such statements, and both sides had a hearing. " Therefore, I confess, I give but halting credit to most histories that are written, not only against the Albigenses and Waldenses, but against most of the ancient heretics, who have left us none of their own writings, in which they speak for themselves ; and I heartily lament that the historical writings of the ancient schismatics and heretics (as they are called) perished, and that partiality suffered them not to survive, that we might have had more light in the Church affairs of those times, and been better able to judge between the Fathers and them. And as I am prone to think that few of them were so bad as their adversaries made them, so I am apt to think that such as the Novatians and Luciferians, and Indians, &c., whom their adversaries commend, were very good men, and more godly than most Catholics, however mistaken in some one point." Baxter's discreet and charitable scepticism has its application to civil as well as to ecclesiastical history. The lost causes have not always been the worst.

Finally, he considers some of the faults of his later

years. He grieves especially over any rash words uttered to those who were near and dear to him. There is a pathos of a beautiful kind in his tender passion of remorse: "When such are dead, though we never differed in point of interest or any great matter, every sour or cross provoking word which I gave them, maketh me almost unreconcilable with myself, and tells me how repentance brought some of old to pray to the dead whom they had wronged, to forgive them in the hurry of their passion." He perceives in himself, and mentions by way of penitent confession, that in his controversial writings he has even of late been much inclined to words that are too keen and provoking. It may partly be that age has soured his spirit, partly that much thought and study has wearied him, and rendered him impatient, partly that he revolts from the flattering humour of the time; but doubtless the principal cause is, that being accustomed to address common, ignorant, and ungodly people, who need the plainest and keenest language, he has acquired a habit which is liable to abuse: "I repent of it, and wish all over-sharp passages were expunged from my writings, and ask forgiveness of God and man." In truth, he cares now less than ever for disputation, and most approves a learning or a teaching way of converse.

Such, reduced from its large dimensions in the autobiography, is Baxter's "Eirenicon." It is no array of intellectual formulæ, no piece of moving rhetoric; it is a simple record of personal experience, an account of the growth of character. When these pages were written the close of Baxter's life was still remote, and he had much work, as a Christian teacher and as a great Englishman, still to do. But he had already learnt the deepest lessons of life, and was ready to depart. "Ripeness," in Hamlet's phrase, "is all."

VIII

JOHN BUNYAN

I

To consider Bunyan merely as a representative of English Puritanism or Nonconformity in the second half of the seventeenth century would be to do an injustice to his genius and his work. Had he interpreted only what was peculiar to a special period and a particular phase of religious thought and feeling, what he has written might still be valuable as a document for historical students, but it could not be a living power with successive generations of readers of every class and in almost every region of the globe. What gives vitality to the "Pilgrim's Progress" is not its Puritanism as such, but rather its Christian spirit and more than this its profound humanity. Yet the "Pilgrim's Progress" is a characteristic product of Puritan faith and feeling; and to bring this fact home to ourselves we have only to imagine what Bunyan would have been if all his life had been passed as that of a member of the Anglican communion; or, rather, we have to put the question to ourselves—"Would an Anglican Bunyan have been possible?" If we desire to see a typical representative of Anglican piety in Bunyan's century we may find such a representative in George Herbert. It is a beautiful type of religious temper, ardent within appointed bounds, spiritual, and finding in forms and ceremonies an aid to spiritual life, exalted without extravagance, regardful not only of holiness but of the visible beauty of holiness, delicate, pure, not driven to passionate extremes, not the prey of intolerable terrors and blissful raptures; a type of piety as it lives and moves in an organised and cultivated community, with a high tradition, and making use of all those adjuncts to the inward life which are afforded by habit and rite and emblem, those regular means of relieving and systematising the emotions, those calculated channels and aqueducts which irrigate and refresh the soul. Gracious flower in the garden of the Master, we are not unmindful of its comeliness or its fragrance.

In such a community there is reasonable scope for the play of individual feeling; yet individual feeling is directed and controlled by a general method and order. In the smaller religious communities a public opinion exists, which is stricter in reference to conduct, and may even result in a close and tyrannous surveillance; but in the drama of the private passions of religion there is often an intenser energy; religion is less of a complex, organised institution, and more of a personal unique experience; the relations of the soul to God are less determined in appointed ways; hence wilder aberrations become possible; but also there may be an incandescence of the inward life, unallayed in its glow, a flame of devout passion which touches heights and depths beyond what can be safely approached in forms suited for the general and habitual uses of religion.

In a great and comprehensive community a place is found for such nobly intemperate souls in some special Order, which converts the *enfant perdu* of piety into the leader of a forlorn hope. All that is best and most characteristic in Bunyan's writings proceeds from that inward drama, in which the actors were three—God, Satan, and a solitary human soul. If external influences from events or men affected his spirit, they came as nuncios or messengers from God or from the Evil One. Institutions, churches, ordinances, rites, ceremonies, could help him little, or not at all. The journey from the City of Destruction to the Celestial City must be undertaken on a special summons by each man for himself alone; if a companion join him on the way, it lightens the trials of the road; but of the companions each one is an individual pilgrim, who has started on a great personal adventure, and who as he enters the dark river must undergo his particular experiences of hope or fear. Yet through what is most personal in each of us we come upon the common soul; let any man record faithfully his most private experiences in any of the great affairs of life, and his words awaken in other souls innumerable echoes; the deepest community is found not in institutions, or corporations, or Churches, but in the secrets of the solitary heart. And because Bunyan, rich as his nature was in our common humanity, put into his writings the central facts of his personal life, his books are not for himself alone, but for all men of like passions, who must each tread for himself the same arduous way. Must tread the same way; but not necessarily

in the same manner. Bunyan's religious history, re-
corded in his wonderful autobiography "Grace abounding to the Chief of Sinners," may be repeated age after
age in its essentials, for it is the history of a soul
struggling from darkness to light, from confusion to
clearness, from self-division to unity, from weakness
to strength, from wretchedness to peace and joy; but
if truths of the seventeenth century remain truths in
the nineteenth, they operate under different conditions;
they mingle with new elements in our minds; they
require new adjustments; they must be translated into
modern speech. And who will say that in the religious
passion of an Englishman of the mid-years of the
seventeenth century the parallax of truth was not considerable? who will assert that gross mists arising from
his own brain did not cloud and distort the light? If
the deep realities of Puritanism remain—its seriousness,
its ardour, its plea for the loins girt and the lamp lit—
yet its exact modes of thought and feeling, which did
their work and have been replaced by others, can no
more be revived than its exact forms of speech. "Grace
Abounding" may truly be described as an awakening
book, and the moment we are really awake we perceive
that if we are to attempt a solution of the problems
and a conquest of the difficulties which beset us, we
must apply ourselves to the task with Bunyan's resolution
indeed, but not with Bunyan's intelligence.

The writings of John Bunyan fill some thousands
of large and closely printed pages. The strength of his
heart and mind are adequately felt in four works—
his religious autobiography, "Grace Abounding," the

"Pilgrim's Progress," the "Holy War," and the "Life and Death of Mr Badman." Among these four there is a marked inequality; the "Holy War" is an allegory rather manufactured,—manufactured with admirable skill—than inspired; the "Life and Death of Mr Badman" is a religious tract of portentous size put into the form of a narrative. These are remarkable books; but the one is an ingenious construction; the other is a study of the vices of middle class English life in Bunyan's day, turned to purposes of warning and edification. Neither of them is an immediate living experience; neither of them is an inspired vision. But these are the words that describe aright the other two books which form the most vital part of Bunyan's work. "Grace Abounding" is a fragment of life; we touch, in reading it, a quivering human heart; the "Pilgrim's Progress" is a vision of a man of genius, the "Divina Commedia" of Puritanism.

II

"Grace Abounding," written while Bunyan was in Bedford gaol, was published in 1666, when he was thirty-eight years old. It is a work of the writer's maturity, not a collection of the reminiscences of old age. The story which it tells was comparatively recent; nothing in it is blurred or faded. Bunyan died at the age of sixty, but if he had lived to be fourscore, and his natural powers had remained with him, he could never have spoken vaguely or faintly about events in the life of his soul which had so deeply branded themselves into his memory, The first characteristic of the book is assuredly its intense realisation of things unseen. Nothing else by comparison was actual to Bunyan; robust, observant, shrewd, kindly, humorous as he was, the external world when set beside the invisible became to him as a shadow or a dream. Heaven and hell were at least as substantial for him as the roads and the Bedford field-paths trodden by his feet. He carried his English plainness and energy into his dealings with the affairs of eternity. Our few mortal years on earth, overwhelmingly important because they determine the issues of life and death, were, as regards all else, lost in the abyss of unending joy or anguish. He must square his accounts with God as a piece of practical business, awful business indeed, but one that must be settled somehow on business principles. He, as truly as the American idealist, but in his own positive British way, must hitch his waggon to a star.

Dormant genius in youth is often awakened by the love of a woman. Bunyan was capable of deep and tender affection. " You must think that my wife and poor children were very dear unto me," Christian confesses ; yet having a wife he must needs be as those who have none. We remember Bunyan's attachment to his blind child. He regarded with honour that mother in Israel, Christiana : he loved his own Mercy for her early devotion to the pilgrim's way and to charitable works ; he felt a manly protectiveness towards Mr Despondency's daughter, whose name was Much-Afraid. But he could not abandon his heart to any creature of earth. Perhaps he feared his own ruder passions. From his first conversion God made him

" shy of women "; it was a rare thing to see him carry it pleasant towards any one of them : " The common salutation of a woman I abhor; 'tis odious to me in whomsoever I see it. Their company alone, I cannot away with. I seldom so much as touch a woman's hand, for I think these things are not so becoming me." And he noticed with disapproval — Butler has said nothing more severe—that others when they gave the holy kiss made baulks, saluting the most handsome and letting the ill-favoured go. For Bunyan the difference between human beings was of another kind than their good looks or their uncomeliness—they were inhabitants of the City of Destruction, or were on their way to the Celestial City. The nobler aspects of human passion he did not attempt to interpret; from one of the most inspiring motives of imaginative genius he was cut off.

Public affairs, which rouse the ambition of manhood, left Bunyan almost untouched. As a young man he served for a short time in the army, doubtless on the side of the Parliament; but, though his marchings and counter-marches may have served to give exactitude to his account of the military evolutions of Emmanuel's captains in the " Holy War," he had no enthusiam for the good old cause ; he was probably a reluctant fighter, who would not of his own accord choose to cut short a human life, whether of saint or sinner ; and his most vivid recollection of that episode of his career was that on one occasion he was himself by special Providence preserved from death at a time when death would have meant the eternal perdition of his soul. At a later date, in Restoration days, whatever interest Bunyan took in public affairs seems to have been connected with the freedom of worship of God's suffering faithful, the Nonconformists ; even for them he would not purchase indulgence at the price of an accommodation with Giant Pope. The degradation of his country in the councils of Europe counted as nothing with Bunyan in comparison with the ruin of a single soul. Preeminently English in the character of his genius, he was lacking in an Englishman's patriotic pride or shame.

The word "otherworldliness" is sometimes used as a term of reproach for such a temper as that of Bunyan; one who devotes himself to the concerns of this earthly sphere is worldly ; is it not the same self-interested habit of mind, fastening on the affairs of futurity, which creates such alarms and hopes, such agonies and raptures as beset the mind of Bunyan ? And thus we are given to understand that there is little real difference between the man who is absorbed in the business of time and him who is devoted to the interests of eternity, except perhaps that the latter is possessed of a superior kind of selfishness. Such a criticism as this may contain a just censure of the fastings and macerations of a hermit in the Thebaid ; yet even he may believe that he serves mankind by his prayers, that a retreat from the evil world is necessary to preserve the regenerating ideal of sanctity, or that, in view of the endless tasks of eternity, his brief days of mortal life may be well spent in processes of self-imposed discipline and education. For one who firmly grasps this earth, and dismisses as a dream the life beyond the grave, worldliness, pursued on his own behalf and that of his fellows, is a virtue. This is to live, at least for an hour, wisely, with his loins girt and his lamp burning. He does well to drink a deep draught of existence while it is still possible. And for one who believes in a life eternal, "otherworldliness," pursued vigorously on his own behalf and that of his fellows, is a virtue; it is at once the highest prudence and the noblest charity. Whoever—was it Charles Kingsley? —spoke scornfully of the anxiety to "save one's own dirty soul" indulged in an idle flourish of rhetoric. St Paul, in a passion of charity, wished that he were accursed from Christ for his brethren; but the very words imply that what he was prepared to surrender, in the heroism of self-abandonment, was an inestimable possession. Bunyan, like St Paul, was no merely egoistic devotee; he was abundant in labours for others; his years of imprisonment were endured because he could not consent to cease from those labours. But he felt that he could not direct others on the pilgrimage, and do the work of a Great-heart, until he himself was acquainted with the way. For one who accepted Bunyan's premises, it was right and it was inevitable to be profoundly concerned about future bliss or woe. Imagine any man of serious and ardent nature, imagine Bunyan, or read his autobiography, and *see* him, possessed by an assurance—though not undisturbed now and again by cold spasms of doubt— that heaven was a veritable fact, that hell was real as his own soul; on the one hand everlasting felicity, purity, light, on the other everlasting torture, darkness, and gnashing of teeth; on this side the presence of God and of his shining ones for ever, on that the perpetual companionship of devils and the damned; imagine him aware of the fragility of human life— a breathing, sensitive, passionate human creature, suspended by a thread between paradise and the pit; imagine this, and applaud him for the fervour of his otherworldliness.[1]

Such was the situation; his own soul overwhelmed by blood guiltiness; death imminent, judgment certain; God inviting him, and a thousand devils waiting to lay hold upon him. What could Bunyan do but put his fingers in his ears to shut out all voices of earth, refuse to look behind him, and run forward with the cry "Life, life, eternal life." But the way that stretched before him was neither short nor smooth. If the most striking characteristic of "Grace Abounding" is its vivid realisation of the unseen, hardly less impressive is the sense it leaves with us of the difficulty and uncertainty of the writer's progress. He was like a swimmer making for shore in a heavy sea, beset by cross and contrary currents. Now he strikes out with resolute arms, and makes a slight advance; instantly he is overwhelmed by some violent wave, is buffetted hither and thither, is swept sideways, or is caught by some refluent surge and hurried back

---

[1] In "The Saint's Everlasting Rest" (I. vi.) Baxter considers the question "Whether to make salvation our end be not mercenary or legal?" "It is properly mercenary," he answers, "when we expect it as wages for work done . . . Otherwise it is only such a mercenariness as Christ commandeth. For consider what this end is—it's the fruition of God in Christ, and if seeking Christ be mercenary, I desire to be so mercenary."

against his utmost effort. All the time Bunyan's
mind was working terribly; yet it seems as if no
advance were made. In some records of spiritual
experience we read of an immediate transit from
darkness to light; and who that has an open mind
for facts would doubt the reality of sudden conversion
any more than he would doubt the reality of love
at first sight? We read in other lives of a steadfast
progress towards good. St Teresa could say "This
attainment is at present beyond my reach; but with
the aid of discipline and Divine grace, twelve months
hence I shall be able to do things that are now
impossible." She knew how to labour and to wait;
she knew how to turn to her advantage a season of
aridity. With Bunyan, during the period of which
he has given us an account it was otherwise; we may
call the whole process of his conversion, if we please,
a crisis; but it was a crisis prolonged over what
seemed long ages of agony. Doubtless from first to
last he was making advance; but he could not reckon
on it for an hour; he was the victim of Divine grace,
the puppet of Satanic temptation.

This resulted in part from the undisciplined violence
of his emotions and his imagination. When he wrote
the "Pilgrim's Progress" Bunyan was master of his
imaginative power; the visions which came to him
were controlled and ordered; when he underwent the
experiences related in "Grace Abounding" his imagination mastered him. His fears and hopes haled him
this way or that; his visions attacked him as if they
had an objective life; they were of the nature of

an obsession. One Sunday, in the midst of a game at cat, a voice suddenly darted from heaven into his soul, uttering the words, "Wilt thou leave thy sins and go to heaven or have thy sins and go to hell?" When at his favourite recreation of bell-ringing in the steeple-house, the thought came quickly "How if one of the bells should fall?"; and then "How if the steeple itself should fall?" and he dared not stand there any longer but was forced to flee. Doubting whether he had faith, as he walked between Elstow and Bedford, he felt that he must put the vital question to an immediate test, and he was on the point of determining the matter by the success or failure of an experiment in the miraculous: "I must say to the puddles that were in the horsepads *Be dry* and to the dry places *Be you the puddles.*" The words "Simon, Simon, Satan hath desired to have you" sounded within his soul, and were called after him so distinctly that he turned his head to see the speaker. He compared himself in his temptations to a child whom some gipsy has taken up under her apron and is carrying from friend and country: "Kick sometimes I did, and also shriek and cry, and yet I was as bound in the wings of the temptation, and the wind would carry me away." With a horrible fascination he longed, as it were, to precipitate himself to destruction, so to foreclose all uncertainty, by sinning the sin against the Holy Ghost, and was often ready to clap his hand to his chin to hold his mouth from opening, or to leap with his head downwards into some muck-hill hole to keep his mouth from speaking.

In prayer he was assailed by the Tempter, who dealt with his victim in the way of scornful grotesquerie, presenting to his fancy the form of a bush, a bull, a besom, and bidding him pray to these. The direst of his trials was the terrible suggestion that as Esau sold his birth-right for a mess of pottage, so should he sell the Christ whom he had found. The words "Sell him, sell him, sell him," echoed through his heart for hours together, and in opposing the temptation, "my very body," he says, "would be put into action or motion, by way of pushing or thrusting with my hands or elbows, still answering, as fast as the destroyer said 'Sell him,' 'I will not, I will not, I will not, I will not, no, not for thousands, thousands, thousands of worlds'." His soul was like a broken vessel, driven as with the winds—"I was but as those that jostle against the rocks, more broken, scattered, and rent."

Looking back, when he wrote the "Pilgrim's Progress," Bunyan thought that fear tends much to men's good at their beginning to go on pilgrimage. But fear has its special risks. There was one Temporary, a forward man at one time in religion, who often had tears in his eyes, but now a backslider; his conscience was awakened by the terrors of hell, but his mind was not changed by the desire for heaven for its own sake; the fear of damnation chilled; hardness of heart was left behind; and so the last state of that man was worse than the first.

During these trials Bunyan was in essentials a solitary, or in company with only God and the

Destroyer. If external influences reached him, they were seized by the forces of his own soul, and were converted into part of the secret, inward drama. The parson preached against Sabbath desecration, and Bunyau became a prey to the alarms of conscience. A woman of loose life reproached him for his profane oaths, and instantly he stood in shame, not before her but before the God of heaven : " hanging down my head, I wished with all my heart I might be a little child again, that my father might learn me to speak without this wicked way of swearing." Three or four poor women sitting in the sun, were overheard by Bunyan while they talked about the things of God, speaking of the new birth as if joy made them speak, and he felt his own heart begin to shake. Now and again he tried to break his mind to humble folk of Bedford, and they brought him as a counsellor holy Mr Gifford, but Bunyan seemed only to grow worse and worse. The people of God would pity him, and tell him of the promises ; " but they had as good have told me that I must reach the sun with my fingers as have bidden me receive or rely upon the promise." If he fell into the slough of Despond, " whither the scum and filth that attends conviction for sin doth continually run," no man whose uame was Help came to pluck him out.

In truth Bunyan's case was too complex to be dealt with successfully by the spiritual physicians of Bedford nonconformity. And we may doubt whether a nineteenth-century pathologist could have served him effectually with modern therapeutics. It is more interesting to conjecture how it would have fared with Bunyan had he

come under the influence of some wise old Catholic
director, a master of the learning of the confessional,
skilled in the secrets of the human heart, severe yet
gentle, bold yet full of discretion. Such a director
would hardly have attempted to stem the tide of
Bunyan's passions, but he might have diverted some
of the current into a course of discipline, and so have
eased for a time the onset and turbulence of the flood.
Yet it may have been better that Bunyan should work
his own way to clearness and to calm after the strife.
Certain it is that Mr Worldly-wiseman would have
made the case only tenfold worse; nor could the fair
speeches of that pretty young man, his son, whose name
is Civility, have comforted the pilgrim's agonised heart.
The burden would but have seemed more crushing, and
flashes of fire issuing from the hill would have made
the sufferer's heart tremble within him.

Macaulay, sane and strong for the generous uses of
earth yet not quite a sure searcher of spirits, attempts
to gauge the actual dimensions of Bunyan's burden, and
finds that after all it was not so very bulky; to a
reasonable wayfarer it need not have proved oppressive.
The honest tinker was not vicious; he married when
young and was a faithful husband; he was quickly
cured of swearing; bell-ringing, and playing at hockey
on Sundays were his worst offences. Why should he
have brought railing accusations against himself? On
the whole Bunyan might have been moderately comfortable. But he was ignorant and excitable, and he
lived in an age of excitement. The old director whom
we have imagined, Father Discretion or Father Experi-

ence, would not have spoken thus. He would have known the difference between measuring sin from without and discovering unworthiness in the inward parts. He would have known that the depth of shadow is proportioned to the brightness of the light ; that the consciousness of our own abjectness and defilement is inexpressibly deepened by our apprehension of a righteousness and purity above and beyond our poor attainment. Undoubtedly it is part of the duty of a biographer of Bunyan to show that he was far from being an outrageous reprobate ; such a reprobate would probably not have suffered from Bunyan's griefs. Undoubtedly Bunyan's religious perturbation was extreme ; but we interpret the drama of his soul in the poorest and shallowest way if we ascribe the vividness of his sense of sin to excitement in an excitable age.

Much of Bunyan's torturing alarm, but also much of his blessedness, many accesses of sudden joy, came from the manner in which texts from the Bible fastened upon his imagination and his feelings. He had not learnt to think of the books of Scripture as pieces of Hebrew literature to be approached in a critical spirit. He had not learnt to regard them as utterances of the highest moral genius of humanity. Nor did he attenuate the idea of inspiration to some vague and wandering luminosity. For Bunyan the Bible from cover to cover was the authentic voice of God. It was a living power able to dart forth terrors or comfort. That drama of the inner life, in which the actors were God, Satan, and a human soul, was a drama in which magic played a part, and the talisman instinct with firiest force was the Bible. Bunyan was the martyr, but also the glorified child, of Puritanic scripturalism. He did not ask the doctors or the Church to interpret the dark sayings of the Divine word ; they leaped out upon him, now like angels waving swords of flame, now like winged messengers of consolation. At one season of gloom the sentence fell with weight upon his spirit "Did ever any trust in God and were confounded ?" Blessed words ! and he turned to search for them in his Bible. He could not find them ; yet still they abode upon him. After about a year he lighted upon the sentence, not in the Bible, but alas ! in the Apocrypha, at which he confesses he was daunted. In great distress he feared that the day of grace might be past, or at least that God had already reckoned up the number of his elect in Bedford ; but the words, "And yet there is room" broke in upon his mind, and they were sweet words to him. The terror assailed him that he was predestinated to reprobation ; but the text of a sermon which he heard, "Behold, thou art fair, my love," kindled in his spirit ; "thou art my love" sang itself over and over in his heart, so that he could not tell how to contain till he got home : "I thought I could have spoken of his love and of his mercy to me to the very crows that sat upon the ploughed lands before me." Doubts that his zeal would soon be quenched caused him icy shivers ; but he had a sweet glance from the fifth of second Corinthians, with hints, and touches, and short visits from other words of comfort—"only they lasted not long, but like to Peter's sheet of a sudden were caught up from me to heaven again." For some time he was under the horrible apprehension that he had committed the unpardonable sin, and was an uglier man than Judas. Bodily pain afflicted him; he felt as if his breast-bone would have split asunder; and this perhaps was the mysterious mark of Cain. But once, while he was walking to and fro in a good man's shop and lamenting his state, a noise of wind rushed in upon him, and he heard a voice speaking—" Didst ever refuse to be justified by the blood of Christ?"; upon which that word of God fell on him with power "See that ye refuse not him that speaketh." At length he could venture to come nigh unto some most fearful and terrible Scriptures, and found that their visage was altered—" they looked not so grimly on me as before I thought they did."

These are only a few examples, out of many, of the spells cast on Bunyan's spirit by that mighty book of wizardry, the Bible. He read it not as literature, but as the scroll of doom; yet, unconsciously, it became a literature for him, and acted as the chief formative influence on his imagination and his style. Its words were not only the rallying points for his hopes and fears, but their music lived within the cells of his fancy. The portion which his first wife brought him consisted of two books, which her good father had left her at his death, "The Plain Man's Pathway to Heaven," by Arthur Dent, and Bishop Bayly's "Practice of Piety." Bunyan's biographer, Dr Brown, discovers some traces of the influence of Dent's homely dialogue in the "Life and Death of Mr Badman." The "Acta Sanctorum" of Protestants—Foxe's "Book of Martyrs"—doubtless stimulated Bunyan's heart and his imagination; there he read how many of the kindred of Faithful had played the man; how they had been scourged and buffeted, and burnt to ashes at the stake, and how the chariot and horses had carried them up through the clouds, with sound of trumpet, the nearest way to the celestial gate. In his earlier religious trials the only volume, beside the Scriptures, which wrought powerfully upon him was Luther's commentary on the Galatians. An old copy, falling to pieces, came into Bunyan's hands, and it seemed as if the book had been written out of his own heart: "I do prefer this book of Martin Luther," he writes, ". . . (excepting the Holy Bible) before all the books that ever I have seen, as most fit for a wounded conscience."

The fluctuations of Bunyan's passions obscure the fact that a real though variable progress was being made towards clearness and strength. First came the conviction of sin and the terrors of death and judgment. Then for a time, like his own pilgrim, Bunyan turned aside towards the village of Morality, where Mr Legality dwells; he laboured to establish his own righteousness; he was reputed to be godly, yet he found that, after all, he was nothing but "a poor painted hypocrite." In the end he yielded himself wholly to something without and beyond himself, something which he felt to be the highest; there was some great power of God to which of right he belonged; not by agonised introspection, not by moral manipulation could he save his soul; he must abandon all spiritual egoism, and simply cast himself in with the divine order of things; its meaning was good, its end was righteousness, and he was himself included in its great movement. Bunyan would not have used such words as these; they would have sounded to him like the phrases of Talkative, mere notion, as empty of religion as the white of an egg is of savour; but they interpret the fact of his experience to modern ears. His own word would have been that unless he obtained the righteousness of a man that never had sinned, neither his own nor all the righteousness of the world could save him. It was his way of asserting that the entrance to the blessed life is through deliverance from self; it was his way of hitching his waggon to a star.

"One day," he writes, "as I was passing in the field, and that too with some dashes on my conscience, fearing lest yet all was not right, suddenly this sentence fell upon my soul, 'Thy righteousness is in heaven,' and methought withal I saw with the eyes of my soul Jesus Christ at God's right hand. There, I say, was my righteousness; so that wherever I was, or whatever I was adoing, God could not say of me, 'He wants my righteousness,' for that was just before Him. I also saw, moreover, that it was not my good frame of mind that made my righteousness better, nor yet my bad frame that made my righteousness worse; for my righteousness was Jesus Christ Himself, 'the same yesterday, to-day, and forever.' Now did the chains fall off my legs; I was loosed from my afflictions and irons; my temptations also fled away; so that, from that time, those dreadful Scriptures of God left off to trouble me; now went I also home rejoicing for the grace and love of God.' Clouds of darkness came now and again after this crisis; but a sun had arisen of power to dissipate the clouds.

Amid all his violences of religious emotion, Bunyan never lost a certain saving good sense. Shrewdness and manly energy are written on that face, which is familiar to us through the animated drawing of Robert White. The dreamer of the " Pilgrim's Progress " as little resembled in aspect the visionary of the Divine Comedy as Elstow of the seventeenth century resembled mediæval Florence. He was a sturdy Englishman of the midlands, tall of stature, strong-boned, with ruddy cheeks and sparkling eyes. The voices that haunted him were commonly brought to the test which he and his contemporaries regarded as the most trustworthy— that of Scripture. It was indeed by the same test that Saint Teresa distinguished between diabolic and divine locutions—" that which purports to come from God," she declares, " is to be received only in so far as it corresponds with the sacred writings." As a preacher Bunyan, although it was not the habit of the time, in general avoided controversy and made edification his chief object. During his earlier years he met with some of the Ranters' books, which were held in high esteem by several of his acquaintances; one of his intimate friends, indeed, turned a most devilish ranter, and, on the plea that the saints are delivered from the moral law, gave himself up to all manner of filthiness. Bunyan rebuked the young man for his wicked ways, and then separated from his company. For his own part he held fast to the old plain rules of morality, and cared not if wayward enthusiasts condemned him as legal and dark. That ancient gentleman, Mr Conscience, once recorder of Mansoul, was appointed by Emmanuel subordinate preacher under the Lord Chief Secretary, and was authorised to express his master's will in all terrene and domestic matters. Bunyan did not slight the subordinate preacher's office. His animal appetites might plead on behalf of the " Ranting errors," but he would not suborn his conscience, and he had his safeguard in the words of the Old and New Testaments—" the Bible," he says, " was precious to me in those days." Those keen eyes of Bunyan brought him reports of all the homely facts of life ; his Puritan inwardness was balanced by his faculty of shrewd observation. He had that happy adjunct of common sense—the gift of humour.

> Some things are of that nature as to make
> His fancy chuckle while his heart doth ache ;
> When Jacob saw his Rachel with the sheep,
> He did at the same time both kiss and weep.

So Bunyan justifies the wholesome laughter of the " Pilgrim's Progress." He was no mystic in the vulgar meaning of that word, but a downright, practical Englishman, who happened to be also a man of imaginative genius.

III

With such powers of observation and of insight, he was no mean discerner of characters. The " Pilgrim's Progress " is a gallery of portraits, admirably discriminated, and as convincing in their self-verification as those of Holbein. His personages live for us as few figures outside the drama of Shakespeare live. They are not, like the humourists of Ben Jonson's plays, constructed by heaping a load of observations on a series of ethical abstractions ; they are of a reasonable soul and human flesh subsisting. We are on terms of intimate acquaintance with each of them ; with Talkative, the son of one Say-well, who dwelt in Prating-row, — wherever the notional apprehension of things is taken for the real apprehension, there is that discoursing wit to-day ; with By-ends, always zealous when a good cause goes in silver slippers, a gentleman of excellent quality, though his grandfather was but a waterman, looking one way and rowing another ; with that brisk lad Ignorance, who came into the path by a little crooked lane leading from the country of Conceit ; there is a narrow gate in science and in art as well as in religion, which the kinsfolk of Bunyan's Ignorance decline to enter ; with Mrs Lightmind, who yesterday at Madam Wanton's was as merry as the maids—surely she is cousin to the brothers Jolly and Griggish, who came to an ill fate at the hands of my Lord Willbewill, and so ended their ticking and toying with my Lord's daughters ; with Mr Brisk, who, since Mercy was of a fair countenance and therefore the more alluring, offered her his love, but was dashed when she explained that her needlework was meant to clothe the naked, and decided on reconsideration that she was indeed a pretty lass, but troubled with ill conditions ; with that old pilgrim Father Honest, a cock of the right kind, for he had said the truth ; with Mr Fearing, one of the most troublesome of pilgrims, a chicken-hearted man, yet having the root of the matter in him, and who at last almost dryshod crossed the river, when it was at its lowest ebb; with Mr Feeble-mind, who must needs be carried up the Hill Difficulty by one of the Interpreter's servants, yet bravely resolved to run when he could, to go when he could not run, and to creep when he could not go; with Mr Ready-to-halt, who, despite the crutch, footed it well in view of the dead giant's head, hand in hand with Despondency's daughter Much-afraid, both answering the music handsomely; with Madam Bubble, that tall comely dame, somewhat swarthy of complexion, speaking very smoothly, and giving you a smile at the end of a sentence, while still she kept fingering her money as if it were her heart's delight; with Mr Valiant-for-truth, Mr Standfast, who crossing the river in a great calm, like the saintly John Wesley, when he was half-way in, stood for a while and talked to his companions; with the dozen enlightened jurymen of Vanity Fair, and many another. Yet these are but examples from the drawings of the Holbein of spiritual England.

One book of Bunyan's is, indeed, a detailed study of English middle-class life and of its vulgar vices. Recent criticism has assigned to " The Life and Death of Mr Badman " a higher place in literature than it deserves; but it presents one side of its author's mind more fully than any other of his writings. Having published the first part of the " Pilgrim's Progress," and enjoyed the surprise of its extraordinary success, Bunyan seems to have thought of presenting a counterpart in the story of one who had travelled another road than

that of Christian, the road leading not to the Celestial
City, but to the gates of hell.   The book is not a vision
or a dream ; it lacks the beautiful ideality of the " Pilgrim's Progress," which has made that allegory of universal interest.   It has, on the other hand, something of
Hogarth's naturalism and something of Hogarth's enforce-
ment of morality by means of the tomahawk ; it is the
tale of an Idle Apprentice ; it is a bourgeois Rake's Progress.   The narrative, thrown into the form of dialogue,
is interrupted by discourses on the several species of sin
practised by that rascally provincial tradesman, the hero,
with many examples drawn from real life of God's judgments against sinners.

The book had its origin not in Bunyan's personal
experiences, idealised and purified by the imagination,
but in his observations of the evil that lay around him.
Even as a child Badman was a highly promising pupil
of the destroyer—addicted to lying, a pilferer, abandoned
(like young Richard Baxter) to the joy of robbing
orchards, a blackmouthed wretch who cursed and swore,
a boy who could not endure the Lord's Day, swarming,
indeed, with sins as a beggar is with vermin.   When
his good father would rebuke him, what would young
Badman do but stand gloating, hanging down his head
in a sullen pouching manner, while he secretly wished
for the old man's death ?   As an apprentice he read
beastly romances and books full of ribaldry, slept in
church, or stared at pretty faces and whispered and
giggled during sermon, being thus grown to a prodigious height of wickedness.   His knavish fingers
found their way to his master's cash-box, and soon

his first apprenticeship closed disgracefully in flight. After a second apprenticeship, during which a base-born child was laid to his charge, Badman set up in business, but through dissipation, high-living, idleness, and evil company quickly came to the end of the money obtained from his over-indulgent father. To retrieve his fortunes he sought out a maid who had a good portion, and as she was godly, he made religion his stalking-horse ; but after marriage he hanged his religion upon the hedge, oppressed his unhappy wife, squandered her coin upon his drabs, and towards morning would come home as drunk as a swine. He reached a yet lower depth of degradation, when he turned informer, obtaining a wretched hire by betrayal to the authorities of the nonconformist religious assemblies. Running up credit and paying five shillings in the pound—the neatest way of thieving—Badman in time gained hatfuls of money. He knew all tricks of the trade—the art of deceitful weights and measures, that of mingling com- modities so that what was bad might go off, and he was skilled in misreckoning men in their accounts. So he goes, with hardly an interruption, from bad to worse. During a dangerous fit of sickness, indeed, consequent on the breaking of his leg in a drunken bout, he thought of death and hell-fire, and altered his carriage to his wife, who was now his duck and dear ; but his repent- ance was worth no more than the howling of a dog. The broken-hearted wife dies, and Badman is tricked into marriage with a woman as wicked as himself. At last dropsy and consumption seize their victim ; he lies upon his bed given up to hardness and stupidity of

spirit. " Pray how was he," asks Attentive, " at his
death ? was death strong upon him ? or did he die with
ease, quietly ? " The last and severest earthly judgment
of God is not an agony of remorse ; it is apathy. He
died " as quietly as a lamb." And with this terrible
word Bunyan's book concludes.

Such a narrative as this could not connect itself with
work of an order so different as the " Pilgrim's Progress." The two inventions move on different planes.
The " Pilgrim's Progress " is the poetry of Bunyan's
soul; the " Life and Death of Mr Badman " is the
prose of his moral observation of the world. Successive
generations may in general be trusted to preserve the
heirlooms of literature. " Mr Badman " is not one of
these; but it deserves the attention of a student of
Bunyan, and the attention of a student of Bunyan's
age.

IV

The great allegories of human life commonly make
choice between two modes of representation ; they
describe life as a journey or they describe life as a
warfare. The " Divine Comedy " is a journey through
the realms of eternal life and death ; the " Vision of
Piers Plowman " is a pilgrimage in search of the
highest good ; the " Faerie Queene " is a series of
knightly crusades against the powers of evil. In his
two allegories Bunyan has presented both conceptions ;
the " Pilgrim's Progress " is a journey from the City
of Destruction to the Celestial City ; the " Holy War "
tells of the assault upon the town of Mansoul by

Diabolus, his conquest by fraud and force, the recapture of the town for Shaddai, its lawful possessor, by Prince Emmanuel, its invasion and partial ruin by the enemy, and the final victory of righteousness.

In one respect, and in that alone, can Bunyan's later allegory the "Holy War" be said to surpass the "Pilgrim's Progress"—it is more ingenious in the adaptation of its details. The design was not fortunate; there is no central personage having the parts and passions of a man ; the town, with its walls, and gates, and citadel, is an inanimate abstraction—a generalisation of humanity, not a living and breathing human creature. The multitude of its inhabitants, the multitude of their foes and of their friends, parcel out the powers of good and evil in the soul into fragments and atoms. No single figure interests us supremely ; not one lives in the popular memory. We hardly feel on closer terms of familiarity with Captain Credence, or Captain Goodhope, or Captain Patience, than with the five points of Calvinistic controversy. In the "Pilgrim's Progress" womanhood is presented side by side with manhood ; even in the first Part gracious female forms appear ; in the "Holy War" counsellors and warriors leave no place for women ; half of our human society is unrepresented. The pilgrimage of Christian is an individual experience idealised in art ; it is the *Wahrheit und Dichtung* of Bunyan's spiritual life ; the allegory of Mansoul is a piece of universal history ; it is the work of Bunyan the preacher, who, having taken his side in the warfare of good and evil, was interested in a great cause. But the epic of a cause requires as its representative a champion exposed to the vicissitudes of fortune and in the end falling or triumphant. Bunyan's Emmanuel is too much of a *deus ex machina;* his beleaguered city is an abstraction of humanity; the epic is one without a hero. Bunyan's ingenuity in detail astonishes and fatigues the reader; poetry is replaced by wit in the form of allegory. One episode, indeed, rises to the height of Bunyan's nobler work, but it is difficult to find a second of equal merit. The town of Mansoul has been conquered by Emmanuel, who has not yet made his entrance and remains in the fields. The guilty inhabitants, freed from the tyranny of their oppressors, are still uncertain of the temper of their deliverer. The prisoners, with ropes about their necks, go forth to stand before the Prince; trembling and amazed they hear his doom of mercy; " the grace, the benefit, the pardon, was sudden, glorious, and so big that they were not able, without staggering, to stand up under it." The joy of Bunyan's own heart, when he could have spoken of God's love and mercy to the very crows sitting on the furrows, returned upon him : " They went down to the camp in black, but they came back to the town in white ; they went down to the camp in ropes, they came back in chains of gold ; they went down to the camp in fetters, but came back with their steps enlarged under them ; they went also to the camp looking for death, but they came back from thence with assurance of life ; they went down to the camp with heavy hearts, but came back again with pipe and tabor playing before them. So, as soon as they were come to Eye-gate, the poor and tottering town of Mansoul adventured to give a shout ; and they gave such a shout as made the captains in the Prince's army leap at the sound thereof."

The " Holy War " is a construction, not a vision. The " Pilgrim's Progress " came to Bunyan unsought. His imagination seemed to be the subject of its own involuntary creations. He tells us in "Grace Abounding" how, in the days of his spiritual distress, the blessed state of the poor and pious folk of Bedford was imaged before his inner eye. He saw them set upon the sunny side of a high mountain, refreshing themselves with the pleasant beams of the sun, while he was shivering and shrinking in the cold, afflicted with frost, snow, and dark clouds. A wall compassed the mountain, through which his soul greatly desired to pass ; by and by he perceived a narrow gap, like a little doorway, in the wall, through which he attempted, but in vain, to enter : " at last with great striving methought I at first did get in my head, and, after that, by a sidling striving, my shoulders and my whole body. Then was I exceeding glad, and went, and sat down in the midst of them, and so was comforted with the light and heat of their sun." This parable was no deliberate shaping of Bunyan's intellect or imagination ; it came to him and announced itself. And in like manner arose his dream of the pilgrim, uncalled for and with no laboured research, as if it were the courteous revelation of some ministering spirit.

Bunyan's biographer, Dr Brown, conjectured that the " Pilgrim's Progress " was begun not during his long imprisonment of twelve years in the county gaol of

Bedford, but during a later and shorter imprisonment of 1675-76 in the town prison and toll-house on Bedford Bridge. Mr Thorpe's discovery of the warrant of 1674 confirmed Dr Brown's happy conjecture.[1] Bunyan was engaged upon another book—perhaps "The Strait Gate"—as he himself informs us, when he "fell suddenly into an allegory"; the vision seemed hourly to grow by virtue of its own vitality. When he had set down twenty things, twenty more were in his head; ideas and images rose into his consciousness "like sparks that from the coals of fire do fly;" lest they should distract him wholly from the book on which he had deliberately resolved, he found that he must make a place for them, he must bestow them in a fit receptacle. The "Pilgrim's Progress," he declares, was not written to instruct his neighbours but to gratify himself; that is to say, it was the work of a devout artist, like those mediæval craftsmen who carved a capital or illuminated a missal, and being such a work, done for his own contentment, with no laboured didactic purpose, it is the one book of Bunyan's which has delighted every generation, and edified, while it delighted, more than all the rest. Dr Brown supposes that the portion of the book written in prison closes where Christian and Hopeful part from the shepherds on the Delectable Mountains. At that point a break in the narrative is indicated—"So I awoke from my dream;" it is resumed with the words—"And I slept and dreamed again, and saw the same two pilgrims

[1] See Mr Thorpe's article "How I found the Bunyan Warrant," *Gentleman's Magazine*, February, 1890.

going down the mountains along the highway towards the city." Already from the top of an high hill called "Clear," the Celestial City was in view; dangers there were still to be encountered; but to have reached that high hill and to have seen something like the gate, and some of the glory of the place, was an attainment and an incentive. There Bunyan could pause.

The second part—the pilgrimage of Christiana—was written several years later. Another Christian on the same journey could only have repeated in essentials the adventures of the first with artificial variations, and the book must have been a feebler version of the original narrative. But women and children desire the Celestial City as well as men. It has been suggested that in Christiana we have an idealised portrait of Bunyan's second wife, Elizabeth, who in the Swan Chamber pleaded his cause before Sir Matthew Hale, while Mercy may perhaps have been created from memories of the wife of his youth. The second part is doubtless inferior to the first in its intensity and directness; it was less a record of Bunyan's personal experiences. The terrors of the way are softened; its consolations, if not more exquisite, are more freely distributed—" and one smiled, and another smiled, and they all smiled for joy that Christiana was become a pilgrim." There is no moment in the women's pilgrimage so dreadful as that when Christian in the Valley of the Shadow of Death took the voice of the wicked one, suggesting many grievous blasphemies, for his own utterance. Roaring giants armed with clubs are less appalling than the soft-footed and whispering fiend; and Great-heart is at hand, convoying his weak ones, a conductor sufficiently skilled in the art of decapitating giants or piercing them under the fifth rib.

Yet we could ill spare the second part of the " Pilgrim's Progress." Mr. Froude was surely in error when he called it a feeble reverberation of the first; on the contrary, it is the best of all after-pieces. And the manly tenderness of Bunyan's heart finds expression here as it does nowhere else. He honours Christiana for her courage ; he leans lovingly over Mercy—a little tripping maid who followed God. Beelzebub shoots no arrows at the women as they stand knocking at the gates ; it is bad enough that a dog (and a great one too) should make a heavy barking against them ; while they knock the Master gives them a wonderful innocent smile. If the two ill-favoured ones cause them alarm, the Reliever is presently at hand. The Interpreter, with a " sweetheart " and a " dear-heart " to encourage Mercy, shows them things easy to understand, His garden where was great variety of flowers, the robin with a spider in his mouth, the hen walking in a fourfold method towards her chickens—a simplified text of an Evangelical Æsop's fables. When arrayed in fine linen, white and clean, the women, fair as the moon, had more than joy in their beautiful garments ; they seemed to be a terror one to the other, for in their marvellous humility " they could not see that glory each on herself which they could see in each other." They are comforted in departing with a bottle of wine, some parched corn, together with a couple of pomegranates—delightful fare for pilgrims. Before descending to the Valley of Humiliation they hear the birds singing their curious melodious notes, which had been learnt, as might happen with pious birds, from Sternhold's version of the Psalms. The valley, beautified with lilies, was for them as fruitful a place as any the crow flies over, and there it was that they espied the fresh-favoured shepherd-boy feeding his father's sheep, who sang of the blessedness of a lowly spirit, and wore more of that herb called heart's-ease in his bosom than he that is clad in silk and velvet. Even in going through the Valley of the Shadow they had daylight. They heard the celebration of their sex from the lips of the good Gaius; they had a medical adviser as well as a beloved spiritual conductor; they had the happiness of being interested in several weddings; and instead of lying in the dungeon, nasty and stinking, of Despair, they enjoyed a pious dance around the giant's head; the shepherds decorated them with such bracelets and earrings as Delectable Mountains afford; and it was the men of Bunyan's earlier pilgrimage—so courteous is he—not the adorned women, of the later, who were taken in the flatterer's net. The token sent to Christiana that she should make haste to cross the river was an arrow with a point sharpened with love; and even Despondency's daughter, Much-afraid, went through the waters singing—singing of some incomprehensible consolation, for none on the hither side could comprehend what she said.

Yet the dangers of the way are many and great. Until Paradise is entered wary walking must be the pilgrim's rule. From the moment when Christian abandons the doomed city to the moment when he touches the heavenward riverbank, he is exposed to peril ; at every point of the road vigilance is needed ; the wayfarer's loins must be ever girt ; he must at every instant be addressed to quit him like a man. At the first step Christian is plunged into the Slough of Despond ; he escapes from it only to be sent astray by Mr Worldly-wiseman and to endure the terrors of the mount ; the refreshment at the Interpreter's house is followed by the ascent of the Hill Difficulty, where in an arbour the pilgrim slumbers and lets his roll fall from his hand ; the lions, whose chains are unseen, test his courage as he approaches the House Beautiful ; thence he descends into the valley where he encounters Apollyon ; the Valley of Humiliation leads to the more dreadful Valley of the Shadow of Death, having on the right hand a very deep ditch and on the left a dangerous quag, where in the darkness Christian hears doleful voices and mysterious rushings to and fro ; even the second part of the valley is full of perils, being set with snares, traps, gins, and nets, and abounding in deep holes and desperate shelv-ings ; after the valley comes the wilderness ; and after the wilderness the town of Vanity-Fair, where one pilgrim endures the cage and the other seals his witnessing with a martyr's death ; escaped from Vanity-Fair, Christian enters into discourse with By-ends, and is tempted by Demas to explore the fatal silver-mine ; a little farther on is By-path meadow—" one temptation," comments the marginal note, " does make way for another "— where, sleeping, the wanderers fall into the hands of Giant Despair. Even from the Delectable Mountains terrible things are viewed, men dashed to pieces at the bottom of the hill Error ; men, seen from the hill Caution, walking up and down among the tombs, and stumbling because they are blind ; and, yet more awful, the door in the side of an hill, by-way to hell that hypocrites go in at. The Celestial City is now visible through a perspective-glass, but it is with warnings in their ears that Christian and Hopeful part from the shepherds ; of a sudden they are snared by the Flatterer's net; delivered and scourged by the Shining One, they go for a while softly along the right way, but presently Atheist is at their side, and when he turns from them they have reached the Inchanted ground ; the pious converse by which they resist the invasion of sleep is interrupted by the volubility of young Ignorance ; at length they have arrived at the country of Beulah, where every day the flowers appear in the earth and the voice of the turtle is heard in the land. But still the river lies before them, a river that is very deep ; they set foot in the water ; all the waves and billows go over Christian's head, and he is troubled with apparitions of hobgoblins and evil spirits. Only when the heavenly shore is attained are all dangers at an end ; the City, indeed, is set upon an hill, but up that hill the pilgrims go with ease, for they have left behind them their mortal garments, and the rest is glorious joy which neither tongue nor pen can express. Yet the final word of Bunyan is one of solemn warning. Ignorance, who had crossed the river in the boat of one Vain Hope, a ferry-man, finds no entrance into the golden city; he is bound hand and foot, and thrust through a door that is in the side of the hill : " Then saw I that there is a way to

Hell even from the gates of Heaven, as well as from the City of Destruction. So I awoke, and behold it was a dream."

A dream of terrors, but also of consolations, hope, and joy; more than a dream, the veritable history of a human soul, lifted into a higher reality by the power of imagination. Bunyan's material was given to him by a series of agonising personal experiences, which seemed at times to border on insanity, and by a great deliverance wrought in his own heart.[1] Nothing is more remarkable than the mastery with which his imagination controls and pacifies and purifies his memories of pain and rapture; the humblest realities coalesce with spiritual passions that belong to eternity as much as to time. Every thing verifies itself as actual, yet the total effect is ideal. And thus the book acquired an universal import, and may serve as a manual of the inner life even for persons whom Bunyan, with his Puritan theology, would have classed among heathen men and infidels. All his powers co-operated harmoniously in creating this book—his religious ardour, his human tenderness, his sense of beauty, nourished by the Scriptures, his strong common sense, even his gift of humour. Through his deep seriousness play the lighter faculties. The whole man presses into this small volume. The purport of what he writes in its most general significance is no other than that exhortation of all great spiritual teachers—to live for what is best and highest

[1] Mr Heath, in articles contributed to the "Contemporary Review," October 1896 and July 1897, endeavours to trace much in Bunyan's designs in the Pilgrim's Progress and the Holy War to Anabaptist tradition and history.

and most real, and to live for these with the loins girt
and the lamp lit—" Viriliter age, exspectans Dominum"
quit ye like men.

V

A comparison between the great Puritan allegory
and two other memorable works of a like kind—the
Mediæval allegory of Langland and the Renaissance
allegory of Spenser—naturally suggests itself. " The
Vision of William concerning Piers the Plowman "
deals like " The Pilgrim's Progress " with matter of
abiding interest for every age—the higher life of the
individual soul ; but far more than " The Pilgrim's
Progress " is Langland's poem a study of contemporary
society, a satire, a rebuke, an exhortation addressed to
England of the fourteenth century. In its art it is
primitive, lacking in imaginative unity, deficient in
imaginative construction, resembling some strange page-
ant or procession without a centre, in which one quaintly
disguised figure succeeds another, which itself disappears
to give way to a third, while ever and anon the procession is interrupted or delayed by incursions of a miscellaneous crowd. Its unity is to be found in the moral
spirit which pervades the whole, and in the fact that its
purpose is eminently social. Bunyan's wistful desire
is concentrated on that celestial city which shines very
far off. How shall the pilgrim meet the dangers of the
way so that at last he may part with his mortal garments
and enter those blessed gates amid hosannas of the
heavenly company ? Langland considers the bettering
of man's life on earth, while never losing sight of God

above and heaven in prospect; he sets forth a programme of social reform ; he examines the duties, one to another, of the various classes of society from the king to the peasant ; he protests against the wrong-doings of lord and labourer, of priest and layman ; he warns his countrymen against the danger of unreal, factitious, extravagant virtues pursued to the neglect or detriment of the simple, homely honesties of life, which indeed are not less difficult of attainment and are not less divine. Chastity without charity is of little worth. Depth of theological learning will not produce right conduct, for theology is a "misty" subject, and grows mistier the farther you advance into it. Yet learning is good, and learned men are fortunately placed for their moral welfare. Above all Langland insists on the importance of love and of work. Love and work—these words strike the keynote of his poem. The pursuit of truth, indeed, is named as the chief object of our earthly pilgrimage, but by truth the poet means no statement of abstract doctrine ; he means truth embodied in a life, precious because it tends to action and is quickened by charity.

On a superficial acquaintance with Langland's allegory we may exclaim "What title has this incoherent dreamer to be placed by Chaucer's side?" If we remain longer in his company, we enter into fellowship with a true brother, seeking in his fourteenth century, through all perplexity and amid much moral confusion, for the same truth, the same goodness which we need in this our day, seeking these not for himself alone, that he may escape from some wrath to come, but because men and women on the right hand and the left, straying, suffering, sinning, were dear to his heart ; a man full of fearless indignation because he was full of love, hating evil because he zealously cherished what was good ; a man who must see matters out for himself; who could not put his conscience or his intellect into another's keeping; who must live the veritable life of an individual soul, not a factitious life of forms and ceremonies, or the life of a mere member of a class or an ecclesiastical corporation.

The close of the series of visions, in their best redaction, is peculiarly noble. Piers the Plowman has risen into the ideal representative of all truth and goodness, and Conscience, that which is most inward in man, is seeking for Piers. But does he in the end attain the object of his great desire ? Has Langland a complete solution of the moral difficulties and imperfections of life to offer ? The answer is stern in its honest heroism— "I count not myself to have apprehended." Conscience as the poem closes has not found Piers ; but in the concluding lines he declares his resolve still to forget those things that are behind and to reach forth unto those things that are before. This at least is possible in our mortal life—to seek for what is highest :

> " By Christ," quoth Conscience then, " I will become a pilgrim,
> And walk as wide as all the world lasteth,
> To seek Piers the Plowman, that Pride may destroy."

For who indeed annihilates all our earthly and spiritual pride save Piers ? And with the cry of Conscience the dreamer awakes. It is a conclusion perhaps more full of strenuous encouragement than even

the celestial shawms and trumpets which greet those
happy pilgrims of Bunyan, who are pilgrims no more.

VI

The " Faerie Queene " is an Odyssey of culture—of
culture moral and religious rather than intellectual.
The purpose of the whole poem is to present an
ideal of noble character, and to exhibit the discipline
by which such character is formed. It is an ideal—
aristocratic, not popular—meant for the heroic uses
of earth. Upon the basis of active godliness, manifest-
ing and training itself in generous enterprise, is built
a structure of moral virtues and courtly graces. While
Spenser was essentially a man of the Reformation, in
sympathy—at least in his earlier years—rather with
the Puritan than the high Anglican or Catholic
tendency of the English Church, he was also essentially a man of the Renaissance. Prophets and Evan-
gelists hold hands in his teaching with Aristotle and
Plato, and the group of masters, sacred and profane,
is encircled by a bright arabesque of Italian ornament.
The discipline of virtue is stern ; there is an unceasing
knightly encounter with evil ; the field of virtue is
this world of ours, no place of pilgrimage, but our
goodly habitation, to forsake which were treason against
the queen and mistress of our lives ; a habitation which
we should rejoice to cleanse, to beautify and to
strengthen.

For corporate human life Bunyan had little feeling ;
for national life, for the play of England's sword-arm
among the peoples of Europe he had still less.

Spenser's knights, though each is entrusted with his single enterprise, form a goodly fellowship under their great queen and empress. A strain of lofty patriotism animates them to high achievement. The first to start forth in defence of injured Truth is no other than Saint George, the patron of our land. Spain and the Papacy are not only hostile to true religion but are the foes of that free people, whose avenging might they had lately tempted. And yet while Spenser writes as an English patriot and Bunyan as the member of a despised and persecuted sect, it might be truly maintained that the genius of England is expressed more characteristically in the "Pilgrim's Progress" than in "The Faerie Queene." The union of a high spiritual intention with a homely realism is Bunyan's achievement and is not Spenser's. The strong objective touch is Bunyan's; his pathos is deeper; his passion, less diffused than that of Spenser, is more intense; his humour, though the author of "Mother Hubbard's Tale" was not devoid of humour, is more direct and genial; his personages are more substantial and less abstract—bone of our bone and flesh of our flesh. The endless visions of Spenser's imagination deploy themselves as tranquilly and continuously as the Indian tree, which rises and descends and roots itself anew, and spreads into a forest. Bunyan's gaze is steadied amid the agonies of his fear and the raptures of his joy only by the power of faith controlling his imagination. It may be added that Bunyan's design is happier in its conception than Spenser's, less vast, less liberal in its humanities,

s

but more susceptible of a treatment which respects the law of artistic unity, and that Bunyan accomplished what he designed. Had Spenser completed his twelve books of the Faerie Queene, and added another twelve on the public virtues, few readers would have followed him through the interminable maze of allegory and adventure; no reader could have held before his imagination the varied and interminable prospect. But no one who has started with Christian from his doorway in the doomed city ever failed to accompany him through all the trials of the way; we know every ascent and descent of the pilgrim's path ; we do not find that anything can be added ; we do not desire that anything should be omitted ; every incident and every episode contributes to the unity of the whole.

VII

Such a comparison between the religious allegories of three periods, each exhibiting a different stage in the growth of the English mind, inevitably presents itself to the student of literature. But the moral temper of Bunyan's time is perhaps more vividly felt if we set " The Pilgrim's Progress," the most popular work of the religious imagination of the seventeenth century, side by side with the most popular imaginative work of the generation which followed Bunyan, a work as characteristically English as his, and one which like his has been accepted by the world at large as an interpretation of the genius of our race. The author like Bunyan sprang from the people—a man of vulgar origin ; like Bunyan he belonged to a community of religious nonconformists ; his book, like Bunyan's, professes to be an allegory ; and, if we are to regard it as such, the allegory, like Bunyan's, had a direct relation to his own life. The points of community are real ; yet no two books can express tendencies more essentially different than " The Pilgrim's Progress " and " Robinson Crusoe."

The mundane spirit had invaded Puritanism even before the Restoration of King Charles II. Wars of trade, as Professor Gardiner notices, had succeeded the wars of religion. With the Restoration material interests became predominant throughout the nation. Milton and Bunyan are, in a certain sense, survivals from the past. The temper of the age is represented more truly by Butler's " Hudibras " than by " The Pilgrim's Progress." Theological passion was by degrees in large measure replaced by scientific curiosity. The violent exhortations of the pulpit were succeeded by lessons, in which Tillotson was a master, in Christian morals. A series of political, ecclesiastical, and philosophical compromises served as temporary expedients to smoothe the path of progress. The middle classes advanced in wealth, in power, and in influence. After the jagged precipices and forlorn valleys—scenes of spiritual exaltation or despair—a table land was reached—safe, if unheroic—where men might plough and build. To make the best of both worlds was the part of prudence, and of the two worlds that on which our feet are planted is, at least, the nearer and the more submissive to our control. Divine providence is doubtless to be acknowledged, but it is highly desirable to supplement Divine providence by self-help.

Defoe's narrative of the castaway mariner is the English prose epic of self-help. Crusoe, the forlorn hero, a tradesman's son, with intelligence above the common, yet far from super-eminent, and with a rare force of will, is no pilgrim following after a divine Piers, no Arthur devoted to the service of Queen Gloriana, no Christian struggling through a Valley of Shadow, buffeted in Vanity Fair, climbing Delectable Mountains, or listening to the song-birds in the country of Beulah. He needs a cover for his head, food to eat, tools to procure his food, a home, even if a parrot and a kid are his fellow-lodgers, some appearance of British decency and comfort, and, in order that he may square accounts with heaven, a copy of the English Bible. By-and-bye he will become a colonial governor and an amateur missionary provided with firearms and the Gospel, not indifferent, at the same time, to effecting a good exchange for his " knives, scissors, etc.," with those untutored barbarians whom he would fain convert to the use of civilised garments and a Scriptural faith. The moral is broad and plain—with energy, ingenuity, and resolution it is possible under the most unfavourable conditions to make this life more than tolerable and even to arrange one's future affairs on a satisfactory footing with an offended Deity.

Whatever sense of mystery is to be found in Defoe's narrative must be sought in that deep, irrational passion for wandering which possessed Crusoe from boyhood, unchecked by his good father's warnings and often to the obvious detriment of his material interests; in this and in certain strange premonitions and forefeelings, secret oracles of the heart, which he never could disregard without loss or danger. For the rest, all is the domain of intelligence and will. The island is no enchanted territory of Prospero, full of

Sounds and sweet airs that give delight and hurt not ;

nor has Crusoe any magic book and wand by which to control the elements, or command his airy spirits. His most vivid surprise is to hear poor Poll articulate his name ; his moment of superstitious fear is when he sees an old goat's eyes shining in the dark ; his staggering terror is caused by the imprint of a human foot upon the sand. He is neither a poet nor a sentimental worshipper of nature. The everlasting wash of waves is only a musical accompaniment to the ring of his woodman's axe ; the sunrise lights him to labour and the sunset invites him to repose.

It is the epic of brave human endeavour. " Tools and the man," sings Defoe, with the inspiration of a British muse, vigorous and bourgeois. There is much virtue in subduing a piece of the earth, in sowing corn, in weaving a basket, in shaping a boat. The reckless youth will be transformed into a prudent God-fearing man, and when prosperous days arrive will be saved from mere respectability by that hidden fire of adventure in his heart, which even old age cannot extinguish. We accept him as a hero of our race. Adventurer, trader, colonist, missionary, we give him hail as one of our makers of empire. He it is who will announce laws and establish order. Wild Caribbean and grave Spaniard will acknowledge him—the resourceful, unwearied artificer—their master. To him the world is no Vanity Fair, but a waste to till, a forest to clear, a market for which to cater. And knowing the world and men as craftsman and tradesman, he has learnt the lesson of tolerance. The Spaniards of Defoe are Papists, but they are far more estimable and honourable persons than his wild Will Atkins; and yet Will, being British and a clergyman's son, has it in him, if he is but reclaimed and moralised, to be worth a wilderness of Spaniards. It is the pious Roman priest who points out to Crusoe how improper it is that his subjects should live in adultery with unconverted wives, and it is he who by a pious fraud succeeds in making them honest men and women; otherwise God's wrath might have come upon the island. The gain in tolerance since Bunyan's time was the gain of Defoe's generation. The turning to earth, with its sanities of hopeful toil, was assuredly not altogether loss.

IX

SAMUEL BUTLER

I

THE device of wringing pathos out of the jester's life is common. The circus clown parts with tears from his dying wife, pallid and lean in her lonely garret, and presently he appears in motley with antic and grin amid the roar of applauding spectators. He returns despairful, seats himself on the wretched bed, and the copious tears are renewed. No pathos of this kind forms part of the story of the author of "Hudibras"; but until we have perceived that he was more than a jester, until we have brought home to ourselves the fact that his jests were flashes of merriment which played over a gulf of gloom, we have not known Samuel Butler aright. His wit was a missile, hard and keen as the stones of a sling; we may name him captain of the slingers who fought under the banner of reason and sense.

The life of Butler extended over nearly seventy years of his century—from 1612 to 1680. He saw the rise and progress of the Civil War, rejoiced at the downfall of the Commonwealth, and died in poverty some twenty years after the restoration of monarchy in England. We know too little of Butler apart from his writings to feel

towards him as we do towards authors who have become
our intimates or friends ; nor do his writings commend
him to our affection. We may indeed doubt whether
he ever cultivated the friendship of men ; he was a great
observer, and seems to have kept his fellows at arm's
length, the better to study their aspect and bearing.
He could live and move among Puritans, noting their
infirmities and extravagances, while he himself remained
unnoticed and unknown. He had none of the generous
illusions and gallantries of the cavalier. He did not
write amiable flatteries to be prefixed to the volumes of
contemporary poets. He could join with others in a
sneer at Edward Howard's "British Princes"; he could
tell Sir John Denham that "Cooper's Hill" was bought
to be passed off under a false name, and that "The
Sophy" was borrowed ; but he could not say a word of
generous praise. He held himself in reserve, or he
repelled and was repelled. And, accordingly, we know
little of his private life ; his celebrity was a mask behind
which the man lay hidden. When Lord Dorset con-
trived a meeting with Butler at a tavern, he found the
illustrious wit very flat and heavy, until the second
bottle roused his spirit; at the third bottle Butler sank
into a deep stupidity and dulness. "He is like a nine-
pin," said his lordship, "little at both ends, but great in
the middle." It is evident that Butler was not a person
of light and bright temper ; he needed something to lift
him above himself. He speaks of wine as given to man
in order that he may cherish his frail happiness, given
to teach him judgment, wit, and sense,

And, more than all these, confidence.

We are told that he was a lover of music; but he writes no songs for the lute; his verse, though skilled in its craftsmanship, is mean, and nowhere in all that he composed can we find a strain of noble melody. We are told that he was passionately fond of painting, and thought at one time of devoting his life to that art; but nowhere has he created for our imagination one picture of harmonious and coloured beauty. Living in a time of social and political strife, melancholy in temperament, keen of intellect, an observer and an anatomist of human follies, he used his intelligence as a scalpel in the processes of pathological dissection.

One of Butler's shorter pieces—that "Upon the Weakness and Misery of Man"—betrays the gloomy abyss that lay below his wit. Its mood is like that which grew upon Swift as the world became arid to his disenchanted gaze, the mood of passionate revolt against life. The poem is not a satire directed against contemporary follies; it is a general indictment of humanity. Nature brings us forth only to be found guilty, and at best to be forgiven. What are our offerings to God but begging presents to get more? What is our purest zeal but a pious intention which effects more harm than the worst deeds? What is our devout humility but a vain glory in our wretchedness? What is our birth but a sentence of condemnation, and our life but a series of reprieves?

> Our pains are real things, and all
> Our pleasures but fantastical;
> .   .   .   .   .   .
> Our noblest piles and stateliest rooms
> Are but outhouses to our tombs.

The stars have conspired to imprint a fatal brand and signature of impurity on the human race. Yet the ills inflicted on mankind by nature are as nothing compared with those wrongs which men inflict on their own hated species. If for a moment the heavens forget to seek recruits for death by pestilence, brother rises in civil strife to slay his brother. Or if there be peace, what is peace but luxury and excess, which are more fatal than the earthquake ? What is wealth but disease, discontent, debt, or at most the means to purchase six feet of earth in the parish church ? Yet greater than these curses is the curse of the intellect, by which man shapes out of his own bowels a rack for his sins, or hangs his soul upon subtle curiosities of speculation. The intelligence which was meant to be a sword we break against the anvil on which it was made ; we torment ourselves most to know that which we can never shape into a deed ; we are busy in creating for ourselves the misery of eternal doubt ; we start at the spectres which we have projected upon the darkness ; we spend ourselves in hypothetic dreams and visions, and are sceptics in those things which are evident. In this poem Butler does not jest, or if he jests, the flash only illumines for an instant the surrounding darkness. He writes with a passionate melancholy not far removed from despair.

In this scene of human life, so dim and troubled, where did Butler look for some security, some consolation ? He distrusted the ardours of the heart ; he had no wing for imaginative soaring. The enthusiasm of religious emotion was in his eyes utterly discredited ; he could not abandon himself to either a person or a cause.

He looked for what is best in man to the understanding, limiting itself to what can really be ascertained, to judgment, to good sense. He anticipates the rationalising spirit of the eighteenth century. Human reason is in a high degree fallible; but let us not essay Icarian wings; let us rather use our tolerable crutch. Among Butler's papers were found certain "Reflections upon Reason," which were posthumously published. "Reason," he writes, "is the only helm of the understanding; the imagination is but the sail, apt to receive and be carried away with every wind of vanity, unless it be steered by the former. And although, like the lodestone, it have some variations, it is the only compass man has to sail by; nor is it to be contemned because it sometimes leads him upon a rock—that is but accidental, and he is more apt to hit upon those without it." Reason, and reason alone, is the foundation of religion: "Faith can determine nothing of Reason, but Reason can of Faith; . . . the very being of Faith depends upon Reason." But how little rational is the mass of men! True; and therefore certain lures and frauds are provided by which to practise on their hopes and fears, so to restrain their blind and inordinate passions.

In the eighteenth century reason was not merely destructive; it laid a great basis for construction; it was united with a boundless faith in the progress of science and the progress of humanity; it helped to create a new conception of the material universe and to reform human society. With Butler the work of the understanding was in the main destructive, or, if not destructive, critical. He looked abroad, and saw, or thought he saw, a world of *un*reason; in politics he saw, or thought he saw, no broadening out of great principles, for which to surrender life would be a little thing, but rather civil fury, a rage for democratic licence, a war against established authority; in religion he saw the extravagances of hot-headed zealots, the presumptuous confidence of ignorance, the sanctification and glorification of nonsense, the jar of rival follies, piety made a cloak for ambition and greed. And over against the unreason of the saints he saw another form of human madness— the rage of brutal pleasure, the reversion to the beast. Aloof and detached even from his own party, Butler was a critic of the followers of the exiled King and of the wantons who gathered to the Restoration court. The cavalier who risked everything for loyalty was especially loyal in forsaking all that he could no longer keep, in order to be a burden to his master, and truly and faithfully to eat and drink at his expense : " He forsook his native country because it forsook him before, and cast himself upon the King, who knew as little what to do with him as he did with himself." Raillery and fooling are found to be higher qualifications for statesmanship under the monarchy than the old-fashioned virtues of wisdom and judgment. The degenerate noble is an empty house haunted, to his extreme disquiet, by the ghost and shadow of his ancestors' honour. The decorative courtier is no better than the furniture for a room, a walking picture, a moving piece of arras.[1] It was not Puritanism only that Butler detested ; he

---

[1] Butler's characters of " A Risker," " A Modern Statesman," " A Degenerate Noble," " A Huffing Courtier."

loathed the vileness of the Restoration ; and in the orgies alike of saints and sinners he perceived one and the same phenomenon—violence done to human reason, good sense, decency, and moderation.   Twice the foolish world has been turned topsy turvy ; no sooner was the juggler's pocket emptied of hypocrisy, than the reversed receptacle was filled with impotent iniquity and sin ; the hypocrisy of piety was followed by the hypocrisy of wickedness—pretensions to greater vice than it is possible for human nature to achieve ; Paradise was to be regained, not by grace, but by the newer way of shameless debauchery.   The sectaries had drowned the light of reason in spiritual ignorance ; the voluptuaries and sots of the newer generation tried as laboriously to quench that light in carnal brutality.[1]

II

The second half of the seventeenth century, if it had little faith in religious ardour or in the voice of the higher imagination, had an eager interest in scientific research.   The arrested work of the Renaissance was resumed.   England, isolated for a time by her internal troubles, from the European movement, now took a foremost place in investigation and discovery.   Men of letters were caught into the general stream.   Cowley saluted the Royal Society with a greeting of cheer, and made his propositions for the advancement of experimental philosophy.   Evelyn was one of the earliest fellows of the Society, and in 1672 became its secretary. Butler, although he leant upon the understanding as his

[1] "Satire upon the licentious age of Charles II."

crutch, had too low an estimate of human powers to hope that the mind of man could range through untried regions. Here also he perceived a revolt against good sense and sobriety of judgment; here also were vain pretenders and impostors; here were hypocrites of the intellect; here were the inventors of a novel cant. The bounds of genuine knowledge—so Butler held—are narrow; let us admit our ignorance of what lies beyond our tether; let us occupy our understanding to some profit with such modest truths as are accessible. In the zealots of science he recognised such foes of human intelligence as Swift found in his "Academy of Lagado"; the rest are not madmen but self-interested knaves.

It was a desolating outlook on the world; religion, morals, politics, the search for scientific truth were alike the possession of madmen, knaves, and dupes; everywhere the pretender was enthroned; everywhere good sense suffered violence and outrage. Even in literature the innovations made in the name of reason were essentially irrational. The subjugation of the several species of poetry to arbitrary rules derived from other ages and other countries was another form of unreason; the ridiculous aping of French fashions was a fantastic departure from the old common sense of England. The new school of critics were literary Puritans, who, professing a stricter code than that of nature, were really debasers of wit; they carried things before them by the audacity of their nonsense; they were fierce inquisitors of the new law and doctrine; or, if in themselves contemptible, still like malicious insects they could sting.

Yet Butler clung to reason; he remained loyal to his central faith—the faith in human intelligence. He did not aim at construction or reconstruction ; that, he believed, would come naturally of itself, if only reason had once again its legitimate play. Meanwhile, for his own part, might he not contribute something to the cause of good sense by an onset against the entrenchments of error ? The heavy-shotted battery of argument delivers projectiles which sink into the earthworks and do little damage ; might they not be captured by an escalade of laughter ? No one had a more vivid perception of the ridiculous than Butler, no one had a gift like his for the illustration of absurdity by ingenious analogies. Of that genial feeling for the laughable which is founded on a sympathy with the abiding infirmities of human nature, of that humour which lies close to pathos, the humour of his master Cervantes, he had little or none. His wit was intellectual, a malice of the brain, a light-armed auxiliary of the reason, as Butler himself conceived it. The proper sphere of wit, he says, lies somewhere between truth and those divergences from the straight line of truth which we call error or falsehood. Wit constantly detects and exposes the departure from truth, and exists only by its unfailing reference to right reason. Though wit may seem to incline to falsehood, it does so only to give intelligence of the truth ; " for as there is a trick in arithmetic by giving out a false number to find a true one, so wit by a certain sleight of the mind delivers things otherwise than they are in nature by rendering them greater or less than they really are, which is called hyperbole, or by putting them into some other condition than nature ever did. . . . But when it employs those things which it borrows of falsehood to the benefit and advantage of truth . . . it is of excellent use, as making a deeper impression into the minds of men than if the same truths were delivered plainly." [1] Butler here uses the word " wit " in the extended sense of the seventeenth century, including what we should call the work of the imagination, but it includes also that wit in the narrower sense which characterises his own writings. Ridicule, therefore, should be his weapon. But the laughter which he desired to evoke was not the laughter of high spirits, nor that laughter, closely allied to pity, which smiles at the deep incongruities of human nature ; it was laughter of the intellect, which triumphs in the illumination of truth by the exposure of folly.

An excellent example of Butler's method, on a miniature scale as compared with his long mock-heroic, may be seen in his satire on the scientific movement of the time. "The Elephant in the Moon" is a criticism of the spirit, the methods, the rash hypotheses, the crude theorising — as they appeared to Butler—of the members of the Royal Society. The Society was new, and Butler did not love novelties. It aimed at the extension of knowledge in provinces, some of which were seemingly remote from human life ; and Butler suspected all attempts to be wise above what is granted to the man of average good sense. As he distrusted the inner light of the religious enthusiast, so he distrusted the am-

[1] Reflections upon Reason in Butler's "Genuine Remains," 1759, vol. i. p. 394.

bitious conjectures of the philosophers. As religion
had its contending sects and factions, so had science ;
and as the religious sects had their jargon, so there
was a jargon of the scientific sects. An observer
of men and a critic, holding aloof alike from the
assemblages of the ignorant and the learned, he
nourished a deep suspicion of the *schwärmerei* both
of religion and philosophy ; he believed that these
gatherings heated men's natural folly, set up a state
of unwholesome fermentation, and engendered mon-
strosities of nonsense as strange as those that swarm
in the slime of African rivers. Truth, he held, is
to be found, if at all, by the solitary thinker ; co-
operative effort only pieces or piles together the
fragments of absurdity which lie ready at hand for
every fool to seize.

The members of Butler's learned society one summer
night agree to explore the moon with their telescope,
and to record in their transactions the phenomena
which have been observed. One after another the
philosophers approach the eye-piece of the instrument.
The first, who is known to be the wisest in solving
impossibilities, perceives that the lunar population
are actively engaged in civil war ; an aristocracy,
possessed of luxurious cellars, eight miles in depth,
are opposed by a rude peasantry exposed to the torrid
rays of the sun. The second philosopher applying his
nose to the optic glass—for has he not proved that
the nose is an excellent substitute for the visual organ?
—observes the progress of the internecine strife. The
third perceives with astonishment that from one of

T

the contending armies an elephant has broken loose.
Of a sudden the elephant is seen to race across the
whole surface of the satellite, and in a moment he
is gone.   Rival hypotheses are confidently put forward
to account for the phenomenon.   While the discussion
proceeds, certain foot-boys, attendants on the sages,
are amusing themselves with the instrument, and
notice some object moving in the tube.   A modest
man of science, not yet wedded to theory, forms his
own conjecture, and presently verifies it by discovering
a mouse imprisoned between the glasses of the telescope.
But is he qualified to consider a question involving the
nature of mice?   The further investigation is claimed
by an eminent specialist who has devoted his life to the
study of vermin.   He urges that bare truth is mean
and unworthy of a learned corporation; they are
members of a joint-stock scientific company, and like
other speculators their business is to impress the public
imagination :

> If nothing else but truth we allow,
> 'Tis no great matter what we do.
> For truth is too reserved and nice
> To appear in mixed societies ;
> Delights in solitary abodes,
> And never shows herself in crowds ;
> A sullen little thing, below
> All matters of pretence and show.

In which opinion all agree; for it is surely a nobler
task to create things like truth than to ascertain mere
facts.   Some still swear by the elephant; a few
suspend judgment; a third party is in favour of
deciding the question by ballot; a fourth proposes

to unmount and open the tube. Finally, this last
is accomplished, when the inhabitants of the moon,
a prodigious swarm of flies and gnats, make their
escape, and presently the impostor of a mouse issues
from his trap. The real discovery, for those who are
wise enough to be humbled is this—

> That those who greedily pursue
> Things wonderful instead of true,
>
> .   .   .   .   .   .
>
> Hold no truth worthy to be known
> That is not huge and overgrown,
> And explicate appearances
> Not as they are, but as they please,
> In vain strive nature to suborn,
> And, for their pains, are paid with scorn.

Butler, we have reason to suppose, designed to treat
the problems and experiments of the Royal Society
in a more extended satire, but only a short fragment
seems to have been written. It recites the various
subjects of the philosophers' learned speculations—
matters celestial and matters terrestrial; they hope
to predict the appearance of the next meteor, to
ascertain whether fishes sleep, whether grass be green
and snow be white in themselves or only as the rays
of light impinge upon them:

> And in the braying of an ass
> Find out the treble and the bass,
> If mares neigh alto, and a cow
> A double diapason low.

An intellectual revolution more important to humanity at large than the political revolution of England
was proceeding in Butler's day. He had no sense of
its true significance. The old truths of human life

and human conduct were enough for him; they had all been ascertained long since; why pervert our intelligence with vain ambitions?

In close kinship with "The Elephant in the Moon" is Butler's unfinished "Satire upon the Imperfection and Abuse of Human Learning." Considering man as ruled and guided partly by nature and partly by custom, he would attempt a study of our natural imperfections and our acquired errors. He values that education most which invigorates and does not overload the intellect. Like Comenius and Milton and Cowley he condemns the excessive study of words to the neglect of the study of things. One who can express "no sense at all" in several languages is esteemed as more learned than he who can speak the strongest reason in his own. Foreign rarities may be bought at too high a price. Even the models of ancient eloquence do not afford the best training for an English speaker; let him use his own language to good purpose and all will be well. Butler pleads against the terrors of the school-room—rod and whip —and urges the use of sport as essential to mental clearness and energy. Without intervals of rest and recreation a man is "never broad awake." A mind of native vigour occupied with reality, and sporting between whiles to recover its spring and resilience— such is Butler's ideal. He recurs to his persistent thought of the folly of those who attempt to pass beyond the limits which are set to human knowledge. All the industry of philosophers who delight to stretch their talents towards things beyond their reach is only

an industry to err. Yet precisely in proportion to a
man's abuse of his faculties he grows bold and confident.
Such theorists

> Can tell us easy how the world was made,
> As if they had been brought up to the trade,
>
> . . . .
> When all their wits to understand the world
> Can never tell why a pig's tail is curled.

And the motive alike of pseudo-philosophy and erudite
pedantry is only a pitiful self-conceit. If a scholar cannot
seize the finer spirit and vital power of knowledge, what
is learning but the index to a book ? Such men may
have travelled with the eye over many printed pages ;
but what if they never " bring the world and books
together " ? Yet without this they can never rightly
judge either of books or of the world.

III

To find in brief Butler's indictment of the Puritan we
may turn to his Pindaric ode " Upon a Hypocritical
Nonconformist." Satire, which has in it necessarily
much of the critical spirit, may at times become lyrical ;
the most impressive example in literature is Hugo's
volume, " Les Châtiments." Butler's genius was not
that of a singer ; he was nothing if not critical. The
ode is a winged form of poetry, and Butler's verse in
general trots upon the highway. If the ode be applied
to the purposes of satire, it should be winged with
indignation and have something of the eagle's infallible
pounce upon its prey. A certain power of kindling his
passions lay in Butler's understanding, but his heat is

not the prophetic flame of moral indignation, it is criticism heightened by anger. Butler reduces into a few stanzas a view of Restoration Puritanism, as seen from outside. Naming his own pitiful ignorance and vanity by exalted titles—spiritual gifts and divine outgoings—the Puritan falls down in reverence before himself and is guilty of the grossest form of idolatry. By a pretence of zeal for gospel truths he justifies every folly and barbarism ; he has discovered a new method of sanctifying nonsense and crime. With spurious distinctions of right and wrong he sophisticates the simplicity of the human conscience ; where self-interest or self-will prompts him, he grants ingenious dispensations, and compensates these by a series of vexatious prohibitions in things indifferent. He draws his life and influence from the weak, the ignorant, the credulous, the vain, the factious—" for trouts are tickled best in muddy water." He cries down human learning and plain morals ; he carries the day by the sheer impudence of self-assertion. He sets himself deliberately against the laws of his country, and gladly accepts fine or imprisonment as the best trading advertisement of a saint. What are his prayers but legal suits prosecuted against his Creator, or wrangles and disputes with the Deity ? With zealous agonies and groans he " drowns the nonsense in the noise." He is intolerant in matters of opinion, imperiously orthodox, a persecutor when he has the power, the follower not of Christ but of Mahomet, propagating his creed with fire and sword. In Butler's poem there is little that can be called burlesque ; it is a vigorous statement of the case against Puritanism by one who applied a strong and clear-sighted intelligence to the study of a phenomenon which intelligence alone could not fully explore or rightly interpret.

The form of the Pindaric ode was ill suited to Butler's genius, and he attempted it only on two or three occasions. The ode tends to the generalisations of passion or of thought; and Butler is happiest when he particularises, or conveys his maxim in some hard and definite image. The irregular ode should move to some incalculable law, like that which determines the rise and fall of waves in a broken sea; that verse of which Butler was an accomplished craftsman is made up of a series of calculated jolts. His octosyllable is not that written by Fletcher and the youthful Milton, varied with exquisite surprises of accent and pause, passing at will from an iambic to a trochaic movement, now loitering and now speeding on its way. Butler's verse is conceived in couplets, and in such couplets as admit of no grace, no dignity, no fluctuant motion, no breezelike stay or breezelike sally. To produce variety and to effect surprise he trusts to the special device of which he was master—the ingenious grotesqueness of his rhymes; that is, he arranges his surprise where it will be most obtrusive, where it will force itself on the attention; it is never a gentle surprise of beauty; it is a hard surprise of cleverness, often of clever jugglery. If we could forget that "pulpit drum ecclesiastic" was quoted a thousand times before and has been quoted a thousand times since it served the nightly uses of the ancient bencher of Steele's Trumpet Club, and if we were to read the line for the first time, we should wonder for an

instant how the master of rhymes could pull himself
out of the difficulty which he had himself created ; finding
the verse follow pat, " Was beat with fist instead of a
stick," we should smile only the more because the accent
is misplaced, and applaud the effrontery of Butler's
legerdemain the more vehemently because the jugglery
is undisguised.

In the case of " The Elephant in the Moon " Butler
made a singular experiment ; he wrote the entire poem
in two forms, his characteristic octosyllables and the
longer decasyllabic couplet, preserving in both versions
the same rhymes. It is as if he would demonstrate the
superior efficiency for his own purposes of the lively
vehicle which he preferred ; the longer lines are padded
with superfluous adjectives and nouns ; everything that
has to be said fits into the octosyllabic verse ; the rhyme,
which is the crack of the satiric whip, comes quick,
and signifies that the flagellation is proceeding briskly.
Butler thought less continuously than in fragments ;
a spark, a flash, a snap, and the little electrical sting or
twitch—all are the affair of an instant. A great observer, he kept a commonplace book in which to enter his
comments on life and society, and those ingenious similes
in which his ideas crystallised. Not a few passages of
" Hudibras " were probably constructed by moving side
by side fragments that had originally existed apart from
one another.

When the first part of " Hudibras " appeared, at the
close of 1662 or the opening of 1663, Butler was over
fifty years of age ; he had already accumulated a store
of observations and reflections on his times. The second

part followed in 1664 ; the third part, a belated rear-
guard, emerged to view after an interval of fourteen
years. The heroical epistle from Hudibras to Sidrophel,
printed at the close of the second part in 1674, does
not form an integral part of the poem ; the second
canto of the third part is an interpolation of the author.
unconnected with the story ; it has much in common
with certain prose pieces to be found among his "Genuine
Remains "—the "Two Speeches made in the Rump
Parliament when it was restored by the Officers of the
Army in the year 1659," and "A Speech made at the
Rota," in which the confusion of contending parties is
exhibited in arguments assigned to their several representatives. In writing these harangues, parliamentary
and military, it is not improbable that Butler had the
" Satire Ménipée " before his mind.

The immediate and extraordinary vogue of "Hudibras"
is attested by passages which have been often cited from
the Diary of Pepys. A lover of books, Pepys was reluctant to squander the coin which he collected and
counted with so much diligence and satisfaction. He
lamented his half-crown expended on silly abuse of the
Presbyter Knight going to the wars, and was glad to
transfer the book for eighteenpence to an acquaintance.
But the celebrity of " Hudibras " compelled him to buy
a second copy ten days later, only to find that he could
not bring himself to think it witty. On the appearance
of the second part Pepys prudently looked it over in
Paul's Churchyard, and decided to borrow, not to buy.
It was impossible to escape from a book " now in the
greatest fashion." He confesses that he could not see

where the wit lay; yet it became inevitable that he should again part with his coin; when the King carried "Hudibras" in his pocket and quoted its couplets at table, it was the part of loyalty to bow before the Court favourite.

Heroic satire is resonant with heroic indignation; it has in it something of prophetic faith and fire. "Cry aloud; for he is a god; either he is talking, or he is pursuing, or he is in a journey, or peradventure he sleepeth, and must be awaked"; the scorn of Elijah arises not merely from sight of the ineffectual madness of Baal's votaries, but from a lofty assurance of the power of Jehovah, whose servant he himself is. The satirist of the Restoration was not among the sons of the prophet; there was no fire from heaven which he hoped to call down; there is more of intellectual contempt than of spiritual wrath in his satire. We feel that any enthusiasm, however pure and generous, would have appeared a form of madness to Butler. If in all his writings we could find one outbreak of noble charity, we should value at a higher rate the criticism of his remorseless intelligence.

The romantic epic finds its themes in war and love. Butler's mock-heroic selects the same themes; but the military operations are directed against a bear-leader and his attendant crew—Crowdero, the wooden-legged fiddler; Talgol, the butcher; Magnano, the tinker; Trulla, the tinker's female follower; Cerdon, the cobbler; Colon, the ostler; such is the army opposed to the champion of Puritan morality; and the amorous siege is laid by the ungainly Knight rather against the purse than the person of a not unwary widow. The supernatural element proper to romantic narrative is furnished by the astrologic impostures of Sidrophel and of Whackum, his assistant cheat. The action is trivial and tedious; Butler's invention worked among ideas, not among incidents. The hero and his squire attack the bear-baiting rabble; after an illusive victory they are routed; Hudibras is placed in the parish stocks; the widow visits him in his distress, releases him, and requires as the test of his true love a self-inflicted flagellation. War is waged between the Knight and certain celebrants of the Skimmington, a procession in which a virago and her subjugated husband are led in derisive triumph. Hudibras and his squire, bedaubed with filth and rotten eggs, take to flight. They consult the astrologer, and the interview closes with another battle-royal. The astrologer feigns death; Hudibras flies to his lady-love, leaving the squire, as he supposes, to be dealt with by the officers of justice. The squire betrays to the widow his master's feigned passion and feigned flagellation; she treats her lover to a masquerade of furies and hob-goblins, which is followed by a cudgelling. Hudibras at last invokes the aid of the law against his coy mistress, and with this the story closes. There is little in the paltry narrative that assists the poem as a satire directed against the political and religious parties of Republican England; the action rather tends to reduce the satire to a drollery.

Yet the way in which we should regard " Hudibras " is not as a drollery, but as a work of serious intention, put into a jest of portentous dimensions. Butler, as we have seen, though possessed of great intellectual vivacity, was not a man of gay temper. His outlook upon the world was the reverse of joyous. He rendered homage to human reason before all else, while he was far from sanguine in estimating the capacity of our intelligence. He put his whole mind, as far as it could find literary expression, into this grotesque poem. He wrote it with all his wit, and with seriousness behind the laughter. It is a plea on behalf of what he thought his age most needed—good sense. The purpose of the whole is to put laughter to use in the cause of reason. The chief enemies of human reason in his time, it seemed to Butler, were the religious enthusiasts and the pretenders to religion who had set the State of England in an uproar, who had overthrown the constitution, prohibited innocent pleasures, set up a new tyranny, denounced learning, exalted ignorance, sophisticated morals, and who, after all their follies and their crimes, had ended by a fierce internecine strife of party with rival party, and of sect with opposing sect. It is only by thus viewing the poem as written by a serious thinker, somewhat embittered by the course of events, that we can extract its true meaning. But at the same time we must accept "Hudibras" as a drollery; and the progress of the whole poem is determined partly by its graver purpose, and partly by its author's intellectual pleasure in the detection of absurdity.

Butler's collection of " Characters " in prose forms a long gallery of portraits, which were meant to be types, each one as hard in line and colour as we may suppose those other portraits of his to have been, which, though they attracted the attention of Samuel Cooper, found their final use in stopping broken windows. The opening pages of " Hudibras "—and these are the pages least forgotten and least forgetable—present two characters in verse, those of Sir Hudibras and Ralph his squire. The rhyme forbids us to doubt that some of the features of Butler's " valiant Mameluke " were studied from the Presbyterian colonel, justice of the peace, and member of Parliament, Sir Samuel Luke, in whose house the taciturn observer had found employment for a time. Bunyan's biographer, Dr Brown, thinks it probable that when the future author of " The Pilgrim's Progress " was a soldier in the Parliamentary ranks, he served under Sir Samuel, the chief military leader of his county. Luke was important enough to be in communication with Cromwell, Fairfax, and other Parliamentary chiefs. His Letter-book still exists in manuscript, and gives a reader the impression, says Dr Brown, that he was a man of shrewd observation, of unquestionable valour, of godly life, and of " considerable breadth of humour and humanness." But Dr Brown is mistaken if he supposes that Sir Samuel's appreciation of good feeding, good wine, and worldly gear differentiates him from the fat Knight of Butler's mock-heroic. It concerns us little to identify a living original of Hudibras. In Sir Samuel Luke's house Butler must needs have had abundant opportunity for studying the Puritan species, and out of the infirmities of many individuals he probably compounded his grotesque ideal. The general notion of master and man riding forth on their adventures, and the enjoyment taken in repeated drub-

bings is all that can be said to be common to Butler
and Cervantes ; no contrast can be greater than that
which Butler's gross hero presents to the romantic
Knight of La Mancha ; Sancho Panza's homely good
sense is equally far removed from the pretended inner
light of Ralpho ; and the discreet widow wooed by Sir
Hudibras in no feature resembles the country wench of
Don Quixote's romantic devotion. In all essentials
Butler is wholly original.

In his portraits of the Presbyterian knight and the
Independent squire Butler dwells rather upon intellectual than moral qualities. It is the perversions of
the understanding which he studies in his scornful
analysis, and seems to regard as prime sources of evil.
Hudibras is a man of narrow brain ; if he has wit, as
his admirers allege, he is " very shy of using it." Upon
this narrow brain has been heaped the learning of the
schools, and with what result ? His knowledge of the
tongues—Greek, Latin, Hebrew—only enables him to
be a pedant. His skill in logic qualifies him to be
disputatious, to sophisticate the truth by spurious distinctions, to palter with his conscience. His rhetoric
is of service in dignifying with pompous titles the
absurdities of his speech. His mathematics instructs
him to measure geometrically a pot of ale, or to

> Resolve by sines and tangents straight
> If bread or butter wanted weight.

His philosophy supplies him with mysterious terms
to misapply, or assists him in mistaking his fantastic
notions for the truth of things. His Puritan school-

divinity has made him a master in twisting theological ropes of sand, and in solving unprofitable questions in the wrong way. His religion of the Covenant and the cause is not that of peace, but of pike and gun. The Church reformation at which he aims is one which must still be doing, never done—

> As if Religion were intended
> For nothing else but to be mended.

His devotion lies in perverse antipathies; he seems to worship God for spite ; by proscribing what is innocent he compensates the indulgence of his peculiar sins—

> As if hypocrisy and nonsense
> Had got the advowson of his conscience.

In brief—for this is the sum of the matter—he represents the dominance of discursive and disputatious unreason in temper, in intellect, and in will.

But unreason may be intuitive rather than discursive. Ralph, the squire, a sectary of a rival school, by birth a tailor, owes less to human learning misused than to immediate inspiration. He has received special gifts and new-lights from heaven, which cost no pains of industry or study. He supplements his inspiration by a certain lore in all things mystical and supernatural, in all things which do not admit of comprehension by the intellect. Hudibras acquires the learning of the schools, and renders it worse than barren. Ralph, with a bolder flight of folly, soars into the region of cloudy nonsense ; master and man are agreed in deserting the modest way of good sense, and in employing their powers, whether derived from spurious learning or false new-lights, to the satisfaction of their lusts and greed. The poem is a satire or a libel of Puritan ideals; but no one can study the history of the time without acknowledging that there were materials at hand apt for the satirist; and in pleading for reason and sense Butler was not a common libeller of religion.

We summon all our fortitude to endure the rough-and-tumble incidents of the narrative, the mêlées, the cudgellings, the flights of stones and rotten eggs. But the dialogues between the two chief worthies, knight and squire, the love-making by ratiocination of Hudibras, the widow's argumentative entrenchments and sallies make amends. As for bear-baiting it is demonstrated by Hudibras to be a form of strife which serves neither the Covenant nor the good old Cause; it results neither in the sequestration of the property of malignants nor in the seizure of church-lands by the saints. The precedents for the practice are anti-christian and heathenish —Indian, Egyptian, Roman. Ralph is of the same opinion, and with a first, secondly, and thirdly proves that the name is unscriptural and the thing is human and idolatrous—as much so, indeed, as Presbyterian synods (for Ralph does not spare a thrust against his master's friends), which have much in common with the popular sport. Hudibras, in addressing the rabble, recalls to their minds those purer days, the memory of which is wronged by this profane and carnal recreation, blessed days when tinkers bawled aloud to settle Church discipline, and

> Oyster-women locked their fish up
> And trudged away to cry "No Bishop";

days when the gospel-preaching minister invented honied

tones to win the women, thereby to draw in the men, or directed Providence what it ought to do, or informed the Deity of news arrived by the latest express, or, acting as plenipotentiary of the saints, made overtures and propositions to heaven,

> Such as the army did present
> To their creator, Parliament.

The fiddler and his instrument fall into the power of the reforming knight; conquest, as Ralpho explains, cannot give a right to the property of the defeated party, but the wicked never had a title to worldly possessions; the saints must inherit the earth and the fiddle.

When the tide of battle has turned, and master and man are in the parish stocks, Hudibras comforts himself with cold scraps of philosophy; his legs are prisoners, but his mind is free; it is perturbations alone that can enchain the spirit; drubbed soundly he has been, but as the field of battle is for the slain a stately bed of honour,

> He that is beaten may be said
> To lie in honour's truckle-bed.

Whereupon the captives beguile their time of durance with a learned disputation of Ralph's pronouncement that Presbyterian Synods are mystical bear-gardens. Bears, argues Hudibras, go on four legs; synod-men have but two; it may be admitted that teeth and nails are common to both species; but can the Independent disputant prove that synod-men have tails? Moreover bears are licked into shape, but it is of their own will and inclination that Presbyters become what they are. Ralph's retort convicts the knight of mere

U

human learning—learning that cobweb of the brain which encumbers gifts and darkens the inner light. And Hudibras responds by proving that learning and Presbytery are worlds apart from each other.

The coy widow advances, recognises her imprisoned lover

> Not by his individual whiskers,
> But by his dialect and discourse,

and the conversation passes from ecclesiastical to amorous topics. Hudibras, while frankly admitting that his affections are inflamed not by her person but by her better part—goods and lands—rises to poetic raptures of which his mistress makes small account :—

> She that with poetry is won
> Is but a desk to write upon,
> And what men say of her, they mean
> No more than on the desk they lean.

Let the lover's sincerity be brought to a test; she does not exact any of those cruel martyrdoms which lovers profess with pride; all she exacts is that for her sake he will try the toughness of his back with one simple scourging; there is much virtue in whipping; there are noble precedents. The fat knight ardently swears assent. But, with time granted for reflection, he perceives that the moment of castigation may lawfully be postponed; and, after a night's repose, in that dewy hour

> When like a lobster boiled, the morn
> From black to red began to turn,

certain scruples arise in his mind. The act to which he has pledged himself is carnal; to be forsworn might be the lesser offence. Ralpho luminously explains that the strife between soul and body should be of a mystical nature ; our vessel, the body, is sanctified ; it suffers enough at the hands of the wicked; self-inflicted penance is Papistical, and is therefore sinful. As for forswearing, saints may claim, and often have claimed, a dispensation; oaths are only words, a whipping is an act, and the weaker should yield to the stronger ; the devil to serve his turn can tell the truth ; should saints prove inferior to Satan, and be unable to tell an advantageous lie ? Besides for a saint to break an oath is really a form of self-denial ; the examples of devout perjury are many and recent; oaths are meant to restrain the unrighteous, not to check the liberty of a free-born conscience. Finally the widow is one of the wicked, and to the wicked no faith is due. Hudibras admits the truth of these views which, however, partake of the nature of mysteries, not to be communicated to profane men. An oath, so far as it is an oath, remains itself intact even when it is formally broken, just as the law remains law though it be violated ; indeed law is of no force until its efficacy is proved by its violation ; and so an oath receives its truest honour by a breach. Admit that there is a court of conscience ; like other courts it requires a vacation. Still there would be a convenience in being able to affirm that the flagellation had been inflicted ; would Ralph kindly submit his own back, and allow his master to take the whipping by proxy ? Ralph is disinterested, but he cannot be the occasion of sin ; how should he permit a Christian knight to maltreat the saints ? So proceeds the discussion ; Butler's intellectual ingenuity serves him better than moral vehemence could have done, in winding his way through the tortuous paths of sophistical casuistry.

We follow the hero through his later astrological adventures and debates with a growing sense of fatigue. The catechetical examination in the first principles of morality and religion through which Hudibras is put by the disguised Ralpho rewards the reader of the first canto of the closing part. "Pulpit, drum ecclesiastic" has hardly delighted the lovers of grotesque rhymes more than the question and answer on the infallible method of theological illumination has delighted the lovers of straightforward reasons :

> What makes all doctrines plain and clear ?
> About two hundred pounds a year.
> And that which was proved true before
> Prove false again ?   Two hundred more.

But hardly less effective a thrust is the answer of Hudibras when his catechist inquires why human morality is an offence to the saints :

> 'Cause grace and virtue are within
> Prohibited degrees of kin ;
> And therefore no true saint allows
> That they be suffered to espouse :
> For saints can need no conscience
> That with morality dispense ;
> As virtue's impious when 'tis rooted
> In nature only, and not imputed.

No wonder that Butler's satire was the favourite piece of wit with the courtiers of the Restoration. It provided them with a quiver of epigrams to be shot against all who professed a stricter way of morals or a more serious spirit of religion than that of White-hall.   It seemed, no doubt, to some of them a storehouse of arguments in favour of licentious living.   But they abused Butler's gift to his time, they failed to understand his spirit, and they left him to die in poverty. The Duke of Buckingham—Dryden's Zimri—on one occasion was engaged by Wycherley to meet Butler with a view to rendering him a service at court. The meeting took place, but as ill-luck would have it, on the moment a follower of the Duke tripped past with a brace of ladies ; instantly his Grace was gone, having other business to pursue than the patronage of letters. Once, and only once, in his collection of characters Butler presents not a type but an individual ; it is Dryden's Zimri. He is " as inconstant as the moon " ; he is " governed by some mean servant or other that relates to his pleasures " ; he has " dammed up all those lights that Nature made into the noblest prospects," and has " opened other little blind loopholes backward." It was not for such spirits, whose laughter is the crackling of thorns under a pot, that Butler wrote. His " Hudibras " is not directed against the decencies of morality, but against the follies and frauds, as the satirist conceived them, of pretended piety ; it is, in its own way, a plea for reason and good sense. Incapable as Butler was of comprehending the true significance of religious passion, his work remains as a document of value to the historian of the English mind, a document which tells us what aspect Puritanism presented to a man of keen observation, who viewed it wholly from outside, and who feared the madness of extremes.

What personal influences went to form Butler's mind we cannot tell. It is stated that in early life he was acquainted with Selden, and even acted as that great scholar's amanuensis. The authority of age and the authority of learning—learning wielded with judgment and penetrated by intelligence—must needs have made Selden a power with such a youth as Samuel Butler. Did materials for investigation exist we might find that Selden was for a time the master of his mind. With a broader intellect and a more generous temper than Butler's, Selden had a rationalising turn of thought, an independence of parties in state and church, a shrewdness, a felicity in witty metaphor, a zest in exposing the ignorance and folly of adversaries which must have won admiration from the young observer of men. As we read his "Table-Talk" we seem to see Butler listening with a smile upon his silent lips. "They [divines] talk (but blasphemously enough) that the Holy Ghost is president of their General Councils ; when the truth is, the odd man is still the Holy Ghost." "We look after religion, as the butcher did after his knife, when he had it in his mouth." "Religion is made a juggler's paper; now 'tis a horse, now 'tis a lanthorn, now 'tis a boat, now 'tis a man. To serve ends, religion is turned into all shapes." In such sayings as these perhaps we approach one of the sources of "Hudibras" not less important than the "Satire Ménipée" or "Don Quixote."

X

TRANSITION TO THE EIGHTEENTH CENTURY

I

THE interval between the publication of the second part
of the " Pilgrim's Progress " and that of Swift's " Tale
of a Tub " is only twenty years. Yet in passing from
the one to the other we seem to enter another country ;
we are sensible of an altered climate. And this is not
merely because the individual genius of the one writer
stands so wide apart from that of the other. The
questions which occupied the minds of the younger
generation were new ; the way of regarding them was
different ; the temper in which they were dealt with
was a different temper. The entire view of life, both
individual and social, had undergone a considerable
modification. In place of absolute dogma and unqualified conclusions, we find a sense that truth is
relative ; in place of passion driving men to extremes,
we find a spirit of compromise, a willingness to accept
provisional arrangements.

In politics the doctrine of the divine right of kings
and the doctrine of the divine right of the saints to
rule the earth were replaced by constitutional expedients.
At the Revolution the crown, as Hallam expresses it,
gave recognizances for its good behaviour, and the several

parts of the Constitution were kept in cohesion by the tie of a common interest in its preservation. The Revolution was based not on absolute ideas, but on political expediency. One party in the State might now cry for improvement; the other might plead for conservation; each might revile the other with all the bitterness of party spirit; but both were agreed in the maintenance of the constitution. The reigns of Anne and the first two Georges formed a period of comparative tranquillity in the constitutional history of England. At one time the authority of the crown and of the executive seemed to be enlarged; at another, the power of the people and their representatives; in the main a certain balance was maintained. "Happy is the nation," exclaims Mr Leslie Stephen, "which has no political philosophy, for such a philosophy is generally the offspring of a recent, or the symptom of an approaching revolution. During the quieter hours of the eighteenth century, Englishmen rather played with political theories than seriously discussed them." The political philosophy of Locke, founded partly on utilitarian ethics, partly on the theory of a social compact, is a doctrine of compromise. But it served well as a provisional resting-place—it gave the word for a much-needed halt.

The temper of moderation, reasonableness, detachment from the violence of party, appears conspicuously in the writings of Halifax, the literary merits of which, Macaulay justly said, entitle their author to a place among English classics. The book which Halifax found the most entertaining in the world was that translated by Cotton in 1685—the "Essays" of Montaigne. A constant lover of Montaigne may be a sceptic; he can hardly be a bigot. It has been shown that Halifax's most characteristic pamphlet, "The Character of a Trimmer," was a retort upon an article of Roger L'Estrange, which appeared in "The Observator" of December 3, 1684. A trimmer, says L'Estrange, is an advocate for liberty of practice in the State and for liberty of conscience in the Church—"a man of project every inch of him, and one that, for the ease of travellers toward the New Jerusalem, proposes the cutting of the broad way and the narrow, both into one." [1] To explain and justify the position of the trimmer in Church and State was a task which precisely suited the genius of Halifax.

He would not add to the race of scribblers were it possible to let the world alone; but when madmen in the two extremes agree to make common-sense treason, he cannot but speak. Names of reproach are invented in order that those who cannot frame an argument may have something which their dull malice can throw at the heads of those they do not like. But in reality the word "trimmer" in its right meaning "might do as much to put us into our right wits as 'Whig' and 'Tory' have done to put us out of them." In a boat one part of the company may choose to weigh it down on this side, while another would make it lean as much to the contrary; but there may possibly be a third opinion, that the boat should go even, without endangering the passengers; they who hold this heretical opinion

[1] The Life and Letters of Sir George Savile, Bart., first Marquis of Halifax, by H. C. Foxcroft, II., 273.

will set themselves to trim the boat, and will therefore be accounted criminals.

The trimmer venerates law, but he also honours liberty. He accepts and approves of monarchy, but he recognises a natural right of self-preservation in a people, and would have a king, feeling himself part of a whole made up of king and subjects, reign in his people's hearts rather by love than fear. The trimmer perceives that no government is free from imperfections, and would rather keep our own with all its faults than suffer it to be shattered to pieces.

He recognises that religion is not only good in itself, but needful for a state ; nor among religions is that of England the least to be esteemed. Among the graces of religion, as our trimmer bears in mind, charity holds a place. He would, if it were possible, draw back by ways of gentleness and love those sheep that stray from the Church's fold. He fears that in some of the Anglican clergy there may be " a too great eagerness to extend the ecclesiastical jurisdiction." He thinks that a nation will hardly be mended by principles of religion where morality is made a heretic ; " and therefore, as he believeth devotion to be misplaced when it getteth into a conventicle, he concludeth that loyalty is so too when it is lodged in a drunken club." He holds that even on the right side some knowledge may fitly go along with zeal. He has no relish for the impertinent wanderings of those who pour out long prayers upon the congregation, yet he considers that too great restraint may be put upon men whom God and nature have blessed with a happier talent, a powerful utterance, and, withal, good sense,

beside whom the regulation "Pray-wees" look like so
many statues or men of straw. As for the other re-
cusants, we must distinguish between the Popish priest,
with whom it is impossible to make a treaty, since he
has pinned himself to a principle which has no mean,
and the laity, who are not pledged to extremes, who
have an interest in the realm, and often the feelings of
true Englishmen. With these latter our trimmer would
deal discreetly and even gently; nor would he enact
against them any passionate laws. Trimmer as he is,
he has one idolatry, which he is willing to confess : " He
doth not worship the sun, because it is not peculiar to
us ; it rambleth about the world, and is less kind to
us than it is to other countries. But for the earth of
England, though perhaps inferior to that of many places
abroad, to him there is divinity in it, and he would
rather die than see a spire of English grass trampled
down by a foreign trespasser." The conclusion of
Halifax's pamphlet sums up the whole in a series of
statements, in which the writer's seriousness is heightened
by touches of humour. He ventures to assert " That our
climate is a Trimmer between that part of the world
where men are roasted and the other where they are
frozen ; that our Church is a Trimmer between the frenzy
of fanatic visions and the lethargic ignorance of Popish
dreams ; that our laws are Trimmers between the ex-
cesses of unbounded power and the extravagance of
liberty not enough restrained ; that true virtue hath
ever been thought a Trimmer, and to have its dwelling
in the middle between the two extremes ; that even
God Almighty Himself is divided between His two great

attributes, His mercy and His justice. In such company,
our Trimmer is not ashamed of his name, and willingly
leaveth to the bold champions of either extreme the
honour of contending with no less adversaries than
nature, religion, liberty, prudence, humanity, and common sense."

The fierce passions which encountered one another in
the civil wars of the seventeenth century were in a
measure assuaged, or they had contracted themselves
within the bounds of party strife under the overarch-
ing unity of an established constitution.   Reason, not
perhaps in its highest deliverances but in its meanings
of temporary expediency, had been applied to public
life, and the result was a conciliation which made
political order and political progress possible, and party
warfare not quite intolerable.   A conciliation was also
effected in the religious life of the nation.   Here also
reason was applied to circumstances, not perhaps in the
form of a theory four-square and coherent, but in a way
that worked sufficiently well for practical purposes.
The Toleration Act exempted from penalty such persons
as took the oath of allegiance and subscribed the declaration against Popery ; it secured from vexatious
interference such ministers of religion as could bring
themselves to accept not the thirty-nine articles, but
thirty-six, or, to speak more exactly, thirty-five and
a half.   As Locke provided the political Revolution
with a theory of compromise which was its justification
for the intelligence, so in his Letters on Toleration he
supplied a doctrine, not invulnerable in its logic but
eminently workable, of religious liberty.   He held that

in religion and morals certitude is attainable, but that
the bounds of certitude in matters of theology are
narrow. His Christian faith was sincere, but he divested
religion of mystery, he suspected enthusiasm, he reduced
the essentials of belief to the single tenet of Christ's
Messiahship, he attached more importance to conduct
than to the acceptance of creeds and catechisms, he
placed the basis of belief not in the authority of
Churches, of Fathers, of Councils, but in the reason
of the individual, seeking and accepting whatever shows
itself to be reasonable. He would exclude from toleration those who are themselves intolerant, those who
profess allegiance to a foreign power, and those who,
denying the existence of a God, are, as he conceived,
lost in universal scepticism as to the order of the world
and of human society, and are thereby disqualified for
the duties of citizenship. In his interpretation of the
Bible the reasonable temper, characteristic of Locke's
entire habit of thought, is strikingly manifested. The
sacred writings were not for him, as for the theologians
of a preceding generation, a vast treasury of elaborated
dogma ; they did not constitute for him, as for Bunyan,
a living book of magic, from which darted forth fiery
sentences of terror or words of irresistible consolation.
He tried to place himself in the position of each writer,
to follow the writer's track of thought, to put to use the
aids of history ; he distrusted the inner light of private
inspiration or enthusiasm ; he recognised the misleading
parallax of personal passion.

The better spirit of that movement which transformed our literature in the interval between the

Commonwealth and the age of Queen Anne found its chief representative in Locke, whose aims were not those of literary ambition, but the aims, large and yet modest, of a simple seeker for truth. It was a movement of concentration, of retirement within a limit intellectual and emotional. Truth was now to be pursued, if at all, not by any winged flight into the empyrean, but by careful treading of the substantial earth. The passions were to be retracted within the bounds of what is reasonable. To ascertain facts, to observe phenomena, to analyse known combinations of things, seemed better than to manipulate mysterious words or to start from magnificent assumptions. The "Essay on Human Understanding" had its origin in a discussion which took place, probably in the winter of 1670-71, between Locke and a few friends concerning the principles of morality and of revealed religion. There were systems of ethics and vast treatises on theology in abundance for those who could find satisfaction in them. Locke could find no such satisfaction. He must first ascertain what knowledge really means, what are the bounds of certainty, what is the field of probability; and in order to do this he must look into the mind of man, bringing no preconceived theory, relying on no pretentious phrases, but viewing the human understanding as a phenomenon to be scrutinised and analysed like any other fact in nature: "I thought that the first step towards satisfying several inquiries which the mind of man was very apt to run into was to take a survey of our own understanding, examine our own powers, and see to what things they were adapted. Till that was done I suspected that we began at the wrong end, and in vain sought for satisfaction in a quiet and secure possession of the truth which most concerned us, whilst we let loose our thoughts into the vast ocean of Being, as if that boundless extent were the natural and undoubted possession of our understanding. . . . These men extend their inquiries beyond their capacity, and letting their thoughts wander into the depths, wherein they can find no sure footing, 'tis no wonder that they raise questions and multiply disputes, which never coming to any clear resolution, are proper only to continue and increase their doubts, and to confirm them at last in perfect scepticism. Whereas were the capacities of our understanding well considered, the extent of our knowledge once discovered, and the horizon found which sets the bounds between the enlightened and the dark part of things, between what is and what is not comprehended by us, other men would perhaps with less scruple acquiesce in the avowed ignorance of the one, and employ their thoughts and discourses with some advantage and satisfaction in the other." In these sentences we have in brief the spirit of Locke's effort towards truth, and the spirit which was to preside over much of the work of the eighteenth century. It was a spirit of sobriety, of courageous moderation; a spirit opposed to the dogmatism of philosophers and theologians; a spirit no less opposed to the enthusiasm of the sectaries. From authority, from the tyranny of words, from the visions of an inner light, Locke turned to a patient examination of facts. His programme was modest, yet without any inordinance of ambition he

became for successive generations an acknowledged legis-
lator of thought. It would be difficult, or rather it
would be impossible to reduce the philosophy of Locke
to a perfectly coherent system ; but he aimed less at
becoming the builder of a system than at investigating
facts. His polemic against innate ideas, his empirical
turn of thought did much to reduce the pretensions
of philosophy, to deprive it of a certain mysterious
grandeur, and to bring it nearer to the general intelligence. The " Essay on Human Understanding " was an
eminent example of the application of reasonableness
—though not perhaps of reason in the highest sense
of the word—to the subjects of speculation.

Locke's early training had been in a Puritan household, where the boy was carefully instructed by his father.
At Oxford his college was presided over by that great
systematiser of Puritan theology, John Owen. But the
young student had small satisfaction in what seemed to
him the trifling and the sophistry of the schools. The
minds of many men were turning away from the elaborate systems of the schoolmen of the Reformation and
from the mystic illumination of religious enthusiasts to
the investigation of nature. Locke was eager in the
study of chemistry ; he filled his commonplace books
with notes on meteorology ; he made careful inquiries
in the phenomena of bodily diseases. If the student
of literature is forced to confess that the years from
the Restoration of Charles II. to the accession of Queen
Anne were marked by a decline in the imaginative
genius of England—for Milton and Bunyan belong
to the formative influence of an earlier period—there

is compensation in the fact that these years were eminent in the history of science. While the courtiers plunged into a mad whirl of sensual pleasure, and the wits were shamelessly gay, or grossly saturnine, or spuriously exalted, the serious mind of England held its own course. If the reaction from Puritanism hurried the shallower spirits of the time into an extreme opposite to that of the saints, and for many the extravagance of the pietist was succeeded by the extravagance of the voluptuary, so that an age of unreason might seem to be followed by a counter-age of unreason, in truth the main tendency of the second half of the seventeenth century was not towards the senses but towards reasonableness, and the bases of a great development of science were securely laid.

In that remarkable chapter of Macaulay's History in which he describes the state of England in 1685, he puts forward a theory—already old in the days of Addison's "Spectator" [1]—to account for the passionate interest of the time in scientific investigations. The revolutionary spirit in politics was dammed up by the settlement of the Restoration; that spirit, ceasing to operate in politics, began to exert itself with unprecedented vigour and hardihood in every department of physics: "The transfusion of blood, the ponderation of air, the fixation of mercury, succeeded to that place in the public mind which had lately been occupied by the controversies of the Rota. Dreams of perfect forms of government made way for dreams of wings with which men were to fly from the Tower to the Abbey, and of double-keeled

---

[1] See "Spectator" No. 262.

ships which were never to founder in the fiercest
storm.   All classes were hurried along by the pre-
vailing sentiment.   Cavalier and Roundhead, Churchman and Puritan were for once allied.   Divines,
jurists, statesmen, nobles, princes swelled the triumph
of the Baconian philosophy." It is perhaps true that
the excitement of the public mind caused by the
great political struggle roused men's faculties to exer-
tion in many fields.   But the scientific movement
of the time was a European, not merely an English,
phenomenon.   In 1660 the Royal Society came into
existence ; two years later it received its charter.   But
the Royal Society of England was a younger sister
of the Experimental Academy of Florence, and only
by a little the elder sister of the Academy of Sciences
at Paris.   In truth natural and experimental science
had advanced to a point which rendered a sudden
expansion possible, and, as it were, inevitable.   Crude
observations, chance - medley experiments, fantastic
theorisings, though these might still be found, had
in large measure given place to regulated methods
and reasonable inference.   The Restoration of monarchy in England, and the check to revolutionary
politics exerted no influence on the chemical investigations of the German Becker or the French Lémery,
on Redi's studies at Florence, on Malpighi's anatomical
inquiries at Pisa and Bologna, on Swammerdam's
dissections at Amsterdam.   But England took an
active and a distinguished part in the European movement, and a power at once enlarging and tranquillising,
after the turmoils of politics and the passions of

religious strife, lay in the pursuit—patient and courageous—of truth as presented in the phenomena and the
laws of the external universe. The comedies of Ether-
edge and Sedley, the tragedies of Lee, the poetry even
of Dryden and Otway do not represent the best mind
of England in their day. It is represented on the
one side by Locke, in his faithful and laborious inquiry
into the facts of the intellectual and moral world, and
on the other side by those eminent students of external
nature who observed and collected, who arranged and
methodised, who rose to theory from a basis of reality,
who revealed the laws of phenomena, and perceived a
cosmos emerging from the chaos of accident and of
miracle. The roll of illustrious names—Boyle, Flam-
steed, Halley, Willis, Sydenham, Ray, Morison, Wood-
ward, Grew, Newton—has been often recited. Such
a recital is indeed inspiriting to the student of science ;
for the student of literature it may seem of little importance. But in fact its importance is great. It serves,
in the first place, to account in part for the comparative
barrenness and frivolity of the literature of pleasure
which followed the Restoration ; that literature stood
apart from the higher mind of England, which had
been drawn away in another direction. It serves, again,
to account in part for the claim made by reason and
sense to control imagination in the literature of the
early eighteenth century. In the development of the
critical spirit the principles of the understanding, or
what were held to be such, were directly applied to
literature. "Return to nature" was inscribed upon
the banner of the classical school no less broadly,

though with a different meaning, than upon the banner of the romantic school a hundred years later.

II

If religion was to hold its own in an age when the understanding became the leading authority, it must be shown to be in harmony with the understanding; religion must be rationalised. The God of nature was seen as the first cause in a vast and orderly chain of causation; He was the President in a constitutional system, acting through general laws, which formed, so to speak, His executive. The God of revelation must, if possible, be identified with the God of nature; his methods must bear some analogy to the methods which preside over the constitution and course of nature. The motives to a religious life must be exhibited as addressing themselves to the rational part of human nature, to the intelligence, the common sense, the prudence of men; the temper in which religion is set before men must be a temper of reasonableness and moderation. If the revelation of Christ be an intervention of the supreme Ruler of the world, it must prove its divine origin by evidence establishing at least a strong probability in its favour; miracles and prophecy must be supported by such witnesses or such historical evidence as could be tested in a court of law; Christian doctrine must justify itself as consonant with man's moral nature, and as tending to promote his welfare. Christianity must appear as the religion of good sense. " He that takes away reason to make way for revelation," wrote

Locke, "puts out the light of both, and does much-what the same as if he would persuade a man to put out his eyes, the better to receive the remote light of an invisible star by a telescope." In order to retain an enlightened intelligence on the side of Christianity, it might be well to place no emphasis on any distinctive doctrines which seem to be repugnant to human reason. As in our own century the Oxford movement has held many persons—so it is alleged—within the Anglican communion by its Catholic exhibition of truth, persons who otherwise must have found satisfaction for their spiritual needs by passing over to the Catholicism of Rome, so in the eighteenth century an attenuated Christianity was held to be the prophylactic against Deism. It is certain that Deism was deprived of much of its aggressive force by the tendency of Christian writers to pursue a *via media*.

Robert South stands midway between the older and the newer generation. He preached good sense and good morals with masculine force, but he was not a reconciler, rather he was an unflinching combatant, and a too truculent victor; among his gifts the grace of charity can hardly be reckoned; he sets forth his gospel of good morals with great intellectual clearness and energy, but rarely with what we understand by unction. The supreme faculty of the soul, he tells us, is reason; the state of grace is that of reason grown adult, reason forsaking the childish things of the senses and attaining, through Divine assistance, the highest, that is, the most rational happiness. The ways of

wisdom are ways of pleasantness; and therefore "such
as are not ways of pleasantness are not truly and properly
ways of religion." He that thinks to expiate a sin by
going barefoot does the penance of a goose; if our religion lies no deeper than the skin, self-scourging may,
indeed, effect a great improvement. To exhort men to
be religious is only in other words to exhort them to take
their pleasure—"a pleasure high, rational, and angelical,
. . . a pleasure made for the soul, and the soul for that;
suitable to its spirituality, and equal to all its capacities." [1]

South's preaching was not dry or cold; through
the vigour and perspicacity of his intellect, aided by
the power of a strong rhetoric, he rises at times to a
kind of rational enthusiasm. New lights, sudden im-
pulses of the spirit, extraordinary calls, irresistible
motions, are only the whimsical cant of the ignorant;
yet South can contemplate the greatness and strangeness
of the future beatific vision, marvelling "how a created
eye should be so fortified as to bear all those glories
that stream from the fountain of uncreated light, the
meanest expression of which light is that it is inexpressible." He has no toleration for the "popular,
rambling, incoherent stuff (seasoned with twang and
tautology)" which passes for moving preaching—"such,
indeed, as a zealous tradesman would even live and die
under;" but he can speak nobly of the rational illumination which carries with it authority: "The sun is said
to rule the day, and the moon to rule the night; but
do they not rule them only by enlightening them?

[1] "The Ways of Wisdom are Ways of Pleasantness," Sermons I.
p. 21 (ed. 1842).

Doctrine is that that must prepare men for discipline ; and men never go on so cheerfully as when they see where they go." Our religion, he declares, is a religion that dares to be understood ; true teaching is not a flow of words, nor the draining of an hour-glass, but "an effectual procuring that a man comes to know something that he knew not before, or to know it better." [1] As for prayer, it also is a reasonable service to be rendered with premeditation of thought and brevity of expression. God does not need that we should supply Him with a notification of facts ; how can ignorance inform omniscience ? Nor will He be wrought upon by rhetoric and pathetical harangues ; nor is He to be wearied into acquiescence by our importunity : "men may tire themselves with their own prayers, but God is not to be tired. The rapid motion and whirl of things here below interrupts not the inviolable rest and calmness of the nobler beings above. While the winds roar and bluster here in the first and second regions of the air, there is a perfect serenity in the third." Prayer is prevalent because it is the fulfilling of that condition upon which God has freely promised to convey His blessings. Decency, sense, and reason are expected in our prayers ; God does not command sanctified grimace, solemn wink, or foaming at the mouth ; nor "to set forth our prayers with dress and artifice, to flourish it in trope and metaphor, to beg our daily bread in blank verse, or to show anything of the poet in our devotions." Can any sober person think it reasonable that the public devotions of a congregation should be

[1] Sermon on "The Duties of the Episcopal Function."

" at the mercy of a pert, empty, conceited holder-forth,
whose chief (if not sole) intent is to vaunt his spiritual
clack, and (as I may so speak), to pray prizes." The
only necessary prayer which is not found in the Anglican
liturgy is this—that God would vouchsafe to continue
the liturgy itself in use, honour, and veneration in this
Church for ever. So concludes the second of South's
sermons "Against Long Extempore Prayers," in which
it pained him—though the pain seems courageously
and cheerfully borne—to have to "rake into the dirt
and dunghill" of other men's devotions.

Reason and conscience—these are the true lights
which lighten every man that cometh into the world.
Gifts of the Spirit there are; but amongst these divine
gifts South has to declare that he cannot find "the gift
of canting and whining, and making faces ; that is, of
speaking bad sense with worse looks; which yet those men
used to call the language of Canaan." [1] The generality
of mankind, blind to the lights which should show them
the plain and safe way, "is wholly and absolutely
governed by words or names." Two or three popular,
empty words in the mouth of a rabble-driver will serve
to impel the whole rout whithersoever the driver pleases.
"Right of the subject," "liberty of conscience," "Lord
Jesus Christ," will do well enough, although no meaning be attached to any one of these. Thus, the religion
of the Church of England is "Popery" (and South
himself has many swashing blows to deliver against the
"Papists") ; those who have schismatically deserted it
are "true Protestants"; the subversion of the Church

---

[1] Sermon on " The Christian Pentecost "

is " reformation " ; the execution of the laws in behalf
of the Church is " persecution " ; a sneaking spirit of
compromise is " moderation." What does one in five
thousand of the exclaimers know of the word " Popery,"
except that it is made up of six letters, that it has rung
in their ears since infancy, and sounds big in the mouths
of carmen, broom-men, scavengers, and watermen on
a fifth of November ? Yet with such words as these,
" well tuned and humoured," the expert demagogue may
whistle his herd backwards and forwards, upwards and
downwards till he is weary, and when weary, adds South,
with the malice of shrewd good sense, the rabble-driver
may rest himself " by getting up upon their backs." [1]

It would be unjust to South to suppose that the
driving logic and bold invective of his sermons are
directed only against religious enthusiasts and hypocrites
who assumed the garb of religion. On occasions the
Court preacher could boldly attack the shameless immorality of the Restoration. Among the terms popularly
abused in that day were " ill nature " and "good nature."
Who is an ill-natured man ? Not one who is false
or cruel, revengeful or ungrateful, but rather one who
is unwilling to spend his time, his health, and his estate
upon a crew of idle, spunging sots, and so play the
prodigal among a herd of swine. Who is a good-natured
man ? If the word be used by his superiors, he is
doubtless some slavish, glavering, flattering parasite,
whose business is to fetch and carry ; if by equals, he
is either some soft-headed piece of simplicity, who suffers

---

[1] Four Sermons : "Of the Fatal Imposture and Force of Words," and
"Of the Fatal Influence of Words and Names Falsely Applied."

himself to be led by the nose, or a painful, able, and laborious soaker, whose good nature is born of the pot and the pipe, a good nature which he takes to bed overnight in an abundant quantity, but which, the chance is, he sleeps away before the morning.

South saw around him a practical atheism and a theoretical scepticism and cavilling at religion, and he found in the former the cause of the latter; these "sons of Epicurus," moreover, would pass for the only wits of the age.[1]   Language almost fails him to describe the rage and rampancy of vice; it is "an ocean, which now swells, and roars, and lifts up itself above all banks and bounds of human laws"; it is a monster that walks abroad with a bare face and a brazen forehead, looking down with scorn upon virtue as a contemptible and a mean thing : "we have sinned apace, and at a higher strain of villainy than the fops our ancestors (as some are pleased to call them) could ever arrive to."   Old age encourages greenness of years in wickedness; it is evil-doing which is the best means of preferment to the favour of the great, and doubtless men are well pleased "to serve their interest and their sensuality together."[2] Women, whose proper ornament should be bashfulness and modesty, now brave it in theatres and taverns, "where virtue and modesty are drunk down, and honour left behind to pay the reckoning. . . . This, I say, is the guise of our age, our free-thinking and freepractising age, in which people generally are ashamed

---

[1] Sermon on "Why Christ's doctrine was rejected by the Jews."
[2] Sermon "Of the heinous guilt of taking pleasure in other men's sins."

of nothing but to be virtuous, and to be thought old." [1]
And while vice kept his house like a strong man armed,
South did not perceive that the stronger than he, who
shall come upon him and overcome him, must be another
than reason and good sense.

In 1670 the Rev. John Eachard, who a few years
later succeeded Lightfoot as master of Catharine Hall,
Cambridge, published his admirably witty letter to
L'Estrange on "The Grounds and Occasions of the
Contempt of the Clergy and Religion." It may be
that we are not to accept all its statements as literally
exact; that something must be allowed for the writer's
vein of humorous exaggeration. The value of Eachard's book as a plea for common sense, characteristic of
the time, cannot be questioned. He deplores the ignorance of some of the clergy as a cause of the contempt,
not altogether unjust, in which they were held; undoubtedly there were "Caroline divines" less learned
and less skilled in dialectic than those whom we
remember under that name. How could it be otherwise, asks Eachard, when lads were ordinarily kept to
sixteen or seventeen years of age "in pure slavery to a
few Greek and Latin words?" Why might they not
be permitted to read some innocent English authors, to
write some English themes, and so learn to apprehend
common sense and to judge what is true? But, no: it
seems more important to their wise instructors that they
should be informed how Phaeton broke his neck, or how
many nuts and apples Tityrus had for his supper.

[1] Sermon on "Shamelessness in sin the certain forerunner of
destruction."

Dieted, as the schoolboy is, with rules and exceptions, he somehow comes to regard nine-pins and span-counter as much more heavenly employments than learning; and indeed in Eachard's own opinion the boy who catches frogs or hunts butterflies, though he may not acquire a great reverence for antiquity, is a happier boy than he who is bound to get before breakfast "two or three hundred rumblers out of Homer" in commendation of Achilles' toes or the Grecian's boots. The student may at last acquire the fine art of rope-dancing upon classical phrases, thinning his judgment by academic wit; but academic wit when turned from Latin into English, is a dismally shrimped thing. For the most part an ordinary cheesemonger or plum-seller will write much better sense than these young philosophers whose main business is to hunt injudiciously for curious words.

When the parson mounts his pulpit, too often he conceives his business as that of fastening on some text of Scripture, and tearing and tumbling it for the space of an hour. If he is plain and practical, he may pass for an honest, well-meaning man, but he is evidently no scholar. He therefore finds it more to his credit when addressing farmers and shepherds, to besprinkle his sermon with Greek and Latin, or to swagger over his poor parishioners with the original Hebrew, though nothing in the church, or near it by a mile, unless it be God Almighty, can understand his learning. Perhaps the sound of it may flatter some patron or all-understanding justice of the peace, who reposes in the great pew. And yet one might suppose that simple words and useful instruction were as fit for an esquire, or for one who holds the King's commission, as for him that holds the plough or mends hedges.

Eachard makes merry over the strained metaphors, childish similitudes, and ill-applied tales of the preachers. Our Saviour spoke in parables, but He was pleased to go no farther than the field, the seashore, the garden, and the vineyard. As for our metaphor-mongers and similitude-men, there is little on this side the moon that will content them. But it is in the division of the text that the preacher finds the happiest opportunity for a display of his genius. If the words do not naturally fall asunder of themselves, what notable hacking and hewing takes place, what an exhibition of slivers and shivers. " Weep not for me, but weep for yourselves "—an excellent text of eight words, and obviously consisting of eight parts : (1) Weep not ! (2) But weep ! (3) Weep not, but weep !—and the rest in due order as may be easily distinguished ; that is to say, adds Eachard, " North, north-and-by-east, north-north-east, north-east-and-by-north," with all the other variations of the same quarter of the compass. The censures of the critic are not specially directed against preachers of any one party in the Church ; some of them indeed apply to the highest pulpit eloquence of the elder generation, to such sermons as those of Donne, even to such sermons as those of Jeremy Taylor. South himself was not indisposed to deliver now and again a blow at the style of florid metaphor in which Taylor indulged at the expense, as the younger orator held, of plain and square sense. " ' I speak the words of sober-

ness,' says St Paul, 'and I preach the Gospel, not with
enticing words of man's wisdom.'   This was the way of
the apostles," South comments, "discoursing of things
sacred.   Nothing here of the fringes of the North Star;
nothing of 'nature's becoming unnatural'; nothing of
'the down of angels' wings, or the beautiful locks of the
cherubim'; no starched similitudes, introduced with a
'thus have I seen a cloud rolling in its airy mansion.'
No; these were sublimities above the rise of the apostolic
spirit."

The representative preacher of the new school was
Tillotson. He died in 1694, but his influence remained
as a conciliating power during the first half of the ensuing
century.   He was the friend of Locke and of Barrow;
a member of the Royal Society; a correspondent of the
astronomer Halley.   "More than any one," said Bishop
Burnet, "he brought the city to love our worship"; he
was named by Voltaire the wisest and the most eloquent
of English preachers; D'Albiac and again Barbeyrac translated his sermons into French; Le Clerc celebrated their
merits in the "Bibliotheque Choisie"; Dryden declared
that he had formed his prose style by a study of Tillotson; "he was the best man I ever knew," said King
William, "and the best friend I ever had"; Addison
describes him as "the most eminent and useful author
of the age we live in."   Tillotson's influence is not to
be explained by any extraordinary power of individual
genius, unless it be genius to have caught the better
spirit of the time and to have given it expression.   It
was his part to exhibit the duties of religion as a reasonable service, to set forth the harmony of natural and

revealed religion, to show that piety is a branch of wise living, making, as it does, for happiness and peace both in this life and the life that is to come, to exemplify in his own person the temper of moderation and good sense.

Tillotson, like his friend Locke, had come from a Puritan household. The writings of Chillingworth widened the basis of his theology, and prepared his mind to receive influences from the eminent group of Cambridge thinkers—Cudworth, Whichcote, John Smith, and others—who found in revealed truth rather the illumination of the natural reason than its suspension at the voice of authority. In later years he incurred the reproach of being one of the "Latitude-men," or something worse. His charitable bearing towards dissenters condemned him in the eyes of the altitudinarians. Tillotson, during the reigns of the later Stuarts, apprehended the revival of Roman Catholicism in England, and saw in the atheistical humour and the profaneness and immorality of the time unacknowledged allies of superstition. "Nothing," he writes, "is more natural than for extremes in religion to beget one another, like the vibrations of the pendulum, which the more violently you swing it one way, the farther it will return the other." It was his desire that all sober-minded Christians should "jointly endeavour to retrieve the ancient virtue of the nation, and to bring into fashion again that solid and substantial, that plain and unaffected piety (free from the extremes both of superstition and enthusiasm) which flourished in the age of our immediate forefathers : which did not consist in idle talk, but in real effects, in a sincere love of God and of our neighbour, in a pious

devotion and reverence towards the Divine Majesty, and
in the virtuous actions of a good life." The popularity
of Tillotson's writings suffered an eclipse when religious
enthusiasm revived in the second half of the eighteenth
century. For Whitefield, though he afterwards regretted
his unjust words, Tillotson was "that traitor who sold
his Lord." But if Whitefield had lived in the days of
the good Archbishop his preaching would have been to
little purpose. Tillotson did for his own time the work
that was most needful in the way that was most suitable.
After the orgies of the saints and the orgies of the
sinners he made sanity acceptable to a whole generation.
There is indeed a beautiful kind of enthusiasm in the
long devotion of a life to things that are pure and
peaceable and of good report.

The temper of the lay mind as to ecclesiastical questions a few years after the Archbishop's death is happily
indicated in one of the papers contributed by Addison
to "The Tatler." In an earlier number it had been
announced that Mr Bickerstaff was the possessor of a
political barometer or state weather-glass, which, by the
rising or falling of a certain magical liquor, presaged all
changes and revolutions in government. Addison enlarges
the jest by his invention of an ecclesiastical thermometer,
adapted to the constitution of the Church, as divided
into "high" and "low." The fluid used consists of a
fiery spirit very apt to ferment, combined with a sort of
rock-water, colder than ice and clearer than crystal. At
precisely the middle point of the glass, where the fluid
reaches the mean position, the marking of the thermometer indicates the Church, which stands directly between

Zeal on the upper register and Moderation on the lower. Passing upward beyond Zeal, we find the markings Wrath, Persecution, and Ignorance ; descending below Moderation we come upon Lukewarmness, Infidelity, and again Ignorance. In a *via media* between Zeal and Moderation the Church best flourishes, and it is there that every good Englishman, who is a friend to the constitution, wishes her to be. However, when the fluid rises to Zeal it is not amiss ; when it sinks to Moderation it is still in a most admirable temper. " The worst of it is," says Addison, " that when once it begins to rise, it has an inclination to ascend, insomuch that it is apt to climb from Zeal to Wrath, and from Wrath to Persecution, which always ends in Ignorance, and very often proceeds from it. In the same manner it frequently takes its progress through the lower half of the glass ; and, when it has a tendency to fall, will gradually descend from Moderation to Lukewarmness, and from Lukewarmness to Infidelity, which very often terminates in Ignorance, and always proceeds from it." Excellent and devout spirit as Addison was, he escaped the dangers of zeal, and to him party-spirit appeared to be a deplorable form of madness. He could not understand why multitudes of honest gentlemen, who entirely agree in their lives, should take it in their heads to differ in their religion. We have travelled far from the inflexible temper of the days of Laud and his Puritan antagonists.

Tillotson had been doing for religion the work needful in his own time ; yet we cannot describe it as other than provisional. The point attained was a point of recovery, a halting-place, an indispensable resting-place

for a season.   In one sermon Tillotson tells a story of a
woman who went about with a pitcher in one hand, and
a pan of coals in the other, and being asked what she
meant to do with them, she answered, " with the one
to burn heaven, and with the other to quench hell, that
men might love God and virtue for their own sakes
without hope of reward or fear of punishment." This
woman, he says, may have been devout, but he does
not think that she was overwise.[1]

With Tillotson, whose piety was pure and peaceably
ardent, the motive to religion of self-interest was taken
up among higher motives and was ennobled ; but when
we read the appeals of later preachers to all that is self-
regarding in human nature, and note their deadness to
all that is loftiest in man—his passion for righteousness,
his enthusiasm of self-surrender—we may come to regard
the poor woman of the story as the genius of heroic
piety gone distracted in an age of ignoble good-sense.
The mid years and the second half of the eighteenth
century with its preachings of Whitefield, its growth of
Methodism, its Evangelical revival, its new philanthropy,
are the justification by Wisdom of her distracted child.
The discovery came to religion and to literature that
neither of these is a mere affair of the understanding ;
in the hidden depths of passion and imagination lie
springs which murmur at the right moment to the rod of
the true diviner, and which, when discovered, bring life

---

[1] I borrow the sentences in which the Rev. John Hunt cites the story
(" Religious Thought in England," vol. ii. p. 103).   His reference to
Barker's edition (ix. 49) does not guide me to the sermon in my copy
of Birch's edition.   I have some recollection of having read the story
elsewhere—possibly in Joinville.

and refreshment to the dry places.   The general conclusion to be derived from the history of religion in
the eighteenth century I shall not venture to state in
words of my own.   It has been stated by a writer, who
knew the eighteenth century well, and who can hardly
be charged with the errors of enthusiasm—the late
Mark Pattison: "To abstain from vice, to cultivate
virtue, to fill our station in life with propriety, to bear
the ills of life with resignation, and to use its pleasures
moderately—these things are indeed not little ; perhaps
no one can name in his circle of friends a man whom
he thinks equal to their demands.   Yet the experience
of the last age has shown us unmistakably that where
this is our best ideal of life, whether, with the Deist,
we establish the obligation of morality on 'independent'
grounds, or, with the orthodox, add the religious sanction
—in Mr Mill's rather startling mode of putting it,
'Because God is stronger than we, and able to damn us
if we don't'—it argues a sleek and sordid epicurism, in
which religion and a good conscience have their place
among the means by which life is to be made comfortable."

Fielding, although his standard of masculine morals,
if only "good nature," that is, a benevolent heart, be
present, is not very exacting, was a sincere friend of
religion as it was conceived in the first half of the
eighteenth century.   He ridicules Methodism, to which
sect Mr Blifil attaches himself, after his villainies have
been discovered, adding the estate of a very rich and
devout widow to the two hundred a year settled upon
him by his good uncle.   But Fielding with even greater

zest ridicules the hypocrisy of the free-thinker in the person of his philosopher Square.   The clergy of the Church of England are treated by that great observer of English social life on the whole with consideration and respect, and it is a happiness to learn from Fielding how much of true piety and goodness was to be found among the representatives of the elder school, who dreaded or suspected the new outbreak of religious enthusiasm.   Dr Harrison, the kind friend and father of Amelia and her children, was serving England in his own way less extensively but not less truly than White-field or Wesley ; and, no doubt, there were many Dr Harrisons.   Yet we may doubt whether many conversions were effected in the manner in which Mr William Booth is so pleasingly converted with a view to making Amelia's felicity complete, and qualifying him for the part of an honest country gentleman. Mr Booth was never a rash disbeliever, but he had his doubts respecting religion, of which the chief arose from his notion that, as men act entirely from their passions, their actions can have neither merit nor demerit.   In the bailiff's house he employed his time with great profit in reading Dr Barrow's sermons in proof of the Christian religion, and before long not a doubt remained unsatisfied—" if ever an angel might be thought to guide the pen of a writer, surely the pen of that great and good man had such an assistant." Dr Harrison does not question Booth's assertion that men act entirely from their passions ; but since that is so, surely the religion which applies immediately to the strongest of these passions, hope and fear, must be true ; a religion, writes Fielding, that chooses " rather to rely on its rewards and punishments than on that native beauty of virtue which some of the ancient philosophers thought proper to recommend to their disciples." The utilitarian argument for Christianity was never more nakedly stated.

To make life comfortable was assuredly not the chief aim of the Evangelical Revival, nor has it been the chief aim of the Oxford movement. The one attempted to bring earth somewhat nearer to heaven ; the other, through sacrament and symbol, thought to bring heaven somewhat nearer to earth. Each was opposed to the characteristic spirit of the earlier half of the eighteenth century, the one more in the temper of individualism, the other with a stricter sense of the importance of corporate religious life.